Obsessed

Obsessed

The Autobiography

JOHNNY SEXTON

with Peter O'Reilly

SANDYCOVE

an imprint of

PENGUIN BOOKS

SANDYCOVE

UK | USA | Canada | Ireland | Australia
India | New Zealand | South Africa

Sandycove is part of the Penguin Random House group of companies
whose addresses can be found at global.penguinrandomhouse.com.

First published 2024
004

Set in 13.5/16pt by Garamond MT Std
Typeset by Jouve (UK), Milton Keynes
Printed and bound in Great Britain by Clays Ltd, Elcograf S.p.A.

The authorized representative in the EEA is Penguin Random House Ireland,
Morrison Chambers, 32 Nassau Street, Dublin D02 YH68

A CIP catalogue record for this book is available from the British Library

ISBN: 978–1–844–88520–6

To Laura, Luca, Amy and Sophie

Prologue

Sitting in the kitchen on a grey morning a couple of days after returning from the 2023 Rugby World Cup, I was hit by a sudden realization: I had time on my hands.

In some ways, this was a good thing. The Sexton family hadn't been together for nearly two months. Retirement from rugby meant that I'd be able to drive Amy, Sophie and Luca to school, which was lovely, because it had been such a rare occurrence while I was a player. There were other simple things to enjoy. Like going out for breakfast with Laura. Or going to the driving range. I had great plans for my golf, like getting down to scratch. Why not? I had the time.

But that morning in the kitchen, I had too much time. Laura was out and the kids were at school and suddenly it was just me and the dog and my thoughts.

When you're a player, every minute in your life is accounted for. Even the time that you spend doing absolutely nothing, just lying on a couch recovering from a training session, is all part of a plan designed to make you better at your job. Laura used to laugh that I was 'world class' at recovery. I was tops at basically doing nothing. I could always claim that sitting on a couch watching rugby matches had a purpose. Even if it didn't look like it, it was work.

Now that purpose was gone and it felt weird.

I was suffering from withdrawal symptoms. Only a day or two previously, the Ireland squad had dispersed at Dublin

Airport and we had gone our separate ways. Now I'm sitting in the kitchen, thinking: I wonder what the lads are up to.

The previous summer-into-autumn had been the happiest time of my eighteen-year career. In fact, that comment probably applies to every Andy Farrell camp over the previous two and a half years – ever since we'd started winning consistently. So many laughs, so much positive energy. OK, so our journey ended earlier than we'd planned but that didn't mean the end of our friendship.

A couple of hours after we lost our quarter-final to New Zealand at the Stade de France, we were still in the changing room, still in our gear, drinking beers and trying to come to terms with the finality of it all.

It was never my style to be in a rush to pack up after games. That dressing-room cocoon is special. It strengthens connections. This time I was even more reluctant to leave because, consciously or subconsciously, I knew that my connection to this group was beginning to weaken. You think: I'll never be in a changing room with these guys again. The same realization occurred on the bus back to our hotel that night: I'll never share another post-match bus journey with these guys.

Once back in the hotel bar, we sat around in a big circle, players and partners. We had beers and took turns as DJ. Keith Earls and I were presented with magnums of a fine red wine, to mark our retirements. The bottles were meant to be kept for a special occasion but they didn't last long. This occasion was special enough.

Laura took Luca up to bed at around 3 a.m. – the two of them commuted to France every weekend during the tournament, while Amy and Sophie stayed with Laura's folks. Luca was now like a zombie-child, having been up all day.

I kept going for a while. Part of me wanted to see the sun come up, but sometimes tiredness just gets the better of you. I knew we'd have all of the Sunday together anyway, as we weren't checking out until the Monday morning – players, coaches, back-room staff, partners, kids. It would be like an old-fashioned Irish wake: a big gang brought together in communal sadness, numbing that sadness with drink and song and laughter.

Our hotel was about an hour north of Paris, a golf resort out in the country. That Sunday afternoon, we found a village with a bar that was showing the England v. Fiji quarter-final. More beers. From there, the lads got a bus into Paris but I grabbed a cab back to the hotel to see Laura and Luca. I didn't fancy being around anyone other than my team-mates, coaches or family.

When you lose a big game like a World Cup quarter-final, you go through different emotional stages. That Sunday night, I was in the self-pity phase: raging at the injustice of it all, fuming at decisions that had gone against us. Watching France lose their quarter-final to South Africa by an even narrower margin (28–29) was weirdly comforting. France were hosts and justifiably one of the favourites to win the trophy but they got no breaks that night, with the Springboks getting all of the 50–50 calls. It reminded me that no one has a right to win a World Cup. It cheered me up. Well, a little bit.

The next morning, we had to check out by 11 o'clock, basically to make way for the Springboks, who were checking in. The irony. The team we'd beaten in the pool stages were now preparing for a semi-final, while we were heading home.

If you'd seen us in our private lounge out at Charles de Gaulle, you'd never have guessed that we were in mourning.

Our flight wasn't until that evening so we went back on the beer again. By the time we boarded, the mood was very giddy. In-flight entertainment was provided by Jack Conan and Bundee Aki, who took turns on the public address. Jack invited passengers up to business class to give me a retirement hug. I was in no need of consolation, though. I was feeling no pain.

At some point, I made one final request to the group: even though I was retiring, along with Earlsy and our hugely popular team manager, Mick Kearney, the RWC2023 WhatsApp group would stay intact. It was such a special collection of people.

I was only kidding myself, though. It's over. I need to accept that reality.

It wasn't just me suffering from withdrawal. Laura had grown close to so many wives and girlfriends, so the ending was cruel for her, too. And Luca was miserable after our return. The time when we started our unbeaten run of seventeen games, during the tour of New Zealand in the summer of 2022, was around the time that he had started to understand the game. Ireland losing was a new experience for him. He didn't enjoy it, and he wasn't used to seeing his mum and dad so upset. For someone so young it was a lot to deal with.

He was only nine, a few years younger than Gabe Farrell, Ellis Catt, Ffredi Easterby and Paddy O'Connell – our coaches' sons – but they kindly let him pal around with them over in France, whether in the hotel or sometimes on the team bus to training. They looked after him like a younger brother. Now he was back at school, hanging around with lads his own age again. Or his two younger sisters, who were oblivious to the World Cup. What a come-down.

'Will we still go to the Six Nations?' he asked me, hopefully.

'We'll see,' I answered.

'But we won't be able to go out on the pitch again, will we?'

No, we wouldn't get to go out on the pitch again.

At least Luca got to see the players again soon – only three days after we got home, in fact. Someone lobbed a suggestion into the WhatsApp group: we needed a reunion. I was all over it. I invited everyone to the house that Thursday evening for beers. And everyone came. It was great. From there, we had pints in Ranelagh and then on to Dillinger's steakhouse, before heading into town.

We had a blast – but it was followed by that sense of emptiness again the following morning. Like an addict failing to shake a heavy habit, I was only prolonging the agony.

And all this time on my hands. Time left with your thoughts. I couldn't bring myself to watch the quarter-final back. I don't think I ever will. I don't need to. I've mentally replayed every second, over and over. It finishes the same way every time. Rónan Kelleher still ploughs into Brodie Retallick and Sam Whitelock. Whitelock goes in for the poach, clearly without releasing, but somehow Wayne Barnes awards him the penalty, even though it has all happened under his nose – and it's all over.

And as I stand there, hands on hips, staring in disbelief at Barnes, Rieko Ioane still comes up to me and tells me: 'Get back ten metres.'

Huh?

'Penalty,' he says. 'Back ten.' And then, after Barnes blows the final whistle, he says: 'Don't miss your flight tomorrow. Enjoy your retirement, you c**t.'

So much for the All Blacks' famous 'no dickheads' policy. So much for their humility. I walk after Ioane and call him a fake-humble fucker. It doesn't look great, me having a go at one of them just after we've lost. But I can't be expected to ignore that.

Later, I got in touch with Joe Schmidt to explain my behaviour. Joe was part of the All Blacks' coaching team and we go back a long way. Typically, he'd been gracious in victory that night. He took time to say nice things to Luca, on the pitch, shortly after the game. The Barrett brothers – Beauden, Scott and Jordie – were real gentlemen, too, as was Ardie Savea, who had some lovely words of consolation for me. I appreciated that.

Replaying those scenes from the Stade de France was an inevitable part of the recovery process but it was also a waste of my new-found free time. I decided to put things in order at home. I tidied my office, then went to work on my 'gear room'. It's a small enough space upstairs, originally intended as an airing closet, where I keep all my training stuff – tops, shorts, socks, piles of Adidas boots and trainers. Laura used to keep it in some sort of order. She's a clean freak, borderline OCD – not unlike her husband. Now I had to decide what to keep, what to give away to charity, what to bin. So I folded and I stacked and I categorized and I chucked.

Laura joked that I was nesting, like a woman in the latter stages of pregnancy. I had to look it up to see what she meant.

Nesting was good because it kept me busy and marked the start of a new phase in my life. I no longer had any use for all my old rehab equipment, so I dropped it down to Leinster's training base: recovery pumps, compression sleeves, a 'Game Ready' machine that reduces all the swellings and bruises. I had invested in the best of the best over the years.

Then I considered my next step. I was only thirty-eight – old for a rugby player but still young. I'd planned for afterlife, of course. For the previous two and a half years, I'd been preparing to go into the world of business with the Ardagh Group, a global supplier in sustainable glass and metal packaging, receiving training whenever my schedule allowed. The plan had been to start full-time the January after I'd retired.

Suddenly I was wondering if I'd made the right decision. What about all this rugby knowledge that I've built up over the years? Should I go back to the IRFU and Leinster and ask them about the opportunities that they'd proposed to me? I've been in this game for eighteen seasons. Am I mad to just walk away from it completely? I found I was also being asked by various companies to share my thoughts on leadership and high performance, and I enjoy that type of work.

I decided to consider my options on our family getaway to Dubai over Hallowe'en. There was just one more item on my to-do list, something that had been hanging over me since we'd got back from France. I needed to thank a few people. Lots of people.

During a quiet moment in the team hotel pre-departure, I'd made a rare enough visit to my Instagram page. Normally, I'll only ever see my 'direct messages', those posts sent by friends or people I follow. But this time, curiosity made me check my 'requested messages' – in other words, messages sent by anyone and everyone who'd felt inclined to do so.

This included a few Scots, South Africans and Kiwis who wanted to give me a Rieko Ioane-style send-off. You get used to this sort of toxic waste after a while. Besides, I was blown away by the avalanche of goodwill – literally thousands of messages conveying love and best wishes and thanks and warmth, from people all over the world, including well-wishers from Scotland, South Africa and New Zealand, incidentally, but predominantly Irish. People who said I'd made them proud to be Irish, people whose kids had been inspired to play rugby by watching me play, people wishing me good luck in my retirement, people who just wanted to say that the team – my team (their words) – had given them so much pleasure. I was overwhelmed by it all.

In the days after we got back, many more cards and letters came through our letter box. To reply to everyone individually would have taken months. Laura suggested that I should say something publicly, on social media, to acknowledge all this goodwill. I'd never formally retired from rugby so here was a chance to make it official and thank everyone at the same time.

So I sat down with a pen and a notebook and tried to figure out exactly what I wanted to say and how I wanted to say it. I wanted to express gratitude but I also needed to confront the way that everything had ended, the sense of failure, of incompleteness. I started and stopped and restarted God knows how many times, editing and deleting and struggling to find the right words. It took me about a week to get it right.

We'll come back to my farewell message later. What I found interesting about the exercise was how it forced me to think about things in a broader context. Stuff like: how you want to be remembered, not just by the people who matter – your family, friends and team-mates – but by the public in general, by people who might read this book.

The nature of professional sport and sports commentary is that you are defined by what you achieve – the caps, the medals, the points-scoring records, the Lions tours and so on. I was fortunate to play in some highly successful teams and to work with some outstanding coaches, so by any measure I had a successful career. When I look back, though, I realize that for the majority of that career, probably up until the Andy Farrell era really, it usually felt like a battle.

Of course there were moments of great satisfaction and celebration and laughter. But for the most part, when I was in the thick of it, it felt like a fight – to prove people wrong or to bounce back from snubs and disappointments. For so much of the time, I was at war – with opponents, with rivals, sometimes with coaches, often with myself.

I've never been very good at hiding my feelings, at being anything other than direct. At times this made me a demanding team-mate, I'm sure, but my first and last loyalty was always to the team. I also think that with experience, and guidance, I learned how to be a better leader, and always an honest one. That honesty should make for an engaging story, and hopefully a revealing one.

I

My first sporting arena was the soccer pitch at Kildare Place primary school. It's a ten-minute walk from where I now live – a collection of pebble-dashed buildings with a small patch of green alongside.

That pitch is where I first kicked a ball in anger. Genuine anger. It's where I had my first run-in with sporting authority. This is where I heard the awful words:

Jonathan, you're going in goals for the second half.

First, some context. I'm ten years old and soccer is my main sport. My dream Christmas present is a new Serie A top – preferably AC Milan or Juventus. Every Saturday morning I watch the *Football Italia* programme on Channel 4, marvelling at the skills of Gabriel Batistuta and George Weah and joining in on the catchphrase that signals every ad break:

GOLAZZO!!!

On week nights, we are allowed to stay up past bedtime if Manchester United are on the box. That's me and Mark, my younger brother by two years.

Ryan Giggs, Eric Cantona and Roy Keane – these are my heroes. We've always been a Man U family. Well, Mum and my sister Gillian aren't really that interested. But the boys – Dad, myself, Mark and Jerry Jr, the baby of the family – are all committed fans. We took Dad over to Old Trafford a few years ago, as a treat for his sixtieth birthday.

As a kid, I dreamed of playing for Man U. The first step on my road to stardom was the Mars Skills Challenge, a sort of scouting system set up by the Football Association of Ireland disguised as a skills competition. Kids from primary schools all over Ireland were encouraged to practise a variety of drills: a certain number of keepy-uppies, long passes to a target, dribbling between cones and so on.

The keepy-uppies were no bother to me. I practised them for hours on my own in our small back garden in Rathgar – a busy suburb south of Dublin, also close to where I live now.

Dad set the challenge: twenty quid if I could get to 200, which he soon changed to 300. He'd sit in the kitchen, his armchair angled in such a way that he could keep one eye on his newspaper, one eye on me. Whenever the ball hit the grass, I'd look to see if he'd been watching.

I never caught him out.

I was picked to represent Kildare Place at the 'All-Irelands' that took place in Templeogue College. This was a big deal. You had to bring your own ball and wear your school jersey, do the drills as you were watched by FAI scouts.

I went to bed the night before in the jersey, ball beside the bed, not sleeping a wink. Word was that the winners would be on TV.

After the drills, we were told: *We'll be in touch if you make it.* I waited impatiently. Eventually I stopped pestering my folks to see if anything had come in the post, and I stopped asking Mr Morton, who doubled as school principal and PE teacher.

Mr Morton was the teacher who told me I had to go in goal that time. I was livid. We were leading Taney primary school 1–0 at the break, thanks to a brilliant goal by our number 10: me.

When we came in for the half-time huddle, Mr Morton says he's making me goalie! Goalie? Was he nuts? I told him where to go.

Years later, Kildare Place sent the letter back to me. They still had it on file and someone thought that it might be amusing for me to look back on.

Dear Mr Morton,

I'm sorry for using bad language yesterday . . .

No one thought it was very amusing at the time. Mr Morton was the principal, after all. He came into the class the next day and made me sit in the 'bold' seat, up under the blackboard, facing the wall.

You stay there, Jonathan.

The school had phoned my mother after the incident. Mum was mortified, ate the head off me. But I was more worried about what Dad would say.

In this parenting set-up, he was very clearly defined in his role as bad cop. If we ever misbehaved in his absence, Mum would give us the old line: Wait until your father gets home. When he did get home, and the beams from his headlights were visible in the drive, there would be a race to get up the stairs and under our duvets with the bedroom lights off.

I don't remember him losing his cool over the incident with Mr Morton, though. He told me that I couldn't speak to a teacher like that. Never. But I could see he was stifling a smile.

Later, I overheard him reasoning with Mum. 'Sure what was yer man thinking, putting him in goal? He's the smallest lad on the team, for Christ's sake!'

I was a titch in those days – small, but competitive. Territorial. Mum remembers feeling sorry for me the day she arrived back from maternity hospital with Mark, my new brother. A friend of hers called over to help and apparently when this woman took Mark in her arms, I threatened her with my toy gun:

That's my baby. Put him down!

Mum was probably feeling a little sorry for herself, too. Dad had dropped her home from hospital and headed straight to Lansdowne Road. His brother was making his second appearance for Ireland that day, against Scotland. That's Willie Sexton, my Uncle Willie, a flanker who played for Garryowen and owned a well-known rugby pub in Limerick.

Uncle Willie won three Ireland caps. This was his first Five Nations appearance, which was obviously a massive deal. On top of that, Dad would have to 'wet the baby's head'. Two reasons to drink pints!

Soccer was my first love but I was aware of rugby's importance in the family. A picture of Willie in his first Ireland jersey is still framed and hanging on the wall of my granny's living room in Listowel, County Kerry. That's where Dad's from, a place better known for GAA and horse racing than for rugby.

He learned his rugby as a boarder in Castleknock College, and at University College Dublin (UCD), where he captained the Under-19s to win the McCorry Cup. The winners' pennant was also encased and hanging on the wall in my grandparents' place in Listowel, as a reminder.

From what I'm told, Jerry Sexton – Dad – was a tall, physical scrum-half, good enough to get selected in the first ever Ireland Schools team, in 1975, alongside a handful of future internationals, including Moss Finn, who played in the Ireland team that won a Triple Crown in 1982.

Dad was an international, too, as far as I was concerned. He had represented his country. I'd seen the photo of him in a green jersey, with a shamrock on the crest, and his shoulder-length hair.

I used to love hearing stories about Dad. Syl Delahunt, his old friend from UCD, told me that several Dublin clubs wanted Dad to join them after college. Club alickadoos used to mistake Syl for Dad – they looked very alike – and ply him with pints.

In the end, Dad chose Bective Rangers, in Donnybrook. He never quite delivered on his promise, partly because of injuries, but he stayed involved in Bective, mainly as a coach.

Bective was also his social hub. It was where he met Clare Nestor. Mum.

Mum is also tall, also sporty. There were rugby links on her side of the family too. All her brothers played for Bective or for Palmerston RFC. But the best sportsman in her family was her dad, John Nestor.

Grandad John was an international golfer and held the course record at Milltown Golf Club for years. I still have the framed scorecard at home – 66 shots, 7 under par: Milltown was par 73 back then!

For a while I had plans to go one shot better. It won't happen now. I still have Grandad John's sand wedge in my golf bag. It's the only one of his old Wilsons that I can use. The sweet spot on those old blades is just too small for a six-handicapper like me.

He did show me how to hold a golf club, though. When I play with good golfers they regularly spot that I've a proper grip.

That's probably not all that I inherited from Grandad John. Older members in Milltown recall that he was a stickler for golfing detail – whether it had to do with the rule-book or with technique. He wasn't slow to ring up a journalist if something had been misreported. The golf writer Dermot Gilleece once referred to his curt manner and from then on, whenever Grandad John left a message, he would sign off as 'Mr Gruff'.

Jody Fanagan, a Walker Cup player who broke my grandad's course record, told Gilleece a story about him. He once asked Jody what he looked at when he stood on the tee. Jody said that he looked at both sides of the fairway.

Grandad John said: 'That's wrong. You must pick out an exact spot, just as if you were hitting to a green.' It's like something you'd tell a place-kicker.

I used to do odd jobs for Grandad John – cleaning golf clubs, tidying his garden shed. He had a soft side. He told me I was 'a great lad' and encouraged me to practise my swing. It's one of my regrets that I never got to play with him in Ballybunion, a few miles from Listowel and probably my favourite golf course.

He died when I was fourteen. The post-funeral reception was in Milltown, where I was a junior member. I remember sneaking out for nine holes while the adults were at a reception in the bar but my heart wasn't in it. It didn't feel right.

In my memory of him, health was always an issue. Emphysema got him in the end. He was a drinker and a heavy smoker. When we visited him in hospital in his last days, he was wired up to all sorts of tubes and you could see how his chest was blackened by all the poison in his lungs. I remember the awful rattle in his chest.

Dad told me: That's why you should never smoke.

I've never had even a drag of a cigarette. I used to give Mum an awful time if I ever caught her on the fags. Why would she do that to herself when she could see what it had done to her dad?

*

Mum probably smoked to ease the stress of being a working mother. Mum's a hairdresser who opened her own salon only a matter of weeks after Gillian was born – Rathgar Hair Studio is bang in the middle of Rathgar village, about fifty metres and ten doors away from the house.

They say you should never go into business with friends or family, but Mum and Dad did just that, buying the lease on the premises with a friend. Dad's an accountant, so he put together the business plan. I remember my parents sitting at the kitchen table on a Friday night going through the books while their kids created havoc around them.

It was only when I got older that I began to appreciate how hard they worked and how much stress they were under. Mum had a six-day week and worked late on Thursday and Friday. On those days, Dad would get home before her and cook dinner for us, except on Thursday when he'd be home late too and our childminder would prepare dinner.

He had a stressful routine, too. For a good few years he was with a timber company in Artane on the north side of Dublin, which meant setting off early to beat the cross-town traffic.

He used to drop me and Mark to Kildare Place at around 7 o'clock in the morning, and the school wouldn't open until eight. Child neglect, they'd call it now! At least he gave us an umbrella when it rained.

We'd sit there, wedged into an alcove by the gate, elbowing each other, waiting for the milkman to arrive so that we could nick a couple of cartons. When the caretaker opened the gates, we'd carry in the crate as if to pay for our crime. We were first in, every morning.

Until we were old enough to walk home alone, Mum would collect us. Once, she forgot. I must have been six or seven. Instead of telling someone, I just walked to Rathgar, the guts of a mile along busy roads in a downpour, and then made a dramatic entrance into the salon while Mum was half-way through doing someone's hair.

Imagine her embarrassment as I stood in the middle of the salon floor, a puddle of rainwater forming at my feet, a vision of anger and disbelief:

MUM! YOU WERE SUPPOSED TO COLLECT ME FROM SCHOOL!!

Team-mates of mine will know the look.

I was a fairly intense kid and not a very easy mixer. Worry wart – that's what Uncle Willie always called me. I was shy in unfamiliar company.

I was sure of myself on the soccer pitch in Kildare Place, or in Bective where I played mini-rugby. But if Dad brought me to Bushy Park Rangers for a try-out, I'd hold back, keep to myself.

It was the same on summer holidays in Kerry. He'd take me to try Gaelic football with the Listowel Emmets and I'd hate it. In the garden on my own, I could spend hours soloing and hand-passing to myself, re-enacting entire matches between Kerry and the Dubs, muttering the TV match commentary. But around strangers I was reserved, almost mistrustful. It's a trait that stayed with me as I grew up. It takes me a while to get to know people.

Child psychologists say that the eldest child is typically competitive, keen to win approval from his parents. Only occasionally did I get into what I would have deemed serious trouble and when it happened, I was eaten up with guilt, unable to sleep for nights on end.

I'm thinking specifically of a shoplifting raid with a friend at the Late Shopper in Rathgar, one afternoon when I was old enough to make my own way home from school. This kid was from America, a year old for our class and a bit wild. We walked in to the Late Shopper with an umbrella and used it to collect all sorts of treats. Then we just walked out of the shop with our loot.

The chocolate and sweets disappeared quickly. My guilt didn't. I couldn't live with myself. That night, I'm watching TV with Mum and *Garda Patrol* comes on. They show close-circuit TV clips of hold-ups at petrol stations and identikit photos of robbers. Suddenly I'm genuinely petrified that I'm about to make my first prime-time appearance on RTÉ.

Mum?

Yes, love?

What would happen if you got caught stealing from a shop?

You'd be in trouble, Jonathan.

(*Pause*)

Jonathan, have you something to tell me?

The next morning I was sent down to the Late Shopper with my pocket money to confess my crime. The shopkeeper took the money but seemed to find the whole thing very funny.

Confusingly, I got into more trouble with Dad for what was a lesser crime – taking some glue from the house that I used for making model aeroplanes. The same American friend was involved. We'd found this big tree with a hollowed-out trunk in a corner of the school grounds, perfect for a hideout. We just needed some planks to glue together for a base and a door and we were all set. We had great plans.

But when Dad discovered the missing tubes of glue in my bag, he got the wrong idea. To say he was angry was an understatement. I wasn't allowed go back to my friend's house again after that.

Dad has mellowed with age, but he had a short fuse back in the day and took no nonsense from us. You'd get a hug at bedtime, but if you did something that was unacceptable – or if you didn't try your best at anything – he was angry.

I've no problem with the fact that Dad gave me the odd clip. I probably deserved it and I don't think it did me any harm.

He was a product of the tough boarding-school environment. His parents both had busy working lives in Listowel, so boarding school made sense. His stories about corporal punishment at Castleknock fascinated us. Whenever he would start a sentence with 'When I was in boarding school . . .' our ears would immediately prick up.

He told us great stories about a priest known as the Boxer – so called for obvious reasons. By Dad's account, the Boxer was likely to greet you on the corridor with a smile and a 'Good morning', but if your shirt was untidy or your tie was undone, he'd suddenly snap: 'Your tie is undone, boy!' Then he'd deliver a dead arm. Any misbehaviour and it was a cane across the palm, not just once but several times. Hearing about this sort of thing thrilled us.

But the bit we found most amazing about Castleknock was what happened if you were caught fighting another boy. Your punishment was to scrap it out in the boxing ring in the school gym, with the whole school watching.

No wonder Dad came out of there with a hard-nosed attitude. The irony is that I find it difficult to discipline my own kids – Luca, Amy and Sophie. Laura tells me that I shouldn't let them get away with things so easily, but they have me wrapped around their respective little fingers. With them, I'm a complete softie.

My sensitive side comes from my mum. She went far too

easy on us, and we made her pay – me, Mark and even Jerry Jr. We'd wind her up – answering back, not doing what we were told. Eventually she'd lose her temper.

Once, she took off her slipper and went to slap Mark on the arse. He swung his hips, Mum had a 'fresh air' and we all fell about the place laughing. Then she lost it altogether. She flung the slipper – a chunky enough item of footwear with a solid heel – at us. Me and Jerry both ducked and Mark got it on the temple. He bawled. Mum was in tears, too, especially when Mark's eye started to swell and blacken. We still wind her up about it every now and again.

Mark and I are very close. He turned out to be a fine rugby player – a strong, intelligent centre who won an All-Ireland League title with St Mary's. He was good enough to make it as a pro but was forced to quit because of injury. He's now in the coaching game and helped Ireland's Under-20s win back-to-back Grand Slams. He's someone I consult regularly for his opinions on the game.

It was different when we were kids. We fought all the time. I was protective of him at school, of course. I remember staying with him for his traumatic first day, sitting beside him in Junior Infants while he sobbed away inconsolably. In general he was acceptable company when it suited me, but if I had a better option I would take it. And once we were all indoors of an evening, it could get niggly.

There were six of us in a three-bedroom house. When I was in my mid-teens and when the folks could afford it, they converted the attic and threw me up there. But up until then, bedtime was never a serene, relaxing experience. Gillian, as the only girl, had her own room, and the boys shared a room: myself and Mark in our bunk beds, and Jerry to one side. The whole structure added up to a kind of raft. If one of us moved, the whole thing creaked. Then the arguments and scraps would start.

Eventually we'd hear the thunder of Dad running up the first few stairs. In a flash, the bedroom light would be off and all three of us would be under our duvets, eyes closed.

'If I hear one more peep,' he'd growl. And that would usually do it.

Dad's escape was Bective – escape from the stress of work. His playing career might have finished early but he stayed involved, helping to coach the first and second teams. Basically, the club seemed to occupy nearly all of his time when he wasn't at home or at work.

Mum tells me that as a two-year-old, I often did what I could to stop him leaving the house. As soon as he'd arrive home from work, I'd nick his keys and hide them somewhere, or take one of his shoes and stick it behind the sofa.

This was never going to work as a long-term plan, though. If I wanted to spend more time with Dad, I'd need to go with him to Bective. And that's what happened.

Mum got fed up minding four kids on Tuesday, Thursday, Saturday and Sunday. She insisted that Dad take at least one of us with him. More often than not, this was me. I wasn't complaining.

Bective is in Donnybrook. The small stadium it shared with Old Wesley is something of a spiritual home for Leinster rugby people. It's where Leinster played home matches before the move to the RDS, where I went to watch St Mary's play Schools Cup matches. It's where my dreams were formed, basically.

Donnybrook is an important cultural landmark for generations of Dublin south-siders with no connection to the sport other than the fact that they had their first kiss at a disco hosted by either of the tenant clubs. The grandstand in Donnybrook has been upgraded, so too the terracing. Grass pitches have been replaced by synthetic ones. Wesley have refurbed their clubhouse, but to walk into the Bective clubhouse is to step back into the 1950s. The same floorboards still creak in what was once the dance hall, the same panels in the ceiling still look loose. In a sense, I wouldn't want it to change. That building is a big part of my childhood. The whole stadium is.

It's where I played my first rugby. I still have medals from Under-7 blitzes and a photo from the time we won an Under-10 tournament, where we're wearing club jerseys borrowed from a team many years our senior – so long on us, they'd leak out through the bottom of our shorts. We were the club's first minis section, set up by the late Joe Nolan, club president at the time and a lovely man.

We trained or played games every Sunday morning on a patch of grass outside the clubhouse that's now covered by a car park and some terracing. I remember one of the dads clearing the surface of beer bottles and cigarette packets before kick-off, and whatever other incriminating evidence might have been left over from the previous night.

We were an interesting mix, mostly kids from the kind of well-to-do families you'd expect to find in a club in the heart of Dublin 4 but also a few lads that Joe invited down from Beech Hill estate – like Derek and Scott, who I came across again recently when they came to do a roofing job for me at home. We had a laugh recalling the time on the Under-10s when Scott went missing just before kick-off and was eventually spotted lighting a fire up in the old stand.

I liked that aspect of Bective, the fact that we were from

different backgrounds yet still tight. I reckon it was good for me to experience that before going into a privileged, fee-paying education in St Mary's College.

A lot of my early rugby education took place just from trailing around after Dad on the club rugby treadmill from September to April. Soccer was my favourite sport to play – or at least it was until I went to Mary's aged eleven – but it took up relatively little of my time. Rugby became a way of life.

On Tuesday and Thursday nights between September and April, I'd be at Bective's training pitches in Glenamuck, hassling Johnny O'Hagan for a ball – Hago was Bective bagman, a close pal of Dad. Dad and I wouldn't get home until maybe 9.30 or 10 o'clock, when my siblings were asleep.

Sundays, I seemed to spend the whole day in Donnybrook: mini-rugby from 10 o'clock, then long afternoons when Dad would be 'minding' me. Typically, this meant a game of tip with his mates on the back pitch, followed by a lunchtime pint in Long's pub before watching Bective's second XV.

By then I'd have found a game of my own, probably a two-a-side involving Mark and the O'Flanagan brothers, Stuart and Barry. Their dad, Tim, was the club doctor and our family GP. He and his wife Carol were great friends with my parents. Stuart is now one of the doctors for Leinster and Ireland.

Donnybrook was a vast, sparsely populated playground on those Sundays. Even if there were games on the front and back pitches, there was mischief to be had on the tennis courts, at the back of the main stand or behind the club-houses at either end. If it rained, we could take our rugby matches into the hall in Bective, until a light bulb got smashed and we had to run for cover.

Later, it was home for Sunday dinner. We'd have been eating crisps and peanuts all afternoon and we'd have no appetite. This was no excuse, as far as Dad was concerned. As a boarding-school veteran, he just couldn't accept the idea of food going uneaten. *You'll sit here until you've finished all the food on your plates*, he said. So we sat there, for hours sometimes, broken only by trips to the bathroom, where you could flush away the Brussels sprouts that you'd smuggled out in your pockets.

Saturdays in Bective were best, especially if it was an All-Ireland League Saturday. There was a buzz about the AIL in those amateur, pre-Heineken Cup days. It was the next best thing to watching Ireland in the Five Nations. I can remember the sudden hush in the crowded clubhouse bar whenever RTÉ would show the results from around the country at 5 o'clock.

Bective were only in Division Three, but they were pushing hard for promotion under the guidance of Noel McQuilkin, a gruff Kiwi whose son Kurt played in the centre. Dad was Noel's assistant, and this gave me access all areas.

From the age of eight until I was eleven or twelve, I was part of the scenery in Bective, a regular in the dressing room even when Dad wasn't coaching the team. I'd just nick a couple of Jaffa Cakes from Hago's stash, park myself in the corner and soak up the banter and the fumes from the tubes of Deep Heat.

I'd listen as the chat gradually became more game-focused and the tone got more serious, more angry, the language more earthy. This was normal. I knew the language and I knew the routine. The ref would check the players' studs about fifteen minutes before kick-off, and then those studs would start to beat a rhythm on the smooth stone floor of the dressing rooms as the players jogged on the spot for what passed as a warm-up. Only then would I slip outside. After the game, I'd slip back in and soak up some more.

I couldn't imagine a child being exposed to all that now, but this was the way that I learned rugby's vocabulary, how I learned its basic laws. By this I mean the rudimentary rights and wrongs of the game but also its code – the smart thing to do strategically in certain situations, the right way to react.

I also had an ear for any rugby gossip that was kicking around. One autumn the big news was that Bective had recruited a hard-man from Barnhall, Trevor Brennan. My dad's friend and subsequently his boss, Ray McKenna, had organized a job that sealed the deal. I remember seeing Trevor play in an Under-19s game on the back pitch, soon after he'd joined. He took no nonsense. I remember a fight breaking out close to where I was standing on the sideline and Trevor didn't hold back. He became an instant hero in our house. That would be the season when Bective were promoted to AIL Division Two – 1993/94. I was eight. I remember the game when they clinched promotion, but more for the fact that I got into big trouble with Dad after the game.

We were somewhere up north with a big travelling contingent and the celebrations were massive. Dad gave me £20 to get myself a drink and a bag of peanuts and I went outside with the other kids.

I lost the change. When he came looking for it, I tried lying, saying that I'd already given it to him. He knew this was untrue. He lost the rag with me, in front of everyone. It wasn't that I'd lost the money – although I'm sure he was pissed off about that, too. He was furious that I'd lied to him. I was mortified.

The trip home was a weird experience. The bus was awash with drink and filled with song and there I was, up the front on my own, feeling sore – arms crossed, staring out the window.

The Bective players tried to wind me up – calling my name from the back, then ducking their heads when I looked around. Then one of them would give me the two fingers, in jest, and I'd give them the two fingers back. They called me down, determined to put a smile on my face.

I warmed up eventually, but Dad maintained the cold front. I guess he wanted to teach me a lesson. He had strong ideas about that sort of thing, about doing what's right.

Fortunately, there was one place where I could do no wrong, where I never got in trouble, where I was treated like a king. Listowel.

2

My dad's home town is a picturesque spot in north Kerry, a small place with a big reputation because of its two annual festivals – Writers' Week in May and the Listowel Races in September.

Its most famous inhabitant is undoubtedly John B. Keane, the playwright and novelist. John B. died in 2002 but he is still very much a presence in the town. His pub, now run by his son, Billy, is something of a tourist destination.

John B. is widely remembered for his wit and his insights into human nature. In our family, he's remembered for losing his patience with a young J. Sexton, who was constantly kicking a ball against a wooden gate in the lane behind the pub: *When the hell is dat young fella heading back up to Dublin so we can all get a bit of peace?*

John B.'s is only three doors down from my grandparents' shop. My granny, Brenda Sexton, was still selling clothes well into her eighties.

My dad and Billy Keane were best pals as kids, shared a flat together when they were studying in UCD, and are still best pals. Like his dad, Billy is both publican and writer. He is also my godfather, one of my biggest supporters, and a real character.

He would have seen a lot of me when I was growing up, especially during high summer. My grandparents came to Dublin every July to buy clothes wholesale for their shop. After they'd done their business, one of their grandsons – usually me – would join them on the train journey back down to Listowel. I'd set up residence until the rest of the family joined us in August.

Nothing compared to the weeks I got to spend alone with my grandparents, as an eight-, ten-, twelve-year-old. Spoiled rotten, I was.

They had a house on the edge of Listowel but in summer we'd stay above the shop in William Street, with me often sharing a room with Granny and Grandad. Everything was so relaxed. I didn't have to get up until around 11 or 12 o'clock each day and only then because it was time for a full cooked lunch, always meat or fish with boiled spuds and baked beans.

Granny hired a Sega Mega Drive from the video shop across the street just for the two weeks I'd be there – a real treat, as we'd nothing like this at home. I played video games for hours. Or my grandad – Daddy John, as we called him to avoid confusion with Grandad John Nestor – would take me playing pitch and putt. Most evenings, Daddy John would bring me down to a pub to play pool against the locals. It might have been 10 o'clock, past my bedtime at home. But there were no rules in Listowel.

Those pool challenge games in Flanagan's or the Saddle Bar were my first experience of playing sport for money. We'd be up against farmers, the sorts of characters you'd find in John B's plays. Country cute.

We were cute enough ourselves, a real double-act, taking alternate shots. Daddy John was competitive. He'd consider every shot carefully, whispering strategies in my ear. Winners held the table. No celebrations, just a quiet wink of acknowledgement from Daddy John while the next challenger racked the balls. Hold the table for a few games and you felt like you owned the place.

We mightn't get home until after midnight and if there was golf from the US on the box we'd stay up and watch that until, eventually, my eyelids dropped.

I grew very close to Daddy John. I never called him Grandad, to avoid confusion with my mum's dad. He wouldn't have allowed it anyway. He was determined not to grow old.

He worked well into his old age, in McKenna's yard and hardware store. Even when his leg was at him, he'd refuse a stick. I liked that about him. I didn't even begrudge him the one cigarette he enjoyed every now and again. And he seemed to like me. I provided entertainment for him. I suppose I helped to keep him young.

Daddy John wasn't my only companion during those Kerry summers. When the sun shone, I'd be dropped out to Ballybunion to pal around with my first cousin, Roy Sexton – Willie's eldest kid, only ten days older than me and still a close friend. Willie had a caravan out on the coast so I'd often stay over, wedged into a bunk bed.

Then August would bring a change of pace as the hordes arrived on their holidays – aunts, uncles, cousins, Mum and Dad and, of course, my brothers and sister. We'd stay in my grandparents' bungalow in Caherdown and every morning Dad would drive us out to Ballybunion.

The road to the coast was dead straight but with dramatic dips and humps we knew so well that we could anticipate them in unison from the back seat of the car.

My dad's four brothers would take great pleasure in winding me up about being a Dub, especially when the football championship was on. They'd remind me about the fact that I'm half-Kerry. It's probably the fiery half, the narky half, the half that gets me in trouble.

Ballybunion was great because there was always something on. We had large, ridiculously competitive games of family football on one of the beaches with the pitch markings scraped out on the hard sand with a stick: typically myself, Mark, Roy, a load of uncles and my Auntie Rachel, Mum's sister, who was a great player, the tomboy of her family.

Or there was golf. Mum always insisted that if Dad was going out golfing, then he had to take one of his sons along. That was the deal and there were no arguments. I'd get to caddy for my dad at Ballybunion, where my Uncle John was club captain, and occasionally, when the course ranger wasn't looking, one of my uncles would throw a ball down for me and I'd give it a whack.

Generally my folks seemed at their happiest on those holidays. They always brought a babysitter to look after us in the evenings so they'd get to go out with my aunties and uncles and enjoy themselves.

We didn't take much minding down there, to be honest. Come evening time, we'd wander up the hill from the beach towards the amusement arcades and the bumper cars and we'd have dinner: a bag of chips and some periwinkles, picked out of their shells with a pin. Heaven.

I don't get down to Kerry as often as I'd like these days but I want my kids to experience the magic of the place. My main point of contact is Billy Keane, who still runs the family pub when he's not writing columns in the *Irish Independent*, usually about Munster rugby.

He still goes on about a question I'm supposed to have asked him when I was twelve: When I win my first cap for Ireland, will you frame the jersey and put it on the wall in the pub? I would never have been that presumptuous, but

Billy would never let the truth get in the way of a good story.

My chances of becoming a decent rugby player were helped significantly by being sent to St Mary's College in Rathmines, a twenty-minute walk from Rathgar. Mum says she gave up the fags to help with the school fees, and that it was worth the sacrifice. She always says: 'Mary's was the best thing that I ever did for my boys.'

Rugby was only a small part of the benefit I got from Mary's. I made friends for life there, and had several teachers who had an enormously positive influence on me.

It helped my confidence that I was able to repeat fourth class, which meant I went from being one of the youngest in my group in Kildare Place to being one of the oldest in my class in the junior school at Mary's.

It took me a while to settle, though. There was friction with new classmates and I was the cause of it, for sure. I was determined to make an impression, whether it was in PE class, in the school yard or on the rugby pitch. It wasn't long before people's noses were out of joint.

It wouldn't take you very long to figure out that rugby is pretty important at St Mary's. The school is just off the main drag in Rathmines, a busy area only a mile from Dublin's city centre. Walk in the gate and the first thing you see is a 4G rugby pitch – the 'junior' pitch, where many of my earliest rugby memories were formed.

At ten years of age, I was still a scrap of a thing, a scrum-half like my dad but a confident, aggressive one, determined never to give an inch. This was partly down to something I'd overheard my dad say to his pals at the bar in Bective.

One of them said something complimentary about my

footballing skills and Dad replied: 'Jonathan's skilful but he's a bit small for rugby. He could be a good soccer player. But wait till you see my younger fella, Mark. He's as aggressive as anything.'

It's funny the way these things register with you.

I knew my way around the pitch, from my time with the Bective minis. I was going to let these Mary's lads know it, too, especially the main men on the team, the guys who'd been there since before I arrived, who had older brothers in the school, who had some cred: boys like Eoghan Hughes, Colin Burke and Brian McDermott. I ruffled their feathers, rubbed them up the wrong way.

It wasn't part of any conscious plan. It was just me. It's probably no bad thing, in a physically competitive sport, for people to be on edge. But sometimes your best traits as a sportsman can be your worst traits as a person.

I ended up being best pals with Eoghan, Colin and Brian, but things were tense for a while. They were understandably territorial, and they had numerical advantage over me, so they froze me out where they could, initially. Mum can recall times when I would arrive home from school miserable, in foul form.

Usually being good at a team sport helps your popularity, but it didn't always work out that way for me. One day during my first year in Mary's I was singled out in the sports hall by Dave Breslin, our PE teacher who was also coaching the Junior Cup (Under-15) team in the senior school. He brought five or six of the Js in, mid-class, and threw me a ball.

'Sexton, grubber-kick off your left foot.'

I did as I was told.

'Now off your right.'

No problem, sir.

'Spin-pass off your left.'

Easy.

And so on. He was using me to highlight the level of skill that these older kids needed. I was more than happy to be used. I remember Dave saying: 'This kid is going to be good.'

But you can imagine what my U-10 team-mates were saying behind my back. I was chuffed, of course, but felt even more isolated in the school yard. I was part of neither one group nor the other.

There were other ways to integrate, of course. I played the part of Maid Marian in the junior school's stage production of *Robin Hood*. It was a part that required few lines, but I live in fear that someone recorded it and that the video will resurface.

So it wasn't all rugby at Mary's. Yet rugby was inescapable.

It was a relatively small school, with only sixty or seventy boys per year, but historically we have punched above our weight in Schools Cup competitions. Rugby was part of the ethos of the school, as devised by the Spiritan Congregation, formerly known as the Holy Ghost Fathers. Father Flavin used Spiritan imagery to coach us how to receive a pass:

Hands towards the passer, fingers spread and pointing upwards, thumbs touching.

Our hands were to be shaped like the outspread wings of a dove – the symbol for the Holy Ghost.

None of the priests were still teaching classes, but there was a small community of Spiritan Fathers who lived in a building adjoining the school. Father Flavin and Father McNulty were obsessed with rugby. My guess is that they had a subscription to Sky Sports before most Irish households did.

Father Flavin talked to us about having a saucer-shaped backline in attack. It gave us twelve-year-olds another clear image of how we should align ourselves to run on to the ball. Maybe the St Mary's coaches had figured it out that we had to be smart technically and tactically, because we didn't enjoy the same weight of numbers as some rival schools.

It was in the months of February and March – cup season – that rugby really took over. That's when I got my first taste of really belonging to the school, days when all rivalries were put to one side. Being up for Mary's was all that counted.

We weren't forced to attend cup matches. It was just expected that you'd go along, wear your blue rugby jersey with the white star-shaped crest and sing your heart out.

It helped that the juniors had cup runs to the final in my first two years in the school. Cup weeks were massive. We'd all be herded together in the school yard to practise the various songs and chants. In art class, we'd make posters flagging the match.

Then match-day would arrive. No afternoon classes. Yessss!

Someone's mum would collect four or five of us and we'd grab a chicken fillet roll somewhere on the way to Donnybrook or to Lansdowne Road, where the finals were played. Blue face-paint, school tie wrapped around the head, Samurai style. Then it was through the old turnstiles at the Bective end and straight into the stand, where we'd be packed tightly together, a block of blue, taking a lead from the cheerleaders. We'd be on our feet throughout, belting out the songs, completely hoarse by the end of it all.

My first Mary's hero was Shane Jennings. I have this image of him piling forward, the ball under his armpit, with Belvedere lads hanging off him. Jenno tells anyone who'll listen that I even asked him for his autograph after one game, but that's his imagination running away with itself. I wasn't one for autographs – but I did idolize Jenno. He was a superstar in school. Probably one of the greatest schoolboy players ever. Crowds would turn up to watch him, his reputation was so big.

'Jenno' would be a fairly typical Mary's nickname, by the way. Basically if it's possible to stick an 'o' on the end of your first or second name, that's what will happen. The school and club are habitually referred to as Maro's. Soon enough, I became Jono, and I still am to most who knew me growing up, including my wife.

To everyone else I was Jonathan, until Michael Cheika referred to me as 'Johnny' in a press conference and that stuck. He has a lot to answer for.

Anyway, back when I was in junior school, Jenno seemed like a giant. The Junior Cup, populated by monsters like him, was somewhere off in the distant future. Fortunately, there was a miniature version of it at Under-13 level – the Provincial Cup, as it was called, contested by a handful of Spiritan schools like Willow Park, St Michael's and ourselves, in the first year of secondary school. We tended to have a good record in this competition as well. That was mainly down to the guy who coached the 13s, year in, year out: Richie Hughes.

We all loved Richie. He brought such positive energy, so much encouragement, so much fun. I'm still very fond of him, and we're still in regular contact. He was my English teacher for three years, one of those teachers who can command attention without having to be stern. Richie doesn't really do stern. He's small with soft features, twinkling eyes behind large spectacles and a big walrus moustache, now silver.

His son is Eoghan Hughes – initially a rival, soon a close pal – who still organizes Christmas reunions for our gang. As our house was on the Hughes's route home from training and matches, Richie would often give me a lift. It seemed like we never passed a McDonald's or a service station without him stopping to buy us a Big Mac meal or a Mars Bar and a can of Coke.

I guess what made all of us so devoted to Richie was his own devotion to the school, to the squad, and to doing things right. I have this image of him at one of those cup matches, down at the front of the stand at Donnybrook, celebrating a try with the rest of us. Usually teachers were there to maintain discipline, to keep an eye out for any rowdyism, especially whenever the opposition were taking shots at goal. But in my memory, Richie is just celebrating a Mary's score, going mental like the rest of us.

He was fanatical about rugby. In English class, we'd always sense when he was open to being sidetracked into a discussion on the previous day's cup match in Donnybrook. He'd always have a copy of the *Irish Times* folded between his books, so we'd get him to read out the match report. There's educational value in analysing the quality of the report, we'd argue. He never took much convincing. Soon it would develop into general chat about the game. Richie loved to chat.

Winning was important to him, but it wasn't the only thing. He was inclusive. I'm not sure what the regulations on substitutions were for those games in the Provincial Cup, but he seemed to have as many players on the bench as on the pitch, all them turned out perfectly in the school tracksuit. Some of those lads hadn't a hope of ever making it on to the pitch for the A team, but they had trained all season and he wanted them to be involved on the big days, when we might get to leave class an hour early, to have a pre-match bowl of soup in the school canteen.

Being part of the A squad was hugely important. I remember how distressed Cormac Waldron was when he had to miss a week's training around Christmas time because his family were going on holiday. Richie put him at ease.

You must enjoy your holiday, Cormy, he said. *Bring me back a stick of rock.*

A few weeks later, after Cormy's return, we had a brilliant comeback victory over Belvedere, up at their ground in Cabra, where I landed a conversion from wide on the right to nail the win. Then, a nice moment in the dressing room, when Cormy opened his kitbag and revealed that he'd brought back a stick of rock for everyone in the squad. Richie said he'd keep his wrapped until we'd won the league.

I noticed that Richie wore a Miraculous Medal on a chain around his neck, and this fascinated me for some reason. He presented me with one years later when I graduated from St Mary's, having first asked Mum if this was OK with her.

I've always been quite religious. I trace this back to time spent in Listowel, where my grandparents would never miss Sunday mass. No one missed mass in Listowel. It was a social gathering as well as a spiritual gathering. The rest of the town would be deserted. In Dublin, my parents went to mass most Sundays – I remember how it used to play havoc with mini-rugby in Bective.

Religion was a significant part of life in St Mary's, too. There was an optional mass before school, which we'd always attend on the mornings of cup matches. Sometimes I'd be altar boy. Richie would always be there. He'd never begin class without first blessing himself and then saying a Hail Mary, an Our Father or a Come O Holy Ghost:

Come o Holy Ghost, fill the hearts of thy faithful and kindle in them the fire of thy love. Send forth thy Spirit and they shall be created. And You shall renew the face of the earth. Amen.

My Leinster and Ireland team-mates probably don't realize that I used to say those three prayers in the dressing room, just before we'd huddle up. Or that I used to go to mass on the eve of Test matches in Dublin. I'd slip out of the Shelbourne Hotel and head down to St Teresa's Church on Clarendon Street. It's not a superstition, and it's not a case of praying that I win the man-of-the-match award. It's just part of who I am. I believe. I have faith.

Occasionally Richie prayed for something rugby-related. In 2009, I was cited for kicking Munster's Lifeimi Mafi during a Magners League game in Thomond Park. When I mentioned to Richie that I was in danger of suspension, he said he'd light a few candles in the church in Rathfarnham. I still got a two-week suspension, but Richie did his best for me. As ever.

Mary's U-13s winning the 1999 Provincial Cup had very little to do with divine inspiration. We just had a great team and were very well prepared.

I was now playing out-half and was team captain. We trained Tuesdays and Thursdays after school in Kenilworth Square, a beautiful park with three pitches, set into a square of Victorian red-bricked houses. We had matches on Wednesdays or Saturdays – sometimes both – and maybe circuit training on a Monday.

The front pitch would be jammed at lunchtime, but Father McNulty arranged handling drills in the gap between the junior school and the 'military wall' – St Mary's is located next to an army barracks.

Hands towards the passer, fingers spread, hips square, take and give.

Do twenty minutes of this three or four times a week, and over the course of a school year it adds up to a fair bit of skill acquisition.

Then there were all the ball-hours we spent in the school yard. Rugby balls only – cheap, hard and plastic, but they lasted. Soccer balls were confiscated by the rugby coaches. I was usually in by 8 o'clock, so that was an hour's tip rugby before the bell to start classes. We broke at 11 o'clock for fifteen minutes so you could squeeze a game in then, too.

Richie was all about developing our skills, and in this he was ahead of his time. He was also very accessible. You'd run up to him in the corridor between classes with an idea for a new play, something you'd seen on TV, and even in the mad rush of a school day he'd always give you his time.

He didn't do it all alone. Once a week, the backs were coached by Paul Andreucetti, a former Leinster and Ireland player whose son John was in the team, and Father McNulty was also involved. Coming close to league matches, a couple of the seniors would help out, too, which was a big deal. As in all good coaching set-ups, we even had a video analyst, which means that our victory over Willow Park in the final at Templeville – the home of St Mary's College RFC – was recorded for posterity.

I still have the DVD. The quality of the sound and the picture is poor, but not the quality of the rugby. It was a great game. Willow went in front just after half-time, against the run of play. I had a mix-up with my scrum-half, Brian McDermott, off a scrum near our line. You can see how furious I was.

We kept playing, and eventually scored a peach of a try by our full-back, Killian Browne, which showed the benefits of all those lunchtime handling drills behind the military wall:

the move involved five or six perfectly timed passes. The try prompted a massive pitch invasion from the Mary's supporters. We won 8–5.

Looking back at the DVD, I see a happy kid, in his element. When the ref blew for full-time my first instinct had been to find Richie. I sprinted almost the entire width of the pitch and jumped on to him, wrapping my arms and legs around him and squeezing hard.

The balcony outside the Mary's clubhouse bar was the perfect platform for the presentation ceremony – all of us walking up the steps of the terrace, through the crowd of supporters, to accept our medals. Mercifully, the winning captain wasn't expected to make a speech. I just smiled sheepishly and held the trophy aloft. In the dressing room we sprayed each other with cans of fizzy orange and the famous stick of rock was finally unwrapped. Lovely memories.

My folks were delighted, naturally. Work commitments must surely have prevented Dad from getting to a few matches during my school days, but in my memory he was always on the touchline, home or away, usually wound up to 90. He says he has always been nervous watching any of his sons play. He's calmed down a bit in recent years, but not entirely.

You can hear Dad's voice on that DVD of the Under-13s final, during a tense second half. I'm down on one knee, winded, when he shouts: 'Get up, Jonathan!' I jump back to my feet immediately. It's hilarious.

I'm sure there were loads of times when Dad wanted to intervene during games or training. He was a coach, after all. Only once can I remember him getting narky from the sideline. Father Flavin used to lose the rag with us occasionally, and for a priest he could use fairly colourful language. One day, Dad just told him to shut up, that he couldn't be talking to us like that. And that was that.

If Dad was a constant presence at rugby matches, Mum encouraged other sporting interests. Being the daughter of John Nestor made it easy for her to get me into Milltown Golf Club as a junior member. But when it came to summer sports, tennis took nearly all of my attention. It's hardly surprising, given that Rathgar Tennis Club was literally twenty metres from our back gate.

During the summer holidays, if we weren't down in Kerry, Mark and I could be found in the tennis club from nine in the morning until nine at night, sometimes later. It wasn't a huge club, just ten courts and a small clubhouse. But there were loads of kids, and tennis took up only a portion of the time.

We'd play Manhunt in the woods behind the courts, using our racquets to ping each other with acorns. If we were wanted at home for dinner, Dad would come to the back gate and whistle for us. One whistle was all it took and we'd drop whatever we were doing.

Mark and I were decent tennis players. In fact, for a while I was more obsessed with tennis than with rugby. At thirteen, I was selected for a Leinster panel which meant attending training sessions on Tuesday and Thursday evenings.

I was picked for an academy down in Tipperary, where we stayed in a convent. Up at seven for two hours' hitting before breakfast – not quite the Nick Bollettieri Academy but intense enough. And of course there were ranking tournaments up and down the country.

The biggest of those was the All-Ireland at the Fitzwilliam club in Dublin, not far from home. You had to apply for entry, write out all your results for the year and post it to the Irish Lawn Tennis Association, and if they met certain criteria, you were invited. I was seeded – one of the top sixteen players in the country in my age group. I was knocked out in the early rounds.

Mum didn't just drive me everywhere. She watched every point. Tennis is still her favourite sport. I can still be drawn in by it if I see a good match on the TV. My only problem with the sport back in my teens was the amount of cheating that went on at age-grade tournaments.

You couldn't always be guaranteed an official umpire down the levels and you'd often get parents acting as line judges in games involving their own children. Sometimes it seemed as if their eyesight was affected by the strength of their desire to see their offspring succeed.

It got to the stage where it felt like you had to keep your shots at least a metre inside the line to avoid being called out. There were dodgy calls all the time. It used to drive me nuts.

Mark couldn't handle it at all. At one tournament he just smashed his racquet off the court, hurled some abuse at the offending mum and stormed off. I'd manage to keep a lid on things for the most part, but there's only so much you can take.

The final straw for me was at a tournament in Naas – the fifth major, as we used to call it. I got to the boys' U-13 final. Both Mum and Dad came along for this one. And I was killing it. I won the first set six games to love and was well ahead in the second set when my opponent – I won't name him – started crying and told the umpire he needed to take a break.

He left the court for fifteen or twenty minutes and went into the bathroom where his mum, his dad and his coach tried to calm him down. Meanwhile, I was left out on the court, twiddling my thumbs.

If that toilet break was a desperate attempt to break my momentum, it worked. After all that time spent waiting out on court, I lost my rhythm, lost the next couple of games and then lost the match. A remarkable comeback – or gamesmanship?

I was inconsolable. As runner-up I was presented with an alarm clock. Cheers. Experiences like that test your love for a sport.

Tennis did at least introduce me to someone important. One day during the summer holidays when I was ten, these twin sisters turned up at the club in Rathgar. Identical twins, good tennis players, too. We had a mini-tournament that day and the twins ended up playing each other in the girls' final. I got roped into keeping score and manning the scoreboard. I'm still not sure if this was by accident or design.

It turned out to be hard work. The only way to differentiate between the girls was that one of them was wearing a head-band. They decided not to swap ends, to make it less confusing, but even so I got distracted and lost concentration.

'Sorry, but which one of you won that last point?' I asked the one at my end of the court, the one with the headband.

'I did,' she said. 'I'm Laura.'

3

I don't remember when it first hit me that Mum and Dad were breaking up. It was more of a gradual awareness – a cooling in the atmosphere in the house, fewer occasions when you'd see the two of them together outside the home. For most of my teens and indeed well into my adult life, they lived under the same roof yet lived separate lives.

It's hard to articulate how this made me feel growing up. I still don't feel comfortable talking about it. It was never spoken about – a silent separation, an unspoken rift.

In one sense, I wanted it that way. I knew that things weren't good between my folks but I didn't want to bring up the subject for fear of forcing the issue, of bringing matters to a head. I hoped things would just sort themselves out.

I didn't talk to my siblings about it because I was pretty sure they didn't suspect anything and therefore I wanted to protect them. So I lugged this sadness around with me, sharing it with no one, putting on a brave face, bottling it up.

And things continued that way for a long time. It was only years later, in my late twenties, when I was about to leave Ireland and join French club Racing Metro, that everything came out into the open.

As I'd suspected, my parents' reasons for continuing to live under the same roof for all those years had been similar to those of a lot of couples enduring difficult marriages. They simply couldn't afford to be living apart, not with four kids in private education. It was less expensive and logistically easier to stay in one location, and less traumatic for the children than splitting up completely. They did it for us. Living in the same house meant that they could maintain the appearance of a normal family life.

They'd kept this up for many years, but now there was no longer any need. Jerry Jr, the youngest, was leaving the nest – also heading to France, for a contract with Auch. There was no need for Mum and Dad to remain in the same place any longer, so they told the four of us that they were getting a divorce.

One attraction of going to Racing was that it meant I would be distracted by a new environment, new people. I remember confiding this to Joe Schmidt when he was trying to convince me to stay in Ireland. I told him that I didn't want to have to deal with my folks' separation.

It was a bit selfish of me, leaving Mark, Gillian and Jerry to deal with the emotional fallout, but going to Racing was my means of escape. It suited me to be away for a couple of years.

Mum and Dad settled everything out of court, so it was amicable enough. Mum kept the house in Rathgar and Dad went to live in Listowel. The funny thing is that they get on much better now, when they see each other. Mum keeps in contact with a lot of her former in-laws in Kerry. Dad usually comes up to Dublin for Christmas and everyone gets on well.

I respect their decision to continue living in the same house for so long. It was a sacrifice they made for us. But during those years I knew something wasn't right. Naturally, I felt the need to blame someone and Mum was the obvious target. Why? Well, it's not like I was going to have a go at Dad. I hero-worshipped him. I'd spent all that time with him growing up, going to and from Donnybrook or Glenamuck, all those road trips, all those evenings spent together watching Man U on TV. I didn't want to annoy or upset him.

It was different with Mum, who used to get emotional. According to my naive view of the world, your mum was supposed to be the one who provides you with emotional support, not the one who needs support herself. So I was often impatient with her, intolerant, difficult. One day Richie Hughes took me aside in the school corridor and asked me, in the nicest way possible, to give my mother a break. He didn't want to interfere, but my mum was at her wits' end, he said. She'd gone to him almost in tears, explaining that whenever she tried to talk to me, I'd bite the head off her.

'Cut her some slack, Jono,' Richie said. 'She's your mum. She wants the best for you. She'd go to the end of the earth for you. Don't be so short with her.'

I told him I'd do my best, but his pleadings went in one ear and out the other. I'd probably decided that Mum was to blame for what was going on between her and Dad. I can be pretty black and white like that. I was unlikely to find fault with my dad, not when I craved his approval so deeply.

It's a powerful motivation, the desire for acknowledgement from the most important role model in your life.

In your teens, you seek acknowledgement for sporting achievements wherever you can get them – from coaches, peers, occasionally from newspapers. The morning after Schools Cup matches I'd duck into the newsagent's beside Mary's to make sure that the three-paragraph reports in the *Irish Independent* and *Irish Times* mentioned the penalty and conversion by J. Sexton.

Years later, when I was an established international, I still yearned for positive feedback. Everyone does. And Dad's approval was what I longed for most, not just in my teens. Even now, I still like getting his approval.

You'd think we didn't already get enough feedback from coaches and video analysts. There is loads of it, highly detailed and perfectly packaged for easy assimilation. The problem is you usually have to wait around thirty-six hours after the game. The time in between can be a bit of a vacuum.

Your team-mates don't really fill it for you. They've got their own stuff going on. So you might end up watching the tape on the night of the game, filling the sleepless hours when your body is exhausted but your brain is still buzzing.

I've stopped that now but earlier in my career, I would stay up late after games, remote in hand, re-living every moment, agonizing over mistakes, hanging on every word of praise or criticism from TV pundits and commentators.

Dad's reactions were the ones I sought first, though. Over the years, he was the first person I rang after games, often before we had even left the stadium.

He is rarely one to gush on the good days, but that's fine. I know when I have played well. But it's funny, if I'd kicked nine out of ten, Dad would always ask me about the one I missed!

'Well done, great match. [*Pause.*] Pity about the one you missed in the second half. What happened there?'

He would have been genuinely curious to know. Had the wind gusted? Did I lose my footing? But that one niggly negative – a missed line-kick, a tactical decision that back-fired, a short-range penalty that slid wide of the upright – is what would lodge itself inside my head for the rest of the evening, for the rest of the weekend.

Occasionally when I'd call him, I'd go straight to the

negative, like I was grasping the nettle. Or maybe I was just hoping he'd say: 'Ah, Jonathan, you were great. Forget that one mistake. You did thirty-five or forty really positive things in the game. Focus on them.'

But it was Laura who was and still is best at providing reassurance. Women are probably better at positive psychology. At this stage, she understands the game pretty well, too. More importantly, she knows me, so she can choose not just what to say but how to say it. My brother Mark was also someone I leaned heavily on, particularly in later years.

In Dad's defence, his post-match feedback got better over the years. I suspect he dipped into a couple of the sports psychology books that I'd have lying around at home. But when I was younger, he didn't give praise easily.

In one sense, I should thank him. He turned me into a perfectionist, forever chasing the spotless performance, that game where you can walk off at the end and say: *I've nothing to think about*. Of course, that game doesn't exist.

Being a perfectionist became my biggest strength as a rugby player and also, for a time, my biggest flaw. I eventually got better at ignoring my mistakes, but for most of my career, errors would infuriate me.

It meant I never got complacent. I'd always have something driving me – that desire to make up for a mistake. It's an addictive way of thinking and of course, it's highly stressful. That way of thinking can fry your brain.

Dad's words carried the most weight because he had watched me play more than anyone else, had been there since the start. He set the ground rules, which can be crystallized into five words: *You always try your best*.

This wasn't difficult to carry out, as I was naturally

competitive. There was only one occasion when he took issue with my on-field attitude.

I was in fifth year, chasing a spot on the Leinster Schools team. We had a 'friendly' away to Blackrock College on a Saturday morning. I remember feeling uber-confident going into the game.

The previous Wednesday I'd played a stormer in a Leinster final trial in Terenure College, scoring a couple of tries and kicking well. I reckoned I was a shoo-in for selection and was probably a bit casual going into the game against 'Rock. I made a few mistakes, and when the game began to get away from us I started snapping at my team-mates. I was still giving out about them when I got into Dad's car to head home.

He was having none of it.

'You were the problem today, Jonathan. No one else,' he said. 'You have a good game in the trial and suddenly you think you're God's gift?'

His words hit me much harder than any slap. They stung me into complete silence for the rest of the journey home, partly because it was the first time he'd had a go at me but mainly because I had no answer to them.

He was right. My attitude had been poor. I'd made the mistake of resting on my laurels, and then blaming others for my mistakes.

Dad explained that it's different in a trial match when you're generally surrounded by a better class of player. On your own school team, there was a responsibility on my shoulders to lead by example, to raise standards, to instil belief, but I'd copped out a bit. I had no answer to this because I knew it was true.

My mum wasn't capable of such brutal honesty. She is

Dad's opposite in many ways. Say we were coming home from a tennis tournament in Fitzwilliam where I'd just been stuffed 6–2, 6–0. Mum would try and soften the blow: 'You gave it your best shot, love.' I'd be having none of that.

'Shut up, Mum, will you?'

I didn't want pity. It was no use to anyone. She was doing her best to reassure me, but I didn't want it from her. Subconsciously, I was blaming her for the situation at home.

My solution to that situation was often just to escape. By now I had the attic to myself, but the easiest place to go was to Laura's, about a five-minute cycle away in Rathfarnham.

Laura and I hit it off from that first day at the tennis club. We just got on really well together. We were both sporty, both hated losing. In her case, it probably had something to do with being a twin. She and Cathy could be fiercely competitive as well as fiercely supportive of each other.

Laura was into different sports – tennis, basketball. She lost it one day when I outdid her at basketball – 'her' sport, or so she thought, seeing as there was a basket at the back of the Priestleys' house. This was our first row and it happened in an amusement arcade after a cinema date in the city centre. We were just taking shots at a hoop, keeping score, when I started winding her up – sledging her, basically.

'The pressure's on Priestley now. Can she handle it?'

It worked. I beat her, probably for the first time ever, and I was pretty smug about it. It drove her nuts. She stormed off down O'Connell Street in a serious strop.

Opposites attract? Not necessarily. Laura and I are both worriers, both stressers. The difference is in the way that we handle stress.

Typically I'll bottle it up. I can sit in silence, pretending to watch television, while my brain is whirring away about some injury, some work-related issue.

Laura will talk about whatever's on her mind, put it out there, which is clearly a healthier option. If we've had a disagreement, she can't sleep on it. I can let things fester, but she wants to have cleared the air.

Neither of us are extroverts. I remember shyness on both sides at first. What attracted me to Laura first was her warmth, her generosity. Whatever pocket money I had was usually pilfered from Dad's golf bag or Mum's wallet – tips from the hair salon she might have forgotten about. Laura always offered to pay for things.

Our tastes weren't very expensive. There was enough fun to be had just hanging out behind the clubhouse in the tennis club. As we moved towards our teens the games of Manhunt were replaced by Truth or Dare and Spin the Bottle.

We became proper boyfriend and girlfriend in our mid-teens. Before that there was a period of maybe twelve to eighteen months where we kind of drifted apart. Laura's a year older than me and was a year ahead of me in school. Socially we just seemed to stay in our own age groups for a while. But I was friendly with her brother, Owen, and we were always likely to see each other in the club during the summer. Sport brought us back together, I guess.

Her home life was so different to mine. Her mum and dad seemed to do everything together. It was an even busier house, with five children in total, but they always dined together. Space was always made for me at the dinner table and there was a spare room if I was staying over at weekends. I was treated as part of the family. I was expected to clean up after myself, load the washing machine when necessary.

With Laura's help, I did pretty well academically. But I

couldn't have been described as a model student. I never got into any serious trouble, but I was a bit lippy to certain teachers at times, especially female teachers. My relationships with them were never strong.

Richie Hughes had to give out to me for being mouthy in second-year English class. Typically he did it without raising his voice or losing his temper.

'Jono, go out and take a walk,' he said. 'Go to the end of the corridor and get a drink of water and come back when you're ready.' I did as I was told. Mortified.

Rugby was a release, but it was also the cause of niggles and occasional flare-ups in school. At the start of second year, Dave Breslin asked me to train with the boys in the year ahead of me – the Junior Cup Team, or JCT, or just 'the Js'. The big time, in other words. I was still a titch, so he moved me to scrum-half. This seemed to annoy one of my best friends, Brian McDermott.

Brian and I were close. At one stage we were going out with girls who were sisters. But now I'd given him a reason to be annoyed – not just jumping a year ahead but jumping into his position, too. He didn't talk to me for ages. Then one day, I literally bumped into him in the corridor outside the school church.

It was one of those situations where you've just broken up a bitching session – and you can tell that they've been bitching about you. Someone then pushed me into Brian and suddenly it's a fully fledged fist fight, one on one.

I would never have shown that side of myself until I got pushed into it – but I was happy enough with how I handled myself. The only problem was that one of my punches connected with one of those old cast-iron radiators. This meant I had to miss a match. It was only a friendly, but still a match for the Js. When Father Flavin asked me how I'd hurt myself, I told him we'd just been playing ball in the corridor. He looked at me sceptically.

Brian and I stuck to the same story when we were called separately into the dean's office. Life went on. Brian was soon talking to me again. It may have had something to do with the fact that Dave Breslin had started picking me at 10.

Many years later, England coach Eddie Jones would make a cheap remark about my parents fearing for my safety on the rugby pitch. I'm sure Mum was worried for me during my first season on the Js.

I was still tiny when I was fourteen, so tiny that Dave had to find ways to protect me from bigger opponents like Kevin McLaughlin – a very old pal from the Kildare Place soccer team but now a strapping number 8 for Gonzaga.

Kev's plan was simple: pick from the base of the scrum and run over me, flatten me into the muck. But we were ready. Just as the two packs were engaging, I would exchange places with our own big number 8, Paul Nash, at the back of the scrum. Try and picture the puzzled look on Kev's face as he finds Nasher, and not me, waiting for him.

Having a tiny little thing at fly-half was a sure sign that the 1999/2000 Js were an ordinary enough vintage. We lost more matches than we won in the build-up to the Cup, which always began in early February. No one predicted us getting beyond the first round, seeing as we were up against Terenure, the Cup favourites, in Donnybrook. But Dave had us well prepared, physically and mentally, making sure we understood the history between two schools that were only a couple of miles apart geographically but separated by a rivalry going back decades.

I didn't need any motivating. I became obsessive about this game. Walking to school in the mornings, I'd decide that if I successfully avoided all lines and cracks on the footpath, we would win. When we heard that Ireland international Denis Hickie would be presenting us with our match jerseys, the excitement verged on unbearable.

We were given new shorts, socks and jerseys, with the inscription stitched on the breast: St Mary's College JCT, 2000. I remember the pure whiteness of the number 10 against the blue fabric. Dave instructed us to polish our boots until we could see our reflection in them.

We won, 17–6. 'St Mary's hold on to win thriller' ran the headline on a three-paragraph report in the *Irish Times*. I even got a mention: 'St Mary's put themselves in pole position with an early try by centre Stephen Grissing, after a speedy break by scrum-half Conor Lane and excellent follow-up by out-half Jonathan Sexton.'

This, I could get used to.

Winning was good for popularity, I soon found. A successful cup run usually means time off class for supporters, and we were providing more of that than Shane Jennings's seniors. We went all the way to the semi-final, where we were narrowly beaten by a strong St Michael's side. I remember the emotion of the final whistle, the tears and also the sympathetic hugs of our supporters – there were still pitch invasions in those days.

The Schools Cups have come in for some criticism over the years. Some people feel all the media coverage puts undue pressure on youngsters. Knockout rugby supposedly forces coaches to go for safety-first rugby at the expense of skill development. It's supposedly unfair on those kids who spend all season building up to the cup only to have their dreams crushed in the first round.

All I know is that the cup competitions create strong memories and lasting friendships for lots of the participants. So many of my team-mates at Leinster and Ireland over the years went through the Schools Cup system and can recall their cup experiences in vivid detail.

I had five years of Schools Cup rugby between juniors and seniors – six, if you count the Under-13s Provincial Cup. Those games sharpen your wits, teach you how to work your way around a rugby pitch. Irish rugby has done pretty well out of that system, when you think about it.

Donnybrook continued to be a home from home, even after I'd started going to school in Mary's. There was work to be had in Bective for a thirteen- or fourteen-year-old.

On Sunday mornings after an AIL match, I'd be rooting through bins of empty bottles, arranging them in trays and getting paid £1 per tray returned. On Friday and Saturday evenings I'd be busy collecting glasses – very busy if Leinster were playing in the Heineken Cup. Their crowds were beginning to grow in size. Typically, I'd work before the game, then go and watch with my dad on the terrace until five minutes before the final whistle, when I'd be needed back in the bar.

Leinster were only beginning to get their act together in those days so it wasn't like I was a huge supporter. I remember them beating Leicester, also Toulouse, but they were inconsistent, unreliable.

They had some fantastic young outside backs, of course. I remember clearly the excitement in the Milltown Golf Club bar on the Sunday afternoon that Brian O'Driscoll scored his hat-trick of tries against France.

As well as Brian, Leinster had Denis Hickie, Shane Horgan and Gordon D'Arcy – big backline talents making a name for themselves. When they got some ball, these guys were good to watch. They just didn't have an out-half I could really identify with, mainly because their out-half kept changing.

Munster had Ronan O'Gara, Ulster had David Humphreys, Connacht had Eric Elwood. With Leinster, you could take your pick. One week it was Emmet Farrell, then Mark McHugh, then Andy Dunne, then Simon Broughton, then Eddie Hekenui, then Nathan Spooner and so on.

Humphreys had won a European Cup with Ulster, but O'Gara was the 10 I looked up to most. Probably because my dad was always going on about him. He was a massive Munster fan. (He does come from Kerry, even if he's lived over half his life in Dublin.) He'd pop down to Donnybrook to watch Leinster, but he'd follow Munster anywhere and everywhere.

If he wasn't down in Thomond Park on a Heineken Cup Saturday, he was somewhere in the South of France. When he finally made it home, he'd be full of chat about who'd done what. In his match reports, O'Gara always seemed to be the hero.

Everyone loved Munster back then. How could you hate them? They were giant-killers, out to conquer Europe. The same spring that Mary's juniors went on that cup run to the semi-final, Munster were marching towards a Heineken Cup final at Twickenham, where they lost by a point to Northampton. You could see how devastated they were to lose, see the connection between team and supporters.

Dad was there that day, just as he was at the final in Cardiff two years later when they lost to Leicester. I watched all those games on TV, and rooted for Munster. Of course I did. Wasn't I half-Kerryman? I assumed every Irish rugby fan was rooting for them back then.

O'Gara was an obvious focal point for me, too. Just as he was seen as a brilliant tactical kicker, I would have been seen as a kicking 10 at school. I was soon able to get some distance on my kicks, too. In the summer between second and third year – the summer of my fifteenth birthday – I grew by about six inches.

That was the season when I was first selected for a Leinster summer camp. One of the kids who stood out from the very first drill was a kid from Clongowes called Rob Kearney, who turned up wearing a Queensland jersey that had once been worn by the legendary John Eales. It turned out that Rob's folks were friendly with the parents of Joe Roff, another Australian legend, and Rob used to get sackfuls of kit sent over.

I got on well with Rob. We used to hang around Donnybrook after those sessions. But I was dead jealous of his kit.

This was 2001, the summer that the Lions toured Australia. I watched bits of it from a golf resort in La Manga. We'd stayed with friends in Spain the previous year, but this was plush. The salon must have been doing well, and Dad had started a new job closer to home, so he no longer had that early morning commute across town.

La Manga is lovely. Every second morning Dad would take me and Mark out on one of the courses while Mum minded Gillian and Jerry by the pool. It should have been brilliant, but I don't remember it being a very relaxing experience.

This was around the time of my sixteenth birthday, so I probably thought I was too cool to be hanging around with Mark. We were always at each other's throats. Even when we were getting on, we were causing chaos for others, bombing into the pool, making too much noise. I was in that difficult stage – old enough to babysit, because I remember Mum and Dad leaving me in charge on the odd night when they'd go out together.

They say that family holidays are important because the memories are so strong. La Manga stands out, but only because it was different from the happier trips to Ballybunion of my childhood. It was also our last time to go away as a family.

4

Joan Manning was losing it with fifth-year French. It was probably tough enough teaching the subjunctive without having me disrupting the class. Every time she turned to explain a verb ending on the whiteboard, I'd flick the projector switch off with my foot. Cue laughter. Cue long-suffering sigh from Ms Manning as she came down to switch the machine back on. Again.

It was childish behaviour, I'll admit. But things had never been particularly good between myself and Joan.

Eventually, after maybe the third false start, she caught me in the act of kicking the switch.

'I suppose you think that's funny, Jonathan?'

'Yeah, I do, actually.'

So she told me to take my sense of humour elsewhere. I wasn't welcome in her French class. So that was it – my first red card. And it wasn't like I could just switch teachers. There was only one fifth-year class for honours French.

Dad wasn't best pleased when I explained the situation. I told him not to worry. I could switch to home economics. It was supposedly fairly easy. But he was having none of it.

I was fortunate that if I had any troubles at St Mary's, I could take them to Brian Wall. He was dean of studies for fourth-, fifth- and sixth-year boys, guidance counsellor, and also an excellent teacher of chemistry and maths. I was in his class for both, so I saw a lot of him. He somehow found time to teach in the Institute of Education, a kind of upmarket cramming college in town with a reputation for providing high-quality notes on each subject. Brian used to slip me his Institute chemistry notes on the quiet.

He was a thoughtful guy, a good listener, a good advice-giver. Do the right thing – that was his mantra. It wasn't unlike Dad's refrain: If you are going to do something then you do it properly.

Clearly I hadn't done the right thing in Ms Manning's class, but Brian gave me a sympathetic hearing. I suspect Mum had asked him to keep a special eye on me, maybe tipped him off about the situation at home, because he was always helpful and encouraging. Occasionally he'd politely ask how things were at home, but I'd never open up and he'd respect my privacy.

It wasn't an easy time, but I was fortunate that I really liked Mary's as a school. I liked the intimacy of it, the fact that everyone knew everyone. No one could get lost. I had a tight-knit bunch of friends in my own year, and then there was the wider rugby circle.

Brian impressed upon me the value of channelling my mental and physical energies positively – into study and rugby, basically. You have brains, he'd tell me. Yes, you can play rugby, but you should aim high academically.

This actually suited me. I needed a focus, a distraction. Besides, I knew I'd need to do a good Leaving. I'd decided that I was going to be a doctor.

As a kid, whenever I was taken to visit someone in hospital, I always enjoyed snooping around the wards. My favourite TV programme at the time was *ER*. Later, whenever I was injured through rugby, I was always quizzing my doctors about things. I'd look at scans with them, ask about ways of accelerating the healing process.

What really pointed me towards medicine, however, was the work experience I did in Transition Year with an orthopaedic surgeon, Dr David Moore, an old friend of Dad's from school. Every morning David would pick me up from the house at 6 o'clock and drive into St James's Hospital, where we'd scrub up and go into surgery. I'd get to watch him do all sorts of operations. I was fascinated.

To get a place in medicine required an excellent Leaving Cert, but I reckoned it was within my capabilities. With Laura's help, I'd done a decent Junior Cert – three As and seven Bs, which I was very happy with. I'd been determined to please my parents.

Dad liked the idea of me studying medicine. He was ambitious for me rugby-wise but he wasn't convinced about me putting all my eggs in the pro-rugby basket.

This was the early noughties, still only a few years into the professional era. From what he'd heard, only a couple of players were on decent money – Brian O'Driscoll, maybe Keith Wood. And it was a short career. You can't just be a rugby player, Dad said. You'll need something else.

Rugby was a bit frustrating that season. I had my heart set on being out-half on what was a strong senior team, with a dozen players back from the previous season, most of them now in their final year. These were guys I had looked up to, but I didn't let that show. When I was invited along to training in early season, I wanted to make it look like I belonged so I was vocal, confident – probably too confident for some people's liking. If you want to be the playmaker on the team, you have to behave like one.

I made a good impression in the friendly games I played that season, but when it came to the Cup, there was always the possibility that if it was a tight selection call between a sixth-year boy and someone two years below him, then the sixth-year – in this case, a guy called Joey Connolly – would get the nod. I get that now. I wasn't so understanding at the time.

The bit I found really hard to take was that we drew Terenure in the first round and they had a guy called Conor Gildea starting at 10 for them. Gildea was said to be the next big thing – my supposed mates were always going on about how brilliant he was, just to wind me up. I was dying to have a crack off him. But on this occasion, I just had to stick on my tracksuit and suck it up.

At least we smashed them, and I got on the pitch at the end. Dave Breslin, now coaching the SCT with former Ireland full-back Rodney O'Donnell, brought me on with a minute to go.

It was the same next round, when we beat Clongowes, again fairly comfortably, and in the quarters against Blackrock. I got a couple of minutes off the bench on both occasions. My big chance came in the semi-final, against Castleknock, when Joey got injured after about twenty minutes. And I took my chance.

We won 34–7 and I had a stormer. Castleknock's coach, the former Ireland out-half Mick Quinn, came up to me afterwards, shook my hand and said I'd played brilliantly.

The next morning, I went straight to the Spar on the Rathmines Road to see if the papers had given me a good mention. They had.

I floated into school, pretty much convinced of two things: first, we were favourites to beat Belvedere in the final, on St Patrick's Day at Lansdowne Road; second, I should be the starting out-half. My dad had told me as much, and so had Mick Quinn.

The coaches didn't agree, and Joey got the nod. I had to hide my disappointment, simple as that. I had to see the bigger picture. I'd have two more bites at playing in this competition, in fifth and sixth year.

I was still going to be involved in a game at Lansdowne Road, sitting in the same dressing room that O'Driscoll had been sitting in the previous week with Ireland during the Six Nations. I might even get to contribute.

A storm blew in the night before – I think the meteorologists may even have given the storm a name – and the weather was horrendous. I was completely relaxed on the morning of the game, because the word was that it would have to be postponed. There's no way that game will be played, Dad said. You couldn't put kids out in that.

They did. When we turned up at the stadium, the corner flags were virtually horizontal, the temperature was Arctic, the rain torrential. But there was no talk of a postponement. Ireland were playing there a week later and the pitch would need time to recover. We were going ahead. By the end of the warm-up, our tracksuits were absolutely drenched.

It was never likely to be a high-scoring game. In fact there was only one try – by Joey Connolly! He aquaplaned over about five minutes into the game.

The positive bit was that we were 7–6 ahead at the break, despite having played into the gale. The negative was that I was stuck on the bench, trembling in my wet tracksuit, teeth chattering. For company, I had Ian O'Herlihy, who actually had more reason to feel sorry for himself. Ian was in sixth year and he'd been dropped to the bench after the first-round win. This was his last match as a schoolboy and, like me, he was desperate to get on.

With about ten minutes to go, Mary's were still leading

7–6. Myself and Ian could see that Joey was struggling with a calf injury.

I'm going to come on here and kick the drop-goal that puts us 4 points clear, says Ian.

No, if anyone's kicking a drop-goal here, it's me, I replied.

Jono, if you drop a goal here, I'll kiss your ass. Literally. In the shower, before the whole squad.

Deal.

Two minutes later, I get the nod from Rodney. Joey's calf's gone. You're on, Jono.

The footage can be found online. The picture is wobbly, for the simple reason that the cameraman was struggling to hold his camera still in the wind. You see me running on, shoulders slightly hunched against the elements, number 16 shirt billowing.

I receive low-fives from the centres, Michael Finlay and Michael Ryan. Mary's were on the attack, wind-assisted, with four minutes remaining, still only a point ahead. How about a drop-goal, Jono?

Had I prepared for this? Not in a formal training context. But I'd seen all the great drop-goals on video: Joel Stransky in the 1995 World Cup final, Jerry Guscott for the 1997 Lions, Michael Kiernan against England in 1985, the year I was born, on the same pitch into the same end. I'd kicked one for the Under-13s – against St Michael's on the top pitch in Kenilworth. I can still see the ball flying between the posts and into the old elm trees.

With a drop-goal, there's less pressure than a penalty, as it's open play, on the run. So I was relatively relaxed as the forwards punched the ball up off a lineout, setting up a ruck on the 22, dead in front of the posts at the Havelock Square end. Scrum-half Simon Gibney had to pass the ball back into the wind, meaning I had to stoop to catch it about six inches off the sodden turf – not the worst thing in this instance as there's smaller margin for error with the 'drop' part of the drop-kick. I connected cleanly and it flew straight – not particularly high but high enough – between the posts and into the empty terrace. Boom.

Individual celebrations weren't really the done thing in rugby in 2002 but I couldn't resist a clenched fist to the Mary's supporters as I ran back for the restart. Only a few minutes to survive now.

People who were watching from the stand tell me there were repeated requests on the public address system, pleading with supporters to stay off the pitch after the game. Ireland were playing Italy the following Saturday and the playing surface needed to be protected.

Those requests fell on deaf ears. When referee Alain Rolland blew the final whistle, we were engulfed, hoisted on to shoulders. Through the mayhem came Mark, my brother. He was ecstatic. He hugged me and shouted: 'You're a legend now! You're a legend!'

Looking back, I'm not sure I really appreciated the moment, or took it all in. There was barely a second to stop and reflect, from the cup presentation to the crowded dressing room to the official reception back in Mary's with the whole school cheering us on stage and the place decked out in blue and white and everyone's parents and siblings there. It was all a bit of a noisy, happy blur.

I didn't forget Ian O'Herlihy's promise, though. I held him to his word.

Winning the Schools Cup brought rewards. We were invited to take part in an international schools tournament in Japan the following month. The principal decided that the squad should be made up of boys from fourth and fifth year, as the sixth years needed to concentrate on preparing for their Leaving Cert. Those poor lads missed a great trip.

We stayed in a boarding school in Fukuoka, thirty of us in one small, sweltering dorm, squeezed into triple bunk beds. The very morning we arrived, we were sent out against an enormous side from Wesley College, Auckland. Some of those guys had beards. They gave us a good hammering. We ended up winning something called the Consolation Cup.

We weren't the only Irish visitors to Japan in 2002. This was the summer of Saipan. Like a lot of families in Ireland, the Sexton household was divided on the issue of Roy Keane and his row with the Republic of Ireland manager, Mick McCarthy. You couldn't sit on the fence on this one. It was civil war.

I was on the side of Roy, unequivocally so. By now he was my favourite United player, not just because he was Irish and because he was club captain but because of one incredible performance, in the Champions League semi-final second leg away to Juventus in 1999: the year of the Treble. I'd watched it on my own, on the TV in my parents' bedroom.

I remember going nuts with excitement as United came from 2–0 down to win 3–2, with Keane completely dominating midfield. And the most admirable thing of all? Keane knew from early enough in the game that he wouldn't be playing in the final, having been yellow-carded for a lunge on Zinedine Zidane. That made his performance even more heroic. Now here was a team player.

Yet three years later on, he was being criticized for being selfish, for putting himself before the Ireland team. I argued that Keane was right to stand up for his belief that an international team going to a World Cup should expect the best preparation possible. I admired the way he had the courage of his convictions. Dad wasn't having any of it. He may have been a big Man U fan – and a big Keane fan – but he was firmly in the McCarthy camp on this one.

'It doesn't matter what Roy's pissed off about,' he said at the dinner table. 'You don't walk out on your national team. Your country comes first!'

That was the summer of my seventeenth birthday. My ambition for the following rugby season was to be selected for the Irish Schools side. It would be my last chance at it, as I'd be overage in my final school year, according to the regulations that were in place at the time.

The Irish Schools team played all their big matches towards the end of the season, after the cup campaigns. But you really needed to make your mark in October, with your provincial side. A good interpro series would get you into the 'Probables' side for the all-important final trial around Christmas time. Get on the Probables and the job was half-done. So the theory went, anyway.

I got the first few steps right. I played well in the Leinster trials, was selected for a trip to play Leicester and Yorkshire in November, then started in the victory over Ulster in Donnybrook. We didn't play particularly well but I reckoned I had a good chance of making the Probables if I could put in a decent performance against Munster.

The training session on the eve of the game was going well until I tried to run a switch with a team-mate and he accidentally stood on my ankle, wrecking ligaments. His name was George Byron, from St Michael's. Certain details stay with you.

That put me out of the Munster game. I was replaced by Fergal Lawlor, from Roscrea. He took his chance well, and Leinster won easily in Cork. I feared the worst.

Sure enough, Lawlor was named in the Probables XV for the Ireland Schools trial in Blackrock in mid-December. I was included in the replacements, but it was a cast of thousands and I didn't even get on the pitch. The Ireland team selected to play the Irish U-19s looked suspiciously like that Probables XV, captained by Chris Henry and including other future senior internationals in Kevin McLaughlin and Andrew Trimble, with Lawlor at 10.

I had to content myself with a place in a Schools B side that played against the Irish Youths, plus the knowledge that I had just been unfortunate with injury. Maybe if I had a good Cup campaign with Mary's, I might push myself back into the reckoning for the home internationals in April.

The first half of that equation worked out fine. We had a long Cup run, beating Blackrock in an attritional semi-final replay to ensure we made it to a second consecutive final at Lansdowne Road. As luck would have it, our opponents were Terenure – Conor Gildea and his pals.

Relations with Terenure weren't cordial. On Leinster Schools duty, you'd spend time with some of their guys but it would never get too friendly. You understood that this was an ancient grudge. I certainly had no reason to be pals with any of them. I remember walking with Laura up beside Bushy Park one day and some of the lads from the Terenure team were walking behind us, close enough so that I could hear their attempts at intimidation.

So I took real pleasure the time we managed to win up in their place. It was only a 'friendly' and I wasn't even meant to be playing, seeing as it was the morning after a Schools interpro, and I was supposed to be recovering. You can sit on the bench but you're not to come on, I was told. Only in an emergency, I was told.

Mary's were behind at half-time. That counted as an emergency.

For some reason, we had to change pitches at half-time. This was when I saw my opening. I subbed myself on and the coaches turned a blind eye. I was like a lunatic out there, getting into fights. I gave one of them a black eye and he threatened me with revenge:

I've got an older brother and he's comin' after you, ya prick!

At one stage when I was lining up a penalty kick to touch, I could see Gildea and his mates on the sideline – Conor would have been involved in the interpro so he was just watching the game. I spiralled the kick low and hard, directly at them. They didn't like that.

We won, though. Sweet. Go tell that to your big brother.

Terenure had the last laugh, though. The 2003 Cup final couldn't have been any more different from the previous year. It was played in a heatwave, for starters – about 24 degrees in mid-March! St Patrick's Day fell on a Monday, so it was a long weekend with a holiday atmosphere and a huge crowd came down to Lansdowne Road to watch.

The Transition Year kid who had nothing to lose now felt he had the weight of the world on his shoulders. Almost the entire school watched us warm up on the back pitch, clapping and chanting. Former Mary's pupils spilled out of the Lansdowne clubhouse bars, beer on their breaths. They all formed a sort of a tunnel as we headed back under the east stand towards the main pitch. I could see guys who'd been on the team the year before, roaring encouragement.

It was overwhelming. I felt loads of pressure that day, felt drained by the whole occasion. Even the rugby was claustrophobic. Despite the sunshine and the dry ball, it felt like there was no space on the pitch. Even time seemed compressed. The first half whizzed past. What do I remember? Not a lot. I'd had one shot at goal but my attempt was held up by the wind.

I got just one more opportunity, ten minutes before the end, at which stage Terenure were 3–0 ahead. It was a kickable distance, just about, wide out on the left. I was reminded of the match-winning penalty that I kicked from a similar angle to beat Rob Kearney's Clongowes team in the first round.

But we had this killer lineout play up our sleeves: two pods, one at the front, one at the back, the jumper at the back palming it down for someone to pile through the gap. Terenure's defence had been excellent but Paul Nash, our skipper, reckoned it would work. We kicked to the corner. We spilled the ball in the lineout. We lost. I was inconsolable.

That evening we went through the same routine as the previous year – back to Mary's, walking into a crowded hall with our parents there. This time, though, the applause sounded sympathetic. We were up on stage but there was no trophy. All the while, I was mentally rewinding to that decision to go to the corner.

I'm still not good at leaving stuff behind.

My mood wasn't improved much by what happened the following Saturday in Blackrock – another Ireland Schools trial match, after which the selectors would announce the squad to play France, England and Wales. At least I got to start for the Possibles this time, directly opposite Fergal Lawlor. I played well, too, but it didn't feel like a proper contest.

It was actually a farce.

The Probables side was so much stronger. Lawlor got to play behind a much bigger and better pack, and he looked a million dollars. I never stood a chance of displacing him. It felt unfair. Basically, I was losing out because of a freak training ground accident months previously.

I wasn't even selected on the bench. Maybe because they felt they couldn't justify having two Leinster 10s in the squad, they went for the Munster out-half. I wondered what might happen if they were hammered by France, first up. But no. They won all three games. I tortured myself by going up to watch them beat England in Templeville Road.

Making the Leinster team again the following season was small consolation. I went on the same autumn tour to Leicester and to Yorkshire, played through the interpros, all the while knowing that I was overage for the Ireland Schools side. It was a weird arrangement when you think about it. I decided to aim for the Irish U-19s, who were due to tour in South Africa in March, just after the Schools Cup finals. I fancied the sound of that.

Another strong Cup campaign would help, naturally. We went in as joint favourites with Blackrock. There was just one problem – we'd been drawn against each other in the first round.

I was wired for that game. Completely wired. I was captain that season – my third season on the senior panel, final year in St Mary's, only a few months away from my nineteenth birthday. I was a demanding captain, too.

We had an alcohol ban from New Year until the end of the cup campaign – 'the pledge', as it was known. It was Brian Moore, our coach, who'd come up with the idea, but I was its chief enforcer. We'd taken the same pledge two years previously. Everyone had stuck by it and we'd won the Cup, so obviously it seemed a good idea. Everyone in the squad was given a sheet on which the pledge was printed, with a space for their signature. It was all very solemn. These are the sacrifices you have to make if you want to be successful, Brian told us.

It wasn't much of a sacrifice for me. I'd had a few cans of beer the night of my Junior Cert results, but I didn't drink much generally, not in sixth year. My weeks were taken up with study and rugby, and I saw Laura a lot at weekends.

Not everyone lived such a disciplined life, though. Stories began to filter back to me that five or six of the team had been on the beer one night. I was fuming with them. Gave them the silent treatment for a while.

We were all best of buddies by half-time against Blackrock, though. We led 17–3 and were looking good for our third straight Senior Cup victory over 'Rock – no mean feat. I felt in complete control, too. I was striking the ball beautifully, converting two tries and dropping a goal. According to the *Irish Times*, I was 'the most accomplished player on the field'.

Unfortunately, the report also described the game as 'one of the great cup comebacks'. I remember it better than any other Schools Cup match I played, partly because it was my last, partly because I have been reminded of it plenty over the years – by Leo Cullen, who was coaching the 'Rock side, and by Luke Fitzgerald, a sprightly sixteen-year-old who came off their bench after the break and made a difference.

I won't bore you with the blow-by-blow, but one bizarre moment in the final quarter is worth recalling, as it haunts me occasionally. I had a fairly straightforward shot at goal to go 23–17 ahead, from almost exactly the same spot where I'd landed a penalty a few minutes previously. Just as I began my approach, the floodlights came on in Donnybrook. Not just that, but there was a bang – like a fuse blowing – literally as I was about to strike the ball. I missed. A few minutes later they scored a try and we lost, 20–22.

I was devastated to have lost what was effectively a cup final, yet quietly proud of my own performance, especially during 'Rock's comeback. They killed us with pick-and-gos in that second half so I had a lot of tackles to make. I tried to get stuck in. I remember their big number 8 Darren O'Reilly surging around the corner and me putting a big tackle in on him. It felt good. It felt like I couldn't have given any more in the cause.

On the way home in the car afterwards, Mum tried to console me with pretty much the same message:

You couldn't have tried any harder, Jonathan.

Typically, I gave her short shrift.

We're just losers, OK?

I knew I'd made Dad proud, though. I was upset coming off the pitch and I could see he was upset, too. I've seen that look on his face after other Schools Cup matches my brothers have been involved in, when he was close to tears – tears of pain but also of pride that myself or Mark or Jerry had given all we had to give.

And I saw that look on his face in Donnybrook that afternoon, as people were milling around us outside the Bective clubhouse.

5

About a month before I sat my Leaving Cert, I received a letter from Brian Wall.

Dear Jonathan,

What lies ahead of you may reshape and change your life for ever. Be sure to enjoy all it has to offer. Enjoy the profile. Enjoy the success. Enjoy the medals and trophies. Enjoy the attention. Enjoy the praise. Enjoy the freebies and enjoy the new genuine friends. Cherish this type of success and all it has to offer.

However, be careful.

The game you are about to enter into is drastically different from the one you have played for the last six years. The schools rugby you have played was interested in Jonathan Sexton the person and not the player. You were minded. You were watched over. You were taken care of in a way that will contrast with what you encounter for the rest of your playing career. The game that is ahead of you is not interested in you. It is interested in a player. It is interested in a number to fill a position. It is interested in winning at all costs. It will want you to surrender your mind. It will want you to surrender your body. It will want you to surrender your integrity and sense of fairness. It will want you to say yes at all times. That is what today's game is about. Learn to say no and to say it with conviction.

When it is all over, do not end up wishing you could turn the clock back and do it differently. You are what you are and owe nobody anything except your family and closest friends. In the future everyone will want to be your friend. No matter how well you think you get on with your team-mates, there will always be individual jealousies. Rise above it. Do not confront it. This will only serve to feed such feelings in others. Listen but treat with scepticism the advice offered by your new friends. Their advice is for your benefit but also for theirs. Listen and heed the advice offered by your friends and family, who know you and who you can trust. Their advice is for your benefit and they have nothing to gain from it. Listen to your parents. They have got it right for the last eighteen years.

Always remember that you will need your degree in your later career but that you can only get that qualification at this stage in your life.

Enjoy and be careful.

God bless,
Brian Wall

This gives you an idea of the pastoral care I received at St Mary's. I'm so fortunate to have come under the influence of teachers who were so committed to their jobs and so caring towards their students.

A couple of things jump out from the letter. First, how prophetic it is. Some of Brian's warnings about the life of a professional sportsman turned out to be very accurate. But the thing I'm most surprised by is Brian's basic assumption that I was going to become a pro.

He doesn't seem to be in the slightest doubt that I was about to head down this route. I wasn't so convinced. At least, the person at Leinster who decided these things – Collie McEntee – didn't seem very convinced about me.

McEntee was in charge of the newly formed Leinster Academy. Up until that point, all the best school-leavers had been invited to a centralized IRFU Academy, which came together for camps at various stages of the season. The idea behind regionalizing the academy structure was to ensure that more players got more coaching, and were given fitness programmes that could be monitored more regularly.

I reckoned I had a lot to offer them. I knew that I was a good footballer. I may not have been built like a pro rugby player – I had skinny legs, sloping shoulders – but I was brave, physically committed. I'd played five years of Schools Cup rugby, won a senior medal, made a bit of a name for myself with that drop-goal.

I'd played for Leinster Schools two years running, been to all the summer coaching camps. I was passionate about the sport, too – fiercely competitive and a lousy loser. I wanted to play at the highest level possible. I wanted to be a pro.

Failing to make the Ireland Schools team had stung, though. It felt like I wasn't really rated. Not like Rob Kearney was rated.

Rob played in a different position from me but still, I was envious. It was generally accepted that he would go all the way – Leinster, Ireland, the lot. You could even see it in the way he carried himself – calm, unruffled, old beyond his years. He'd be going straight into the Leinster Academy on leaving school. The word around the traps was that Munster had been chasing him, that they were going to offer him a contract.

Nobody was chasing me.

There was no place for me in the Leinster academy, though McEntee did offer me a place in the sub-academy. I wasn't exactly bowled over. These days, there are school-leavers who would crawl over broken glass for a spot in our sub-academy; back then, I felt like an afterthought.

In the academy proper, you received a bursary – only a few grand but still an acknowledgement that you might have a future as a pro. You also got to train with the full-time pros occasionally.

The sub-academicians didn't get a penny. We'd be expected to turn up for some training sessions but would be excluded from others. Fitness sessions were usually held at the crack of dawn.

Looking back, I guess the idea was to test your dedication. At the time, it felt part-time and half-baked. The snub-academy. I accepted McEntee's offer, but privately I was underwhelmed.

My stock might have been higher if I'd been selected for that Ireland U-19s trip to South Africa in March, three months before my exams. I wasn't. There were a couple of trial matches out at the ALSAA complex beside Dublin Airport, against England selections – though it wasn't like we were representing Ireland. We played in training tops.

There were two Irish teams. I didn't need to be told that I was in the equivalent of the 'Possibles' XV once again; I knew by the make-up of the other team.

I looked for the squad in the paper the following morning, expecting the worst. My name wasn't on the list. Conor Gildea's was. I was seething.

But just this once, I didn't let the disappointment chew me up for long. I was already in Leaving Cert mode. Someone mentioned that I might be in the running for the Irish Schools tour to Australia in the summer, seeing as they were tweaking the age regulations to bring them into line with the Aussies. Whatever.

I'd almost lost interest. It was all about the Leaving now. Mary's getting knocked out of the cup meant I'd had a free run at my mock exams and they'd gone really well. I got 550 points. If I could match that in June, I'd get Medicine in UCD.

Many years later, during my time at Racing, Ronan O'Gara used to call me the Swot. I never missed one of the French lessons organized by the club for their foreign players. O'Gara would want to have seen me prepare for the Leaving. It's an exam system that generally rewards students who are able to process a lot of information and regurgitate it appropriately on the day. This suited me just fine.

In fifth year and especially in sixth year, I did a lot of after-school slog, basically supervised study in the library from 4 till 7.30 p.m. I was never in a rush to spend evenings at home.

When I did go home, I'd work up in my room. Or I'd take the keys to Rathgar Hair Studio and bring my books to the beauty salon upstairs. Once I cleared a table, I could use a nail light as my study lamp and beaver away until around 10 p.m. Saturday mornings, I went to the Institute to study French, seeing as I still wasn't welcome in Joan Manning's class. I ended up getting a C1, which wasn't bad for basically one year's work.

I was lucky in that I had good teachers and I was willing to work hard. I had Brian Wall for chemistry and maths. He chopped down the relevant chapters in each textbook to the essential material and I'd learn that off by heart. Chemistry was factual, formulaic. You just had to do the work. It was similar with maths. I liked the way it was process-driven, with no grey areas. You had it right or you had it wrong.

English was completely different, but once I got into

Denis Murphy's class for sixth year I knew I'd be well prepared.

Denis was strict, had authority – he's now school principal at St Mary's – but he was my dean all the way through secondary school and I always got on with him. He had a tough job getting me to fall in love with the poetry of Seamus Heaney, but he did show me how to get an A2 in Leaving Cert English, which was quite an achievement for me.

For the literature paper, I boiled it down to essentials, as in chemistry. There would be a question on an Irish poet and there would also be a question that would allow you to write about a woman poet. I learned to write authoritatively on a handful of poems by Seamus Heaney and Eiléan Ní Chuilleanáin, how to answer the question and to back up each point with a quote. The same with *Macbeth*. I may never have seen a stage version of Shakespeare – and had no interest in seeing one, either – but I'd all the major themes and characters covered, with supporting quotes.

Having a definite target gave focus to my study. Wherever possible, I'd stay overnight in Laura's, in the spare room. All the while, she was not only my girlfriend but my tutor and also my financial support. She was in first year in university at this stage but worked weekends in a pub, delivering drinks, collecting glasses. Between wages and tips, she was making a fortune, so on the rare occasions that we went out, to the cinema or wherever, it was always her treat.

A less generous girlfriend might have passed comment on my ballooning weight. Once we'd been knocked out of the cup, my average school day consisted of eating, studying and sleeping. Not very healthy eating, either. For breakfast, I'd usually grab a bacon roll from the Spar beside the school.

Come mini-break at 11 o'clock, the sixth-years had the school canteen to themselves, so it was chicken curry or sausage rolls and chips.

At lunch, we could venture out to Rathmines – Fast Food Central. Same after school. As for my evening meal, if I didn't eat dinner at home, I might pop into the chipper six doors down for a cheeseburger.

My old Ireland team-mate Simon Zebo occasionally likes to post unflattering pictures of me on Instagram. Fortunately, he never got his hands on a photo from that summer in which I'm flanked by Gavin O'Meara, our hooker, and Brian McGovern, a prop. It looks like an entire front row.

I weighed nearly 100 kilos – my fighting weight for most of my career was around 92. I'd been consuming between 5,000 and 6,000 calories a day and burning zero. I was a whale.

I'm probably lucky that the Irish Schools selectors hadn't seen me for a while when they included me in the squad for that tour to Australia that August – a pleasant surprise. It was a seven-game tour, culminating in a solitary 'Test' against Australian Schools in Canberra.

The squad included some now-familiar names: Rob Kearney, Devin Toner, Seán Cronin, Darren Cave, Billy Holland, Duncan Williams. I knew I was second- or even third-choice out-half behind Gildea and Conan Doyle, but it turned out that I saw plenty of rugby on that tour, mainly through someone else's misfortune. Tom Gleeson, the highly rated Munster centre, went home mid-tour when his father fell ill, so I got to play against all the state sides at 12. Carrying a few extra pounds may have been a blessing after all.

Typically, I was pretty reserved on tour to begin with. I was never comfortable with the idea of sharing a room with one of the lads from the other provinces until I got to know them. There were stages of the tour when we were billeted out with boys from opposing teams, which put even more stress on your social skills. Now, I can see that it was good for me. At the time, it was uncomfortable.

For the Brisbane leg, I was fortunate to stay with Tony McGahan, who was coaching one of the local sides and who would join the Munster coaching staff a couple of years later. Tony and his wife Libby had a lovely house with a small apartment in the basement, where I dossed down with Peter Shallow, a lad from Rockwell College.

I hit it off with Tony. One night when I couldn't sleep, I was snooping around the apartment when I stumbled on a cabinet stacked with rugby videos – Brumbies v. Queensland Reds, State of Origin, you name it, hundreds of them. While Peter snoozed, I made myself a bowl of cereal and stuck one of the tapes in the VCR.

I got the shock of my life when Tony appeared in his pyjamas. 'I see you found my tapes,' he whispered. I was mortified, but he told me not to worry. He actually ended up showing me a few tries that he liked – two rugby nerds just chewing the fat. Peter snored the whole way through it.

I never made the Test team, but I took confidence from the tour, and from Tony's quiet encouragement. He drove us around that week and watched our game against Queensland Schools. I remember getting properly stuck in. I scored a try, too, after a nice show-and-go.

After the game, Tony took me aside, looked me in the eyes and said: Mate, you can really play.

It was nice, getting a compliment like that on the far side of the world. It stayed with me.

*

The only slightly sour memory from that tour came the day of our Leaving Cert results, which Mum relayed to me over the phone. I got 495 points, 55 fewer than my mocks. It turned out that I'd made a mess of chemistry and maths. In chemistry I'd left out one full question altogether. I still got a B1, but this was my strongest subject and I'd been banking on an A1.

Looking back, it's kinda weird the way things worked out. Missing that question meant that I missed out on studying medicine, but it also left me with a clearer route towards playing pro rugby – med students struggle with the demands on their time. I was offered my second choice, chemical engineering in UCD. A terrible choice, as it turned out, but you live and learn.

From a rugby point of view, the obvious thing to do was to play for UCD. I'd be studying there, plus I'd be part of their rugby academy, along with a lot of other aspiring players. They'd even offered me a scholarship, pending my Leaving results. My fees would be taken care of. I'd have an accommodation allowance and a books allowance.

The only problem was that the academy director told me I'd be playing for the Under-20s in my first season. The senior team already had an out-half, Eoghan Hickey.

I didn't fancy a year with the UCD 20s. My goal for the season was to make the Ireland Under-21s and I'd heard that Mark McDermott, the coach, wouldn't consider any Ireland-based player who wasn't playing in the AIL. So no thanks, UCD.

Bective, my first club, offered me €10,000 to join – a fortune – but Fergal Campion, a former Leinster player, was nailed on as out-half, so that wasn't a runner. My other options were Trinity, who'd also offered a scholarship, and St Mary's, the old boys' club for my school.

Mary's had been in touch before I'd gone to Australia. The coaches, Steve Hennessy and Peter Smyth, explained that the club had just been relegated from Division 1 and that they needed an out-half to guide them back up. They could guarantee me first-team rugby in a team containing players with experience in the professional game – former Leinster players like Ciarán Potts, James Norton, John McWeeney, Gavin Hickie.

They offered me a 'salary' of €4,000, plus €10 per point scored. Happy days! More importantly, I could tell that they believed in me. Smythie told me he thought I could play for Leinster and that he could help me get there. He was a former Leinster player himself, so he knew the ropes.

He texted me not long after I returned from Australia to let me know that they'd be playing a pre-season friendly against Greystones in Kenilworth Square the next day and that I should pop down for a look. I brought the dog down, all casual. Before half-time, my mind was made up.

When I told Smythie that I'd like to play for them, he looked surprised. Playing with one of the universities was the standard route for a school-leaver with aspirations to play professionally. But I liked the rugby Mary's were trying to play. I liked the fact that there were so many guys in the team from the years ahead of me in school, guys I'd looked up to. Guys who knew how to put me in my place, too.

At my first training session, I lobbed my IRFU-branded gear-bag on to the bench in the first XV dressing room before heading for a leak. When I returned, my bag had disappeared. Dave Clare, the veteran loose-head prop and a prison officer by profession, had tossed it into the car park. Unwittingly, I'd taken his place, which provided everyone with plenty of amusement. An ice-breaker, I guess.

I continued to provide them with plenty of amusement. Our first AIL game was down in Limerick, against Old Crescent. The league had lost a lot of its magic since the provinces had been properly professionalized, and there weren't the same bumper crowds. But there was no cap on the number of professionals allowed to play for their clubs and the provinces had no A team fixtures yet. So if a pro was battling to have his contract renewed and needed to make his point, he would do it in the AIL. I remember Crescent had a few Munster players that day – like Mike Mullins, the former international, and Eoin Reddan.

The rugby was more physical than I was used to but we won well, with John McWeeney scoring a hat-trick. This earned him the man-of-the-match award. In the Crescent clubhouse, the custom was that the MOTM had to stand on a stool and down a pint in one.

McWeeney had already left, so I was nominated to take his place. There was no arguing. It was the same on the bus journey home.

Down in one, Jono.

Give us a song, Jono.

I did as I was told. By the end of the journey, I was poured into the Mary's clubhouse in Templeville Road and, later, into Tramco, a bar in Rathmines.

The more we won, the more Templeville became my social hub. No matter how late we might have been out on a Saturday night, we'd reassemble in Templeville to watch the second XV on Sunday afternoons. Then we'd train Monday, Tuesday and Thursday evenings. I basically lived up there.

Weekdays were a grind, though. It would start with sub-academy fitness sessions at 6.30 a.m. in Belvo – Old Belvedere

RFC. I used to cycle down with my bag of college books on my back. From there, I'd cycle to lectures at Earlsfort Terrace in town from 9 o'clock to 12 o'clock. After those, I'd grab a ham and cheese roll before cycling five kilometres out to Belfield for more classes from 2 o'clock to 5 o'clock, before hopping on the bike for a ten-kilometre spin out to Templeville for training, stopping for grub at a service station on route. It was madness.

The Leinster sub-academy was the first to go. It happened one pissy wet morning when Brad Harrington, Leinster's fitness coach and a straight-talking Aussie, had a proper go at me. I had turned up in Belvo wearing runners, expecting to be in the weights room, as we'd been the previous week. But no, it was a speed session that morning. On grass.

'Where the fack are your boots, mate?'

'I didn't know it was a speed session.'

'You didn't know? You can fack off, then. Go on, fack off home.'

So I did.

I'd say Brad thought I was a complete waste of space. I was disorganized and not in great shape – I'd barely lifted a weight at this stage in my life. To be honest, my heart wasn't in it. Or rather, I just had too much on my plate.

The lecturers were telling us that for every hour of lecture time, we should be studying thirty minutes, which added up to around three hours' study a day. This, on top of club training and sub-academy? There weren't enough minutes in the day.

My folks wanted me to take my studies seriously. They actively discouraged me from the sub-academy. It wasn't like I was getting paid for the privilege. By Christmas, I'd stopped turning up altogether. Leinster probably lost interest in me at that stage.

My other problem was that I hated chemical engineering. Thermodynamics and particulate science? Ugh. By the end of the autumn term, I knew I'd had enough. I broke down one night, told Mum I couldn't go on.

It wasn't that I wanted to drop out of college altogether. I still wanted a degree, just not one in chemical engineering. I suggested switching to do a Bachelor of Commerce, starting all over again the following September. The folks agreed, as long as I found a job.

Steve Hennessy was able to help out here. Steve worked for Friends First, a financial services company, and was able to get me a gig. Every morning on his way to work, Dad would drop me to Steve's house for 7.50 and we'd head off to the office in Cherrywood, where I'd spend my day assessing loan applications from farmers looking to buy Massey Ferguson tractors, checking their credit ratings and so on.

On training nights, Steve would drive me to Templeville. We became good friends, though it meant that I had to put up with constant abuse in the dressing room about being coach's pet.

Did I care? I was on a salary of twenty grand from Friends First, plus €500 a month from Mary's, plus €10 per point. I was scoring loads of points, too. Mary's were running the ball and I was scoring tries – ten of them that season. I was loaded. The first Monday of every month, I'd call to the club treasurer's house to collect my earnings.

I even purchased my first car, a Volkswagen Polo. Soon I was driving to work – too soon, given that I hadn't a clue what I was up to. During my lunch breaks I used to head out to the car park to practise basic manoeuvres.

*

That first year out of school was an important year in my rugby development. The coaching we were getting from Steve and Smythie was up a level from anything I had experienced. Every Monday evening we'd have a detailed video review of our previous game and some analysis of our next opponents.

We played good attacking rugby, but because the league was played through the middle of winter, I also learned how to control a game in the mud and the wind and the rain, how to keep the forwards happy, how to protect a lead – the sort of stuff you can only figure out through experience.

For all my aspirations to become a pro, I hadn't the first idea about professionalism. My diet was still terrible – loads of processed food in the canteen at Friends First, lots of late-night visits to the chipper in Rathgar. There was a dingy little weights room up in Templeville, but I only ever went in there for show. The only reason I was in any sort of shape was because we did so much running after training – sprints, shuttle runs and so on.

Looking back, I had no discipline. I hardly ever practised my place-kicking and when I did, there was no structure or goal or routine. The inside of my car revealed my general disorganization – dirty gear and fast-food wrappers flung everywhere.

I lived for the games, though. Steve and Smythie knew how to channel my desire, too. At one pre-match meeting, my chest swelled when Steve turned to me at one stage and said: Jono, Leinster can't keep ignoring you if you keep playing as well as you've been playing.

Steve knew I had the hump about not making the academy. Smythie knew it, too, and privately told me that he was banging the door down at Leinster, telling them I was playing out of my skin.

Smythie and I became good friends that year. He lived pretty close to me at the time and, importantly, he had a subscription to Sky Sports. I'd ring him on a Sunday to see if he was watching Leicester v. Northampton and he'd invite me over, tell me to pick up a sandwich at the deli across the road from my folks' house – his girlfriend Gillian was working there at weekends.

I was impressed by his complete love for rugby, and his encyclopaedic knowledge of the sport. I consider myself a rugby nerd, but Smythie was in a different league. His professional career had ended a couple of years previously when he underwent operations to remove a tumour inside his skull the size of a golf ball. Even now, he was still playing the odd game for us, flinging himself around and starting fights.

I loved his training sessions because they were challenging, different. And I loved the fact that he rated me. He understood my desire.

'You'll play for Leinster, Jono,' he told me. 'You can play for Ireland, too. You just have to keep working hard.'

He would have known that Ireland didn't have a queue of young 10s waiting to take over from Ronan O'Gara. O'Gara was only around twenty-eight at this stage, but Munster were so concerned about their lack of depth that they had flown in Jeremy Manning, a young Kiwi, to qualify for Ireland through residency. Ulster and Connacht had thirty-something playmakers in David Humphreys and Eric Elwood, while Leinster had been relying on foreigners – David Holwell (who'd just returned to New Zealand), Felipe Contepomi, and Christian Warner, the Aussie utility back.

The way to get noticed was to get into the Ireland Under-21s. Coming towards Christmas of 2004, Mark McDermott took a squad of around forty players to Marcoussis to play two training games against French selections and I was included as one of three out-halves, along with Gareth Steenson and Conan Doyle. This despite not having featured for the Leinster Under-21s in the interpros at the start of the season. It proved that AIL form still counted for something.

I knew it would be hard to budge Steenson. He was the most obvious captain for the upcoming U-21 Six Nations, seeing as he'd played in the team the previous season when Ireland had upset the odds by reaching the final of the Junior World Cup.

Sure enough, I didn't make the initial squad for the Six Nations, but when Steenson got injured I was picked on the bench for the game against England at Donnybrook, with Munster's Barry Keeshan starting. I never got off the bench, but just to be sitting there in my shiny new IRFU tracksuit proved that I had leapfrogged kids who had been selected ahead of me in the Schools set-up. I was in the mix. What made it even better was that the game was in Donnybrook – still Leinster's headquarters at that stage. Someone would have to notice.

Mary's kept providing me with big days out in that spring of 2005, days when the media were in attendance – a Division 1B final against UL Bohs at Lansdowne Road, the Leinster Senior Cup final, and the final of the new All-Ireland Cup. But the most important goal of the season had been to gain promotion to Division 1A and we'd achieved that.

We'd also had a lot of fun. You were never allowed take yourself too seriously in Mary's. Team manager Brian 'Rolo' Rowntree once asked me to do a TV interview with RTÉ. I wasn't keen, but he explained that it would help the club game in Ireland and that they'd asked for me, as an up-and-coming player. Just turn up at RTÉ on Friday afternoon in your Mary's top, he told me.

I was nervous enough about appearing on TV without the horrible surprise I got while sitting in make-up. That's when I was told that 'Dustin will be along shortly.'

Anyone familiar with Irish TV in the noughties will know that Dustin is a celebrity turkey with a strong Dublin accent whose catchphrase is 'Go on, ya good thing.' He had his own children's show at the time. Dustin is hilarious, unless you are the butt of his jokes. And I was the butt of his jokes that day. He asked me embarrassing questions about Brian O'Driscoll. He made me show my 'determined face' and my 'ruthless face'. I had no option but to play along.

My only hope was that people would miss it because it was on afternoon TV. But of course Rolo made sure to tape it and show it to the squad. It took me a while to live it down.

Just as Mary's knew how to keep your feet on the ground, they also knew how to celebrate individual success. They made a fuss of me when I was included in the Under-21s squad for the Junior World Cup in Argentina that summer.

Even better, Leinster acknowledged the achievement by including me in the academy for the following season. It was almost as if they'd been forced to include me, despite my apathy towards the sub-academy.

Collie McEntee sat me down before we departed for Argentina and told me I'd have to do a huge pre-season to catch up on my physical development, and warned me there would be no cutting corners.

I reassured him. I blamed my parents for my non-attendance at sub-academy. It would be grand this time. I'd be back in college, so I wouldn't be rushing to work in Friends First any more. I had a car. It would be easier to get to every session.

Go on, ya good thing!

Argentina went well. Mendoza wasn't the most beautiful spot, but just to be involved in a world tournament, and to be challenging for a starting place, was exciting. I could have sat back and accepted my role as backup out-half, knowing I'd be underage again the following season. But I reckoned I could put pressure on Steenson.

We had a decent team with some future senior internationals in Stephen Ferris, Chris Henry, Kevin McLaughlin and Andrew Trimble – I struck up a close friendship with Trimby on that tour. But we were in a tough pool and finished ninth, considerably lower than our pre-tournament ranking as second favourites. I was happy enough with my contribution, which was mostly off the bench, with Gareth moving to 12. I got to start against Canada and Samoa and was happy with how I went.

The real work started when we got home, though. Collie told me I needed to do a twelve-week pre-season to catch up with my peers. Brad Harrington was waiting for me and it soon became obvious that he was going to make me pay for all those missed fitness sessions.

Brad went hard on me that summer down in the gym in Belvo, unbelievably hard. He was constantly on my case.

Say you were doing a set of eight lifts and you had one more to go, he'd bark: Two more! How many more chin-ups? One? Give me two more!

Years later, Brad told me about how he'd been a talented footballer as a kid but pissed it all away. He didn't want to see kids waste their talent, and he'd had me pegged as a waster. At the time, I just thought he was a sadist.

There was one particularly nightmarish training week down in Clongowes, where they worked us into the ground – weights, sprint work, training games. My first experience of training professionally.

I literally collapsed into bed every evening. It was training like I'd never experienced. But because I was new to it, the gains I made were huge. When I turned up at Templeville to watch Mary's play a pre-season friendly, people noticed that my physique had drastically changed. I felt quicker, stronger. I was kicking the ball miles in training. I couldn't wait to flex all these new muscles on the pitch.

But Collie wouldn't let me play in the Under-21 interpros, not until I'd finished my pre-season programme. I pleaded with him but he wouldn't budge. Then Leinster were beaten by Connacht in the first game – virtually unheard of.

Collie, come on. I'm dying for a run here.

I kept hounding him and he kept telling me I was on a specific programme and that I wasn't due to play for another couple of weeks. Besides, I hadn't even trained with the team.

I pleaded with him. If I could train with them Thursday and Friday, I'd be ready for the Ulster game that Saturday, in Donnybrook.

Eventually, probably fearing an interpro whitewash, he relented. I had talked my way into the team.

I played like a dream – dropped a goal early on, hit my wing with a well-weighted cross-kick. We killed them. Five minutes from the end, I was called ashore, pleasantly knack-ered. I was slumped down at the side of the pitch, back against a hoarding, socks around my ankles when I felt a tap on the shoulder.

'That was awesome, mate. See you at training on Monday.'

It was Michael Cheika, the new Leinster coach. Holy Christ.

I could see the old man was down at the Bective end. *Wait till he hears this.*

6

Whatever you thought about Michael Cheika, you couldn't ignore him. Tall, loud, ambitious, charismatic and, above all, passionate. In my memories of those early training sessions down in Belvo, he is in rugby shorts and T-shirt, socks rolled down, barking instructions, losing it with people. But he was a breath of fresh air. The lads loved him.

We'd heard he once ran a fashion business, and on match days he looked smart. But you could tell he'd been in a few scraps. The cauliflower ears and the crooked fingers gave it away. The nasal delivery.

Aw, maaaate, what the FACK?!

He was still in his thirties, still relatively fit, so mucking in at training made sense to him. He had been an aggressive, narky number 8 for Randwick and he made it pretty obvious he wanted the Leinster pack to be a bit narky, too.

I loved the fact that he wore his heart on his sleeve. I made it my business to try and impress him. I'm not so sure how often I succeeded.

Cheiks was the dominant character in our Australian odd couple. Down at the other end of the pitch, our backs coach David Knox was joining in on games of tip, producing outrageous flicks and dummies and snatches of Australian rugby league commentary, with references to players none of us had heard of. A complete madman.

I didn't know what to make of Knoxy at first, and he seemed unsure about me. He probably saw me as a kicking

10, whereas he'd been more of a runner and a distributor for the ACT Brumbies in Super 12. It didn't feel like he rated me much at all.

With Cheika, though, first impressions were entirely positive, mainly because he was so positive towards me.

He said: Mate, any time you wanna come down for a skills session with the senior guys, just let me know.

I could barely believe my ears. Me, training with Brian O'Driscoll?

Then, when I did turn up, sheepishly, and did some kicking off to the side, he'd come over and show some interest. I'd bang a spiral punt and he'd say: Mate, do that again.

So I would.

Mate, that's outstanding!

Soon, it was like he was your best pal. He'd spot you getting out of the car in Belvo and it was 'Sextos, you beauty. How are ya, mate?'

Sextos?

He had nicknames for all of the younger lads. Devin Toner was 'Inkjet' for a while. Toner, ink, printer – you get the idea. Some of his jokey names were corny but we all went along with them. Why wouldn't you? Cheiks was boss.

We kids made a good early impression on him because we won the Under-21s interpro title, beating Munster in the final down in Athlone, with Seán O'Brien scoring the decisive try – a legend, even at eighteen.

Cheiks understood the rivalry with Munster. As an Aussie, he'd grown up with the whole New South Wales v. Queensland thing. He knew that Leinster were living in Munster's shadow at that stage.

He wouldn't have been at Leinster at all if it hadn't been for Munster luring Declan Kidney away at the end of the previous season. I read the rugby pages so I knew this was the second time Munster had done a number on Leinster like this – two years previously, they'd pinched Alan Gaffney in similar circumstances.

Looking back, Leinster was a bit of a mess at the time. We had a massive potential fan base and arguably the best backline in Europe: Chris Whitaker, Felipe Contepomi, Denis Hickie, Gordon D'Arcy, Brian O'Driscoll, Shane Horgan, Girvan Dempsey. Yet here we were training in club grounds, driving down in our gear and showering at home. Compared to the facilities we have now, it was a shambles.

At the time, I knew no better. I was just incredibly excited – and nervous – at the prospect of getting to train occasionally with these legends, to run a shadow backline against them on the main pitch in Belvo. The speed with which they transferred the ball was scary.

Stuff was written at the time about a split in Leinster between the rock-star backs and the mere mortals. As a newcomer, you certainly knew your place. I was lucky to have Denis Hickie there because he was kind and encouraging to a fellow Mary's man. He also set a good example just by the way he looked after himself. You'd see him and Girvan Dempsey with their tupperware containers of boiled chicken and broccoli.

Girve is a gentleman, and he was always available to do extras after training. Chris Whitaker – another gentleman. Both of them took me under their wings and really made a big effort with me. Darce was kind to all the young kids, too. Maybe it was because he'd been through a few difficult years after bursting on the scene so young. He was also on a healthy eating kick, taking vitamin supplements and fish oils. He'd actually employed a nutritionist at the time and I remember he used to share all her printouts with me.

I was in awe of Felipe, of course. Maybe it was because he was the live version of what I'd planned for myself – the rugby-playing doctor.

In some ways, Felipe was a bad example because he made everything look easy. He seemed to be able to come straight from lectures at the College of Surgeons and materialize on the pitch, ready to go, barking orders. Everything was on the run. Place-kicking practice? He'd try a couple of shots from wide out after team training. If they went over, he was happy to leave. His logic was simple: if I can kick them from the touchline, why do I need to practise from in front of the posts?

But appearances were deceptive. Knoxy would show me clips to highlight the subtle nuances to his game – the angles that he ran, how he used footwork, how he cleverly made space for himself and to put others through holes. I sponged up every detail.

Felipe was generous, too. Adidas once sent him boots and runners that were half a size too big for him. Would I be interested in them? Would I what! I didn't have a boot deal at the time so free Predators were a real treasure – two pairs of them, plus two pairs of runners. I never mentioned the fact that I was really size 10. I wore them so often that they fitted me eventually.

I was just twenty – ambitious but insecure. I knew that I was on trial, and that Leinster had a high turnover of out-halves, so I feasted on any scrap of praise. During one session on the back pitch at Lansdowne, I'd been getting great height on my restarts off a hard pitch and afterwards, Malcolm O'Kelly asked me if I'd do a few more so he could practise his receptions. I was chuffed.

Of course the player I wanted to impress most was Brian.

We didn't see much of him in the first half of that season as he was recovering from the shoulder damage that had put him out of the Lions tour the previous summer. He seemed stand-offish, though I realize now that Brian can be shy with newcomers.

This meant that even a hint of positive feedback from him was gold. I have clear memories of one session in the early days when I was part of a second-string backline – the bibs – working in opposition against the seniors. We were running attack plays that they were likely to get from the Scarlets, their next opponents. On one rep, we managed to bust them, with my pass sending Stephen Grissing outside Brian. We were quietly delighted with ourselves.

As we ran back, I could just about catch what Brian said as he analysed the bust with Knoxy. He said that he didn't think the Scarlets would be able to run that play quite so flat or at such speed in a match.

Was that a compliment? Was it intended for me?

Does he even know my name?

Compliments weren't just chucked around Leinster at the time. The initial love-bombing from Cheiks started to dry up. As a young coach, he was in a hurry to make an impression, to build a squad that could challenge in Europe.

Christian Warner was out injured a lot that 2005/06 season, so Felipe started almost every game at out-half. Behind this pair were three apprentices: Eoghan Hickey, David McAllister and me.

The other two lads had been there longer than me and I remember McAllister trying to pull rank occasionally. If I ran a play in training with the shadow backline, he'd step forward, all elbows: I'm in for the next rep. I backed myself against both these guys, but for some reason Cheika usually preferred them for the handful of provincial A team games that were part of the calendar back then.

The AIL was still my greatest source of game minutes. This was challenging enough, given that we were now in Division One. Shannon stuffed us in the first game of the season, at Templeville, with a side crammed with ex-Munster players or members of the Munster academy. Smythie gave me a bit of a pep talk afterwards.

At least I knew that Smythie rated me. Cheiks, I was less sure about. He seemed to be on my case the whole time. He had a bee in his bonnet about the way that I used to run on to the ball, saying that I was stuttering, taking short sharp steps as I was receiving. He wanted me to look at the way Steve Larkham used to stride on to the ball. All his model players were Aussies, naturally.

You need to look at Larkham, he'd say. Glide on to the ball and you'll fix the defender, plus if there's a hole, you can accelerate through it.

I understood what he was saying. Larkham was a hero of mine, partly because he had a similar frame. But I was really struggling to break the stutter habit. I used to wait until the ball was in the air from the scrum-half before I'd set off but Cheiks told me to run and let the 9 worry about putting it out in front of me. He wouldn't let it go, either.

Nah, mate. You're stuttering again.

But . . .

No buts, mate. You're stuttering. Don't expect to get selected if you can't get this right. Now go again.

He could be incredibly tough on the academy guys — demanding, critical, often just narky. Myself, Kev McLaughlin and Ross McCarron used to have good bitching sessions about him, about how he was all palsy with the Horgans,

O'Driscolls and Hickies, how he was sweet on some younger players, like Rob Kearney and Jamie Heaslip.

He most definitely wasn't sweet on us. He was always at us, always finding something to pick apart. Hear enough nagging from the coach and you can easily start to believe that he's laying the groundwork to let you go at the end of the season.

The stutter thing really began to get to me. After one session, I stayed sitting in my car in the Belvo car park, on the verge of tears. Mike Brewer, our forwards coach, spotted that I was upset and came over to reassure me. I hung on every kind word that year.

Out of the blue in January, Cheiks told me I was on the bench for a Friday evening Magners League game against the Border Reivers, at Donnybrook. Leinster had won a Heineken Cup tie in Bath the previous Sunday, so he was resting a few of the rock stars; and Felipe's wife was due to give birth, so I had to prepare myself for the possibility of starting. Mad stuff.

I was a bag of nerves all week. The Reivers were very ordinary but they did have a couple of Scotland internationals and one huge Aussie in the centre called Ben MacDougall. Knoxy was able to tell me all about him. I was crapping myself that I'd have to tackle this giant.

Then I got down to the ground on Friday to hear that Felipe's wife had given birth that morning. There was no sign of him. Holy Christ. I was half-hoping he turned up, half-hoping he didn't. And if he didn't, would Cheiks bring Eoghan Hickey in to start and leave me on the bench?

Felipe arrived eventually. In fact, he did more than that. He scored 20 points as we hammered the Reivers 62–14. Cheiks produced champagne and cigars in the dressing room to wet the baby's head.

Dev Toner and I had sips of bubbly, too, seeing as we'd both made our senior Leinster debuts.

I got eight minutes off the bench — completely pumped, desperate to make an impression. At the first opportunity, I flew into a ruck like a madman. I can still hear Mike Brewer's voice in the half-empty stand: 'Great clean-out, Johnny!'

I was feeling pretty good about myself when I turned up at Templeville the next day, too. St Mary's v. Dungannon was one I'd put in the diary months back — me against Gareth Steenson. I felt I'd a point to prove against him. And I did. We stuffed them and I scored 26 points, including a couple of tries.

The bit I remember most clearly is running at Steenson off the side of a ruck and stepping him before running behind the sticks to score. Mark McDermott was right in front of me, leaning on the rail.

Actually, I resisted the urge to open my gob. But things weren't great between myself and McDermott, and they wouldn't get much better.

I should have been an asset to him, seeing as I'd played in the World Cup in Argentina the previous year and seeing as Leinster had won the interpros. I should have been one of his 'senior pros' with the Ireland U-21s. But I think we just rubbed each other up the wrong way.

Maybe it was because I sensed that he didn't rate me. Macker got some credit when the 2004 team made it to the World Cup final, but it seemed to me that he put a lot of emphasis on brute force with not much focus on imagination. He also liked picking Irish-qualified guys who'd grown up in England and were now studying at Loughborough or somewhere. They might have been physically well-developed athletes, but as rugby players some of them were pretty average. I thought we had much better options in Ireland.

Macker and I had fallen out in Argentina the previous summer, too. It was stupid, over nothing important, but it had festered. One day after training I was practising some spiral punts down the centre of a pitch, towards the posts. Normally, you'd use the touchline as your guide but one side was a water-logged area while the other was a fenced-off vineyard. Macker marches over, clearly unimpressed.

Are you trying to prove a point?

I told him I was just practising my punting. You're practising what you're good at, he said. Plus I should be working more purposefully, using a touchline. I explained the limitations of our training area, how I didn't have an option. And I explained myself pretty aggressively.

Looking back, I should have been more respectful. But this is how I reacted when someone got confrontational with me. I generally wouldn't be quick to seek reconciliation, either. This was one player–coach relationship that was going nowhere.

He did pick me for the first couple of games of the Under-21 Six Nations, but I should never have played. The week before the opener against Italy, I took a heavy bang on the patellar tendon playing for Mary's. I should have got it properly sorted, but I limped through the games against Italy and France and duly lost my place for Wales, when he picked Conan Doyle to start at 10.

I got back in for Scotland, and Cheiks and Knoxy came along to watch. I still wasn't properly fit and it didn't end well, with the Scotland out-half scoring late while I was in the bin for killing the ball. Cheiks and Knoxy were supportive but still, I'd been hoping to make a big impression on them.

Losing to the Scots meant that we had lost three on the trot. That left one game, in Worcester, against an England team that was chasing a Grand Slam. Macker chose Conan to start again and put me on the bench. I didn't play a minute. Maybe it was a blessing. James Haskell and his pals put 40 points on us.

Things were not good. Yes, I'd made one brief appearance for Leinster, but playing for the 21s was my best opportunity to make a mark, and I hadn't done it. I was hearing whispers that Macker was finished with me, that he wasn't even going to pick me for the World Cup in France.

There had been an incident in Worcester, and I wondered if he was going to use it against me.

A few days after we'd returned from the UK, I'd received a phone call from the 21s team manager, Niall O'Shea. A complaint had been made to the IRFU by some girl from Worcester. Some damage had been done to her car. He wanted to know who was responsible. I admitted personally to being there but I wouldn't give him the names of the others.

My memories of the night were a little hazy. The team had gone out for drinks, to celebrate St Patrick's Day and maybe to celebrate the fact that our crap Six Nations campaign was over. When we fell out of the nightclub in our leprechaun hats, there wasn't a taxi to be found in sleepy Worcester.

The girl in question agreed to take a few of us back to our hotel, but of course there wasn't enough room for all of us in her tiny car. It became a drunken challenge, to see how many of us could pile in or on, how many could fit on top. People were messing with windscreen wipers and mirrors. Eventually she pulled off without me. My desperate attempts to get back in the car left a bit of a dent, apparently.

I confessed my guilt to Niall. He told me the cost to repair the damage was £2,000. This was going to put a hole in the fund I'd built from playing for Mary's, but I could put up with that if it made the problem go away. Could my professional career be over before it started?

I was paranoid that Leinster would hear about it. Our kitman Johnny O'Hagan knew – the same Hago from Bective all those years ago. He told me he'd heard that I'd been 'up to no good in Worcester'. Hago was never going to say anything, but it wasn't good that news had reached him. I told Niall I'd pay.

He wanted to take it further, though. He wanted to know who else was involved. When I refused again to give him any names, a meeting was called. Suddenly it had become an investigation: Niall and most of the team, all of us sitting in a big circle. He told us that one person had owned up. When I smiled, the sniggering started. Then Niall asked one of the lads if he had been involved. When he denied it, someone else said: 'Well, I've got a photo of you climbing on top of her car!' At which point everyone collapsed laughing.

Thankfully the problem fizzled out. I never had to pay the money, and it was not mentioned to me again, at least not by anyone in Leinster or the IRFU. It became a private joke for the lads who'd been involved – the Worcester Ten, as we referred to ourselves.

We still have an occasional giggle about it, but I wasn't giggling much at the time. I'd learned an important lesson about alcohol, and about behaviour in general, that stood with me for the rest of my career.

Macker picked me for France after all, though I had to play in a trial match pre-selection. I could tell from early in the trip that he wasn't interested in starting me in the games that counted. He air-dropped in a guy from Bedford Blues called Kieran Hallett, who now works for Leinster as a development officer. Kieran and Conan Doyle shared the out-half duties for the first few games, which we lost. I was given a run against Georgia, and we smashed them, but then Kieran was brought back in for the 5th/6th-place play-off, against England. They stuffed us again.

I was hurt, naturally, but determined not to sulk. Instead, I tried to keep it upbeat. Too upbeat, probably. I became almost the court jester, cracking jokes at training. That probably pissed Macker off even more. He probably thought I was being disrespectful. But I felt like this had become a feud.

It wasn't like there was anyone on the management team I could complain to. I did get on pretty well with Nigel Carolan, who was in charge of the backs. I felt he was sympathetic to my situation. Without spelling it out, he kind of let me know that he wasn't having much say in selection.

That summer of 2006, my reassurance came from Leinster, who showed some faith in me by giving me a development contract for the following season. Knoxy tried to comfort me, too. He told me that I couldn't be expected to make a difference because we weren't functioning as a team.

Still, I felt that the Six Nations and the World Cup had set me back in Cheika's eyes. I was annoyed at myself for playing through an injury, annoyed at Macker. Then, when my contract letter arrived, I noticed that it was for €12,000 and not €15,000 like my pals Kevin McLaughlin and Ross McCarron.

I asked Dad to call Mick Dawson, Leinster's CEO. I think Mick explained that I was a year younger than Kev and Ross and that's I why I was being paid less. But Dad kept at him and Mick agreed. I was bumped up to €15K. It wasn't the last time that I'd haggle over a contract!

When I look back at my younger self, I see a pretty antsy twenty-one-year-old. Nothing seemed to run smoothly for me in the early days at Leinster. I was fuelled by impatience, envy, strong feelings of injustice.

Part of me thinks this was good for my development, that the habitat suited me. Leinster was an angry, narky club at the time, going through its own growing pains. Yes, they had over-achieved in Cheiks's first year, getting to a semi-final in Europe for the first time since 1996. But that semi-final was a galling experience: a heavy defeat by Munster, and at Lansdowne Road.

Then Munster went on to capture their first Heineken Cup title, which only upped the ante for everyone associated with Leinster – players, coaching staff, administrators, supporters.

It had become a place of conflict, of disputes, of bollockings. Cheiks could fly off the handle, especially in the dressing room after a poor performance. Referees used to dread being confronted by him after matches. We needed this, though. Poor standards in any form shouldn't be tolerated, and Cheiks made this clear. He wanted to fight for everything. Eventually that rubs off. His drive was contagious.

You could also see the friction between Knoxy and Mike Brewer. They shared a desk when the centre of operations moved to David Lloyd Riverview, up the road from Donnybrook. This wasn't just an Aussie v. Kiwi thing. I think Mike thought some of the rock-star backs needed to be taken down a peg. He reckoned they took the foot off the gas as soon as they came back to Leinster from international duty.

He also wanted to stick up for the forwards, who were almost second-class citizens.

Knoxy, meanwhile, was pals with the rock stars. He knew how to wind Brewser up but also knew to stay at arm's length.

With Cheika, Knox and Brewer running the show, the atmosphere was always going to be fiery. But this was my natural milieu.

My role model at Leinster, Felipe, was another hothead. That Latin temperament was occasionally his undoing, but it was part of his genius and I loved him for it. Even on the day Munster beat us in Lansdowne Road he was fighting for every inch even when the game was lost. This wasn't lost on me. He played differently to me, but I learned so much from watching him every day at training.

Felipe was clearly out on his own as first-choice out-half. The contest for next-in-line had become a bit more complicated. Hickey and McAllister had been let go but in their place came Andy Dunne and Ian Keatley.

Dunne was quite experienced, having been on Leinster's books previously before spells at Harlequins and Bath. The Leinster committee presented him to Cheika as someone who could deputize when Felipe was away on Argentina duty in November or if he got injured.

Keatley was the next out-half through the academy system. He was on the Ireland Under-20s – as they had become – and they won a Slam that season. He was being touted for great things and wasn't short on confidence. I heard Richie Murphy, Leinster's skills coach, going on about him. That got up my nose a bit. I would find motivation anywhere I could.

I had my opportunity to put Keatley in his place when Mary's played in UCD that season. I went through him to score a try, then flung the ball into the crowd. I didn't mean to hit anyone, but clearly I wanted to make a point and then underline it.

Whatever about winning my private duel with Keatley, I was apparently no nearer getting a run with Leinster, and that was beginning to eat me up. Eventually I lost it with Cheiks.

This was early November, when Felipe was away with the Pumas. The A team was due to fly to Sale for a Monday-evening game, and pre-departure I got a tip-off from Emmet Farrell, our long-serving video analyst, that this could be my big opportunity. The senior team was due to play Glasgow in Donnybrook that Friday and there was talk that if I played well in Sale, I could get a run in the Magners League game. Emmet told me that Cheiks was flying over with team manager Paul McNaughton to watch me specifically.

We won easily and the game went well for me. Sale had a strong side out and we had plenty of senior players, too, so I was pleased. I landed maybe nine out of ten shots at goal on a pretty dirty night, including a couple of long-range kicks. After the final whistle, I had a quick glance up at the coaches' box but there was no sign of Cheiks, only McNaughton. I was fuming.

At least Emmet was there to film the game, so I knew there would be a review the next day. The good news was that Cheiks was going to take the review. This was his opportunity to big me up.

The first clip showed me launching a bomb that resulted in a Leinster try after the Sale full-back spilled the ball. It was the perfect start, but Cheiks was unimpressed.

He turned to me: 'That bloke was under no pressure at all from our chasers. Do you think that kick is going to be good enough against Shaun Payne [the Munster full-back]?'

That's how it started and that's how it went on. He ignored anything I'd done well and seemed to pounce on any opportunity to have a dig.

No doubt he'd say he was trying to set high standards. I get that now. At the time, I took it personally. It looked like he was seeking excuses not to pick me against Glasgow. I was fuming.

So I knocked on his door.

All right, mate? Did you get what I said in there?

Yeah, I replied. But I was told that you were coming over to Sale to watch and you didn't even bother. How come?

He tried to stay calm but I could see his face darkening. He suggested that maybe I could look after my job and he'd look after his. But then I went back at him again. I'm not sure what I said because the red mist had descended, on both sides of the desk. I just know I ended up storming out.

Years later, Cheiks revealed that he'd been impressed by the way I'd fronted up to him. It showed balls, he said. But at the time I was afraid that I'd blown it with him. I told my dad about what had happened, told him I was afraid Cheiks was going to tell me to pack my bags the next day. Dad reassured me, told me to keep my head down and work hard.

It turned out that he was right. Cheiks was grand the next morning.

It was: You all right, mate? All good?

He told me he was going with Andy Dunne for the Glasgow game but that my chance would come. I just needed to keep plugging away. I was just relieved he wasn't kicking me out.

My impatience must have been plain for all to see, though. Even opponents in the AIL seemed to be picking up on it. When Mary's played Shannon down in Thomond Park the following week, their out-half Tadhg Bennett was constantly taking the piss out of me.

I'm taking Contepomi here!

Or: It's OK, lads. I'm marking Felipe.

He had a right old giggle at my expense. Years later, myself and Tadhg had a good laugh about it when I was introduced to him at Seán Cronin's wedding. At the time, I wanted to smash him.

I couldn't understand why Cheiks could bring Luke Fitzgerald in straight out of school and throw him on the wing for a load of games that season, but when Felipe came back from Argentina duty with an injured knee, Cheiks refused to take a chance on me.

When he was talking to the press, he was always going on about how he wanted to promote Irish talent. When he listed his options at out-half, he always gave me a mention – 'Johnny', as he started calling me.

Just before Christmas, Cheiks shocked me. I was driving out of Templeville after some kicking practice on a Tuesday night when his name came up on my phone. He told me I'd be starting against Munster the following week, 27 December. Holy fuck.

Felipe's knee wasn't right yet. Christian Warner also had some sort of niggle. I wasn't even in the Heineken Cup squad, but suddenly I'd leapfrogged Andy Dunne.

Cheiks just said: I told you you'd get your chance.

I rang Dad, who was delighted. I didn't know how to feel. I'd been on my way to John Kilbride's house when Cheiks had called – John was the St Mary's scrum-half at the time and a good mate. I'd been sworn to secrecy, so I couldn't talk to John about the only thing that was on my mind.

When the team was announced, I got texts from my uncles in Kerry. *Hope you're man of the match but Munster win.* That would become the standard pre-match message from Listowel whenever we played Munster.

Seeing the Leinster line-up in print only spooked me: Dempsey, Horgan, O'Driscoll, D'Arcy, Hickie, Sexton, Easterby. Hundreds of international caps, an all-Lions three-quarter line, and me. Christ.

And that's before you considered the Munster team. Heineken Cup champions. At Thomond Park. I'd played there a couple of weeks previously with St Mary's against Shannon, and the place felt empty. Now it would be heaving to its 13,000 capacity – this was before the stadium was redeveloped. It was Christmas time, so the whole country would be watching. And instead of Tadhg Bennett standing opposite me, it would be Ronan O'Gara.

We had a training session under lights in Belvo on Christmas Eve, and I was very jittery. I went to throw a long pass to Brian off my left hand and it flew miles over his head. He threw his eyes to heaven and then gave me a look of utter disgust. I shrivelled inside.

I can't have been great company on Christmas Day or St Stephen's Day – the longest days of my life up to that point. Kicking on Christmas Day – Mark and I went to Donnybrook – was a first.

Strangely enough, I was grand once I got out on the pitch at Thomond. At some stage on the journey to Limerick, it had twigged with me: Cheiks wouldn't be starting me here unless he'd seen something in me. I'd been moaning about not getting an opportunity. Here it was. Get on with it. It's time to show what I'm made of.

I was lucky to get a shot at goal very early in the game, also lucky that it wasn't a particularly easy shot. Say it had been from twenty metres out, straight in front? That's wet-your-pants stuff, with the crowd eerily quiet as you line it up. With this shot from wideish on the right, I'd almost a licence to miss. But I didn't. The surge of confidence from seeing the ball sail between the sticks was incredible.

A good start got better when Girvan scored off a lovely move. From a scrum to the left of the posts, I shaped to feed Brian coming on a hard switch-line, then hit Denis with a long pass off my left – basically, the pass I'd screwed up in Belvo a few nights previously. This time it was on the money. Girve scored in the corner and while I missed the conversion, we now led 8–3 and I'd been central to all 8 points. Even Brian gave me the thumbs-up.

But that was our purple patch over and done with. The Munster pack steamrolled us after the break and O'Gara kicked five penalties. Final score: Munster 25, Leinster 11.

Cheiks was furious with the referee, Alan Lewis, and the mood on the bus journey back up was muted. But secretly, I was delighted with myself. I could feel a bruise developing on my chest where Denis Leamy or Anthony Foley had stamped on me when I was on the wrong side of the ruck, but it would be a badge of honour. I hadn't shirked the physical challenge. The feedback from my team-mates had been positive, too. When I came off twelve minutes from time, to be replaced by Felipe, I knew I'd given a good account of myself.

It was late when I got home that night, but I couldn't wait to watch the tape of the game. I must have watched and re-watched the first half about twenty times over the next few days.

There was more good news when we came in to River-view for rehab the morning after the game. Cheiks took me aside and told me that I'd be starting against Ulster on New Year's Eve; Felipe still wasn't right and Christian Warner wasn't 100 per cent either. Besides, he reckoned I'd earned another crack. I was beginning to warm to Cheiks.

The Ulster game was a massive fixture and a historic occasion – the last game at Lansdowne Road before it was knocked down for redevelopment. They marketed it as the Last Stand and 48,000 people turned up, which was a record for the Magners League. Both teams had their internationals all on parade.

Cheiks had a right go at me before the game. I'd been out on the pitch, practising my punting on halfway, when Andrew Trimble and Stephen Ferris came over to say hi. There were high-fives, some hugs and jokes. When I turned away, there was Cheiks, fuming.

What the fack, Johnny? We're going to war with these guys and you're high-fiving them?

By the time the game was ten minutes old, I'd already levelled Trimby twice. I was pumped. I had to prove to Cheiks that what happened before the game wasn't me.

David Humphreys went off injured early, so I was directly opposite Paddy Wallace, who was now officially Ireland's second-choice out-half. I was happy with how I went. It was blustery – appropriate conditions for the last game at the old stadium – and I coped well. We won, which helped. Afterwards, Cheiks admitted to the media that he'd left me on longer than planned.

'We probably wanted to give Felipe longer off the bench, but I thought the other kid was playing well,' he said. 'We decided to leave him on. He was taking the ball to the line. His defence was great, his kicking was good. I just thought: Leave him in there.'

I was actually sitting alongside Cheiks as he said this, maybe blushing a little. We did a press conference together a couple of days after the game – him sitting alongside me in case I said anything untoward!

He needn't have worried. I was suitably modest and respectful, saying how fortunate I had been to have been given the opportunity to play opposite O'Gara and Wallace, how lucky I was to learn from Felipe every week, how much I still had to learn. 'I just want to keep working hard in training and try and improve all the time,' I said. 'I suppose Michael will decide when I get my next opportunity.'

No doubt I had a wry smile as I said this. Did Cheiks take my words as a cheeky challenge? His quotes suggest that maybe he did.

'I don't think we've crossed any major bridges yet,' he said. 'Johnny knows that. We'll just keep working away. He's got heaps to learn but if he keeps evolving his game, he's going to get more opportunities. Johnny's given me some dirty looks from the crowd sometimes when he's been on the bench and I haven't given him any game-time. He's given me the dead stare. He's got some time now so that should keep him happy for a while!'

He didn't know me as well as he thought he did.

7

The only other time I made headlines that 2006/07 season, it was for the wrong reasons. In April 2007, the *Irish Sun* ran a picture of me on their front page, along with a story that I'd been stabbed in an incident outside a nightclub the previous November. Mercifully, this caused barely a ripple in the other papers. Clearly I wasn't box office.

The incident seemed a big deal at the time. It had been a standard AIL Saturday, finishing up with the Mary's crew in Tramco. A dance-floor argument turned into a full-scale bust-up on the Rathmines Road, between a bunch of rugby players and a bunch of lads from God-knows-where.

I was relatively sober and playing the role of peacemaker. Just as I was trying to talk sense to someone, I got smacked from the side a couple of times. Mayhem. During the next 'break in play' I noticed that I had blood coming from wounds in my head and chest. I could see that my team-mate Darragh Fanning had a chest wound, too. There was blood all over his shirt. It turned out that he had a punctured lung.

By the time the cops arrived and everything had been broken up, we discovered that three of us had been stabbed. CCTV footage showed a young woman moving through the crowd, slashing at people.

It turned out that she'd used cosmetic scissors, her hand in a fist with one of the blades protruding between her index and middle fingers. She'd jabbed at anyone she reckoned might have hit her boyfriend.

I gave a statement to the police the morning after, but decided not to attend when the case went to court. From what I heard, the woman expressed contrition for her actions. She was given a suspended sentence, community service and a fine.

It was a nasty business, but those of us who were involved can see a certain comedy in it now. We slag Mark, my brother, who lost it when he heard that I'd been attacked and grabbed his chief suspect by the throat. I liked his loyalty.

The problem was that the bloke he grabbed turned out to be an undercover cop. Mark was about to be handcuffed until I explained the misunderstanding. Thankfully the cop relented.

Then there was Darragh, our war hero, who was fine until he saw blood on his chest. That was when he collapsed. He had the oxygen mask on in the ambulance, as the three of us were carted off to Accident & Emergency. He was grand. We were taking the piss out of him before we'd arrived at the hospital.

The rest of the gang piled into taxis and followed us out. But the excitement soon faded. One of the cabs might have even gone to A&E via McDonald's. I seem to remember eating a burger while waiting to be stitched. We were all fine. By that stage I was more concerned with how I was going to explain my wounds at work on Monday morning.

There was no hiding the evidence: three stitches in my chest, two at the side of my head. I'd have to explain what happened – to Leinster's doctor, the late Professor Arthur Tanner, and of course to any of the players I bumped into that morning. For a day or two, there was talk of little else.

I was an innocent victim, of course, but I knew it didn't look good, especially coming so soon after the Worcester incident. Irish rugby is a tiny community, so everybody gets to hear everything. This only strengthened my determination to stay out of trouble from then on. Stay away from town. Stay away from anything that could put me in a situation like that again.

It's not like I gave up drink altogether. The odd beer was no harm, especially for someone who needed to be brought out of himself occasionally. But I cut right back on the Saturday nights out. For a few years, most of my team-mates probably thought that I was no craic at all.

I didn't have too many excuses to celebrate for the remainder of that season, except for the small matter of landing my first full-time professional contract for the 2007/08 season. A few of us had been given one-year deals: Dev Toner, Kev McLaughlin, Ross McCarron and myself. I even hired an agent, John Baker, to negotiate my salary. I started on €50,000.

Brian Wall had been right after all. I was a pro rugby player. And I was delighted with myself. I knew there was a good chance I'd see some game time the following autumn, when Felipe would be away with the Pumas at the World Cup in France. It couldn't come quickly enough.

The spring of 2007 had been a slow crawl. For all Cheiks's talk of playing me alongside Felipe during the Six Nations, it never materialized. He preferred to play Christian Warner and Mick Berne. I survived on a diet of AIL and the odd game for Leinster A.

It was as if Cheiks felt that by giving me a couple of starts, he had ticked a box. Having given the local lad a run, he could now get on with trying to win trophies.

As it turned out, Leinster went backwards in his second season, results-wise. Wasps walloped us in the quarter-finals of Europe and we finished third in the Magners

League – one slot lower than the previous year. Suddenly, Cheiks was beginning to get some heat.

Seeing as I was out of his plans, my aim for the remainder of that season was to feature in the Churchill Cup. This was a short development tournament with A teams from England, Scotland and Ireland mixed in with USA, Canada and the New Zealand Maori, to be held in England that year.

I made the squad but my performance was only so-so. Jeremy Staunton of Wasps started at out-half in our first game, against Canada, and I filled in for the injured Ross McCarron at full-back. When Eddie O'Sullivan called Jeremy out to the senior tour in Argentina, I got to start against a strong Maori side, who beat us well in Exeter. I was happy enough with how I played, but my goal-kicking on a windy day was poor. I held my place for the plate final against Scotland A at Twickenham but coach Michael Bradley brought Ian Keatley off the bench far too early for my liking.

All told, it was a forgettable trip. The previous year's Churchill Cup, in Canada and the US, had become known as the Churchill Stag – essentially a drinking tournament with occasional breaks for rugby. Twelve months on, it was as if guys felt they needed to maintain standards of partying. I wasn't up for that, not with my new regime of self-discipline and lessons from previous experiences.

I was never one of those happy-go-lucky tourists, to be honest. I wasn't comfortable with the idea of rooming with someone I'd never met before, who snored in the middle of the night and woke you up. I was probably seen as being very serious.

Looking back, I wish I'd made more of an effort to be

sociable, to lighten up a bit. But I guess it shows that I had serious aspirations. I wanted to make a breakthrough.

The remainder of that 2007 summer was a happy time. For the first time since fifth year in school, I was on holidays by early June. Laura and I had a lovely fortnight in Portugal, thanks to the generosity of Girvan Dempsey, who gave us the use of his apartment in Praia da Luz. It was also the first time I did a proper pre-season, so I came into the new season in good shape, carrying some new-found muscle.

I turned a corner with Knoxy, too. I can pinpoint the moment when it felt like he started to believe in me. It was during a mini-tour to the Basque Country, a week or two before the start of the Magners League, culminating in a friendly against Biarritz.

In training, we had been toying with this attacking play borrowed from rugby league, involving a couple of forward runners, and two passing options for the out-half: one 'front-door', one 'out the back'. We had no plan to use it against Biarritz, but a couple of minutes before half-time I pulled it out of the bag.

Miraculously, the two forwards went where I ushered them and then I hit Mick Berne with a no-look pass to send him in under the sticks. When we got back to the dressing room at the break, it looked as though Knoxy was on the verge of tears.

Sexto, you facking genius!

He was jumping around the place, ranting all sorts of random stuff about Greg Inglis and the South Sydney Rabbitohs. Cheiks had to tell him to pipe down. The lads were puzzled, but Knoxy often had that effect on people. I was chuffed. It was as though his entire perception of me had changed. He took me under his wing from that point.

I was given a good run at the start of the Magners campaign, too – five straight games where I wore the number 10 jersey. We didn't get a lot of attention that autumn. The eyes of the world were on France, where Ireland were flopping badly at the World Cup. You could have fooled me, though. When I ran out to make my first start at the RDS, against Edinburgh, it felt like this was the centre of the rugby universe.

It was a lovely evening and we got a decent crowd – the RDS was now our permanent residence, seeing as we had outgrown Donnybrook. We beat Edinburgh fairly comfortably and I scored my first try for Leinster.

With the internationals away, there was a different atmosphere about the place. New voices. Leo Cullen and Shane Jennings were back from their spell in Leicester and they commanded respect simply by the fact that they had won things with the Tigers – a Premiership title and an EDF Cup. They'd both played in a Heineken Cup final, which was further than Leinster had ever gone in the competition.

I warmed to Leo. He was quiet-spoken but had natural authority, which Leicester had acknowledged by making him captain, plus he was a pal of Smythie. Jenno was Mary's, so I was inclined to like him anyway, but he and Leo brought a directness that I loved. They were Leinster through and through. What they'd learned in the Leicester culture started rubbing off on us.

Before our second game, away to Cardiff, Leo and Jenno introduced a concept that was probably new to Leinster dressing rooms: we needed to beat the shit out of Cardiff. It was simple – they'd be looking to bully us so we'd need to bully them. Leinster teams weren't known for having a hard edge back then.

Cardiff were decent. They'd only been pipped by the Ospreys for the Magners title the previous season. But we tore into them, stuffed them 30–12. I made twenty-two tackles, scored the bonus-point try, got a couple of touchline conversions. It felt like I was beginning to belong.

It all came tumbling down the following week when the Scarlets put 50 points on us – still Leinster's biggest defeat at the RDS. I cringe at the memory of some mistakes, like not taking due care with a short-range conversion and seeing it rebound off the upright. Schoolboy error.

But things went better for me in Glasgow, and better again in Belfast when some of the internationals started to filter back after the World Cup. This was my first experience of playing alongside Ollie le Roux – a big man with a big personality.

Johnny, you must give me the ball early.

Ollie had opinions on everything, but when it's someone who has over fifty caps for the Springboks, you listen – especially when he had positive things to say. There were a few compliments on the bus back to Dublin after our 16–16 draw with Ulster. Darce was really positive about my performance.

'You were up against David Humphreys and you looked the part. You looked like an international player in the making,' he said.

The more time you spent with the Ollies and the Darces and the Dricos, the harsher the withdrawal symptoms when you were yanked out of the team. Which is what happened a week before the Heineken Cup.

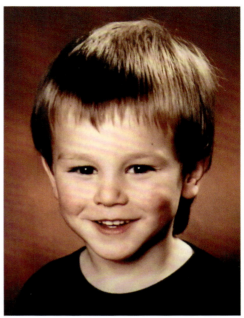

With my parents and my mother's parents, John and Sally Nestor – rugby ball already in hand.

First day of first class.

Golf runs in the family – my Grandad John held the course record at Milltown for years – and I started early.

Celebrating my third birthday with my parents and my Kerry grandparents, John and Brenda Sexton.

With my siblings: Jerry (on chair), Gillian and Mark (with Dad).

Bective Rangers was Dad's club, and from a young age it became my club too.

Giving a speech as captain of the St Mary's College Under-13s, after winning the 1999 Provincial Cup.

In fourth year at St Mary's, I came off the bench late in the 2002 Leinster Schools Senior Cup final against Belvedere at Lansdowne Road and hit a drop-goal that turned a one-point lead into a four-point lead. (Inpho/Billy Stickland)

On holiday with Laura, aged sixteen.

In 2004, my final year at St Mary's, I was team captain and we were joint favourites with Blackrock College for the Senior Cup. But we were unluckily drawn against them in the first round, and lost after leading by 14 at half-time – which meant my schoolboy career ended in the low-key Plate competition.

I'd been frustrated about not getting an opportunity to start for Leinster when Michael Cheika picked me to start away to Munster just after Christmas 2006. We lost, but I gave a good account of myself. (Inpho/Lorraine O'Sullivan)

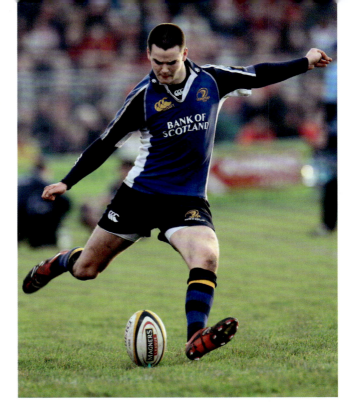

'We probably wanted to give Felipe longer off the bench, but I thought the other kid was playing well': so said Cheika at a press conference after my second consecutive start against an Irish province. (Inpho/Dan Sheridan)

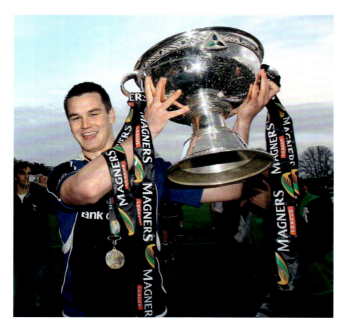

When we won the Magners League in 2008, it was Leinster's first trophy in a number of years. But Munster had just won their second Heineken Cup, and that was the trophy we really wanted.
(Inpho/Dan Sheridan)

Away to Castres in the Heineken Cup in December 2008, I was taken off at half-time, even though I'd scored a try and we were ahead. We went on to lose the game and got hammered in the media. Humiliated, I started thinking about where I would play my rugby next season.
(Inpho/Dan Sheridan)

Ronan O'Gara's words to me – 'You're useless, a nobody' – had been running through my head in the weeks leading up to the 2009 Heineken Cup semi-final at Croke Park. On the day we finally lived up to our potential, something was released. (Inpho/James Crombie)

As I set up to take a long-range drop-goal early in the 2009 Heineken Cup final against Leicester, everyone watching – family, friends, team-mates – thought it was a bad idea. But I nailed the kick and we went on to win our first European Cup. (Inpho/Graham Stuart)

With Laura after winning my first senior international cap, against Fiji in November 2009.

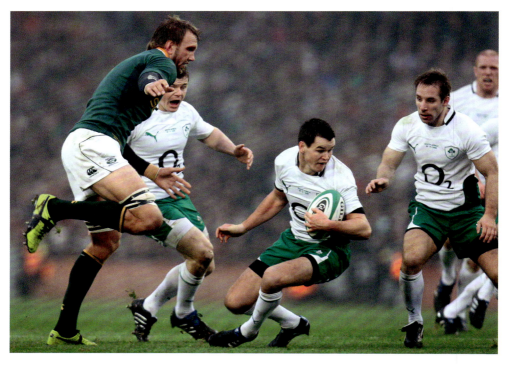

After I started against Fiji, I expected Declan Kidney to pick O'Gara to start against South Africa at Croke Park – but I was wrong. (Inpho/James Crombie)

I'd been hopeful of featuring in Europe, mainly because there was no sign of Felipe. The Pumas had made the last four of the World Cup and then he'd popped home to Buenos Aires for his brother's wedding. Naively, I'd allowed myself to think Cheiks might start me against Leicester at the RDS, with Felipe on the bench, or at least that he might include me in the twenty-two.

But no, he moved Christian Warner to 10 against Connacht the week before the Heineken. Warner kicked seven out of seven. I got two minutes off the bench.

He made me twenty-fourth man against Leicester. A gesture of inclusion? I didn't see it that way. I remember it was a lunchtime kick-off because I was there for the build-up before going to play for Mary's in UCD. I was there for the pre-match meal, for the jersey presentation by Fergus Slattery, for the warm-up. I was out on the pitch as the crowd grew, practising my kicking with Felipe. Then it was cheerio, grab your bag, hop in the car and head up to Belfield.

To be driving out on to an empty Simmonscourt Road, just as the noise inside the stadium was building to a crescendo, was soul-destroying.

I couldn't tell you if Mary's won that day. I was suffering from separation anxiety. I was fixated with getting back to my folks' house to watch the highlights of the Leinster game. They hosed the Tigers. That only pissed me off more.

Does this sound disloyal to Leinster? Unprofessional? If I heard a junior player say something like this now, I'd tear strips off him. But let's be honest. This is what ambition looks like. And if you asked the O'Driscolls and Horgans, they'd probably tell you that they wanted young players with a bit of hunger coming through, guys with an edge. They were sick of kids who were happy to have the contract, the sponsored car and the tracksuit. They liked the fact that kids like myself, Seán O'Brien and Fergus McFadden were aggressive in training, competitive in the gym. They liked that we put ourselves about. They could see it meant something to us.

So while I wasn't exactly cheering as Toulouse beat us 33–6 the following week, I wasn't heartbroken either. Nor was I unhappy when Darce was a late withdrawal from the Magners game against the Ospreys. Leinster got back to winning, with me at 10 after the reshuffle. The week after that, I got lucky again, as Brian limped off thirty minutes into the game against Munster in Cork. Another opportunity, another win.

A significant win, too – our first on Munster soil since the turn of the century. It was a horrible night, freezing and wet, exactly the sort of night when Leinster packs were supposed to run out the gate. The forwards actually outplayed a full-strength Munster pack that night, and this was when Munster were at their peak. It must have been sweet for Stephen Keogh, who formed a double act with Trevor Hogan – our Munster cast-offs. They were chippy about having to leave their native province, but that type of chippiness was what we needed.

We were still way off the pace in Europe, though. Any chance of qualification virtually disappeared when we lost in Edinburgh in Round 4. Again, I was absolved of any blame, as I only played a minute off the bench.

In the Magners, however, we looked almost unbeatable. At Christmas time, Cheiks tried a 10-12-13 of me, Felipe and Darce against Ulster at the RDS. In some quarters, it was written up as a face-off between myself and Paddy Wallace to decide who was second in the Ireland out-half rankings. We won 29–0 before a full house and while Felipe took the place-kicks, I took the MOTM.

Things were looking up.

Two weeks later, it was the Ospreys in Dublin and Cheiks stuck with me and Felipe at 10-12, with Brian replacing Darce at 13. Leinster 26, Ospreys 15.

Reporters noted that Felipe had given me a tongue-lashing at one stage during the game. 'The odd time he lets his Latin side come through,' I told them afterwards. 'But that's fine, I'm the same, I get a little bit angry sometimes.'

Toulouse were due at the RDS the following Saturday, and when I was announced as Leinster's Player of the Month for December, there was media pressure on Cheiks to start me, especially given that our chances of qualifying from our Heineken pool were negligible. He resisted that pressure.

But there were some amazing whispers from Darce and Brian at training. They told me I'd a good chance of being on the bench for the Six Nations opener against Italy. What?!

They explained. With Ireland having gone so badly at the World Cup, Eddie O'Sullivan was under enormous pressure to bring in some new blood. Weirdly, it was beginning to look like I'd a better chance of playing international rugby than I had of playing in the Heineken Cup.

Sure enough, on the Tuesday after the Toulouse game, Eddie announced a squad of thirty-three for the Six Nations and my name was included as one of three out-halves, along with O'Gara and Paddy Wallace.

I'd never spoken to Eddie. I met him on the day of the squad announcement at a press conference to publicize the IRFU's High Performance Select Group – myself and Cian Healy had been included in this, as well as the Ireland squad.

We had an awkward elevator experience with him, where he shook our hands but said nothing, before walking out into the hotel foyer.

Did he actually know who we were?

The cynic in me wondered if Eddie had felt pressurized into including us. Or did I have a genuine chance of featuring as O'Gara's understudy? Paddy had been playing centre for Ulster, and Ulster had been struggling.

Just to be in the extended squad was unbelievably exciting. I was fascinated to know what the Munster players were like close up. I couldn't wait to pick up all that new kit when the squad assembled in Killiney Castle the following Sunday evening. But I never made it to Killiney.

That Saturday I was in Leicester, on the bench for what was a meaningless Heineken Cup game. Cheiks threw me on when the game was virtually over but I found time to break my thumb tackling someone. I was put in a cast for six weeks – the entire Six Nations, in other words.

I saw it as a catastrophe. What if this had been my chance and I didn't get another? Laura did her best to console me. Felipe was thoughtful, too. He called and asked me to meet him for coffee. He managed to convince me that my injury wasn't the worst thing. I was better off not being with Ireland for this campaign. The pressure on Eddie was building. The camp wouldn't be a positive environment for a young player. And he was right. Eddie got the bullet at the end of the tournament.

Other things worked in my favour. Darce had broken his arm badly against Italy and would be out for the guts of a year. His career was even under threat at one stage. I felt for Darce as he had been so good to me, but when you're in the thick of it you are more concerned with what his absence means for you. I was fit to play again by the end of the Six Nations. With Darce gone, Felipe would move to 12. This was my opportunity.

By now, Leinster had one goal only: the Magners. With six games remaining, we needed four wins to clinch the title. This was in the days before play-offs and grand finals. Our fourth-last game was at home to Munster.

In theory, Munster had a score to settle. Having lost to us in Musgrave Park before Christmas, this was when they'd put us back in our box. But whereas they had one eye on a Heineken Cup semi-final against Saracens the following week, we had no distractions.

All we had was an axe to grind. Cheiks kept reminding us in the days leading up to the game: Jenno and Keith Gleeson hadn't got a look-in with Ireland during the Six Nations, despite being in great form all season; meanwhile Munster had four back-rowers in the squad. Leo, our skipper, had been inspirational, and yet he, too, had been overlooked; Eddie had preferred Mick O'Driscoll – Munster's third-choice lock. What were we going to do about it?

It was a dogfight, played on a pissy night. I was as fired up as any of the forwards, determined to stir things up. I clipped Denis Leamy with my shoulder just after the whistle had gone for half-time – he chased after me and pushed me through the advertising hoarding near the tunnel.

Naturally I wanted to play well opposite O'Gara. What I noticed about him was how aggressive he was towards his own forwards. At one stage, Alan Quinlan had to be held back from him but O'Gara kept snapping at him, telling him to shape up. Cheiks was always at me to get into team-mates, to push my weight around, not to worry about someone's age or reputation.

Mate, if you are going to be the number 10 in this team you need to learn to give it to someone when they don't do what you want.

It was instructive to see O'Gara in action, close up. And it was especially enjoyable to have the decisive say that night. Near the end, I dropped a nice goal to put us two scores clear. Felipe gave me a big high-five to celebrate.

I've happy memories of playing alongside Felipe during that Magners run-in. He was still taking the place-kicks, so that took some pressure off me. It was educational. For each set piece, I'd consult with him before sending in the call – do we box-kick to put the pressure back on them or do we play? I learned a lot about managing the team, managing the scoreboard.

I grew in self-assurance, too, even though we stuttered on the home straight. Needing just one win with three games to play, we lost in Edinburgh – typical of Leinster in those days. In the review, Brian, Shaggy and Mike Brewer all had a go at me over my game management. We'd been leading by 9 points with ten minutes to go and I had moved the ball from deep. It was a five-on-three but someone spilled the pass. All three of them agreed that in the circumstances, I should have kicked long.

I was up against a heavyweight trio – two Lions and an All Black – but I stood my ground. It shouldn't matter where we were on the pitch, I argued. We had numbers, we had pace. Why give the ball away? They weren't having it. Play according to the match situation, they said. It got quite heated. They won the argument but I hadn't backed down. Knoxy gave me a wink and a thumbs-up afterwards.

Lots of the players seemed to walk on eggshells around some of the senior players in particular. The deference probably annoyed them after a while. But what Brian in particular used to say was: 'We won't win anything until we start holding each other to account, and that includes me.' Maybe he saw the Munster players in Ireland camp doing this. I took it on board.

The only positive about losing against Edinburgh was that we avoided clinching the title at Murrayfield when it felt like there was nobody there. Instead, on a balmy evening at the RDS, we walloped the Dragons 41–8 before a full house to win the league. They erected a presentation platform on the pitch and we sprayed ourselves with champagne and cider.

I remember the leaders saying in the dressing room that this was only a stepping stone. The Magners was fine for now but it wasn't the trophy we really wanted – Munster had just won that, for the second time. Still, it was an emotional evening. This was Keith Gleeson's final game for Leinster, a fitting send-off for a great pro and great person. Ollie le Roux was heading back to South Africa, and he signed off with a couple of tries.

It was a massive moment for me, too – Leinster's first trophy in a while, and I had worn the 10 jersey. I was happy, finally.

I made my first senior appearance for Ireland a few weeks later, although you'll struggle to find mention of it anywhere in the record books. It was against the Barbarians at Kingsholm, a warm-up for the tour to New Zealand and Australia but without the Munster contingent, who were still celebrating their Heineken win. I replaced Shane Horgan in the seventy-ninth minute of an uncapped match.

You may laugh, but I was happy with my minute or two on the pitch. Before the game, I'd spent some time with video analyst Mervyn Murphy, who was a vital player in a few Ireland coaching set-ups. Merv showed me clips of Dan Carter, focusing on how he passed and then ran support lines up the middle, sometimes ahead of the ball, backing himself to get on the end of something. Against the Baa-Baas, I got one opportunity to run a similar line and almost got that critical second touch. Merv spotted it, too. I've always been good at learning. When coaches I respected told me something I made it my business to implement it into my training. This piece of advice would serve me for the rest of my career.

The Churchill Cup was in North America that summer: pool games against USA and England Saxons in Ontario before finals day in Chicago. Compared to twelve months previously, I felt confident and secure – and determined to make an impression on Declan Kidney, who'd just been announced as the new Ireland coach and who'd be watching the action on TV.

We were well beaten by a strong Saxons side but I was satisfied with my general performance, except for carelessly missing a short-range conversion. The Plate final was against an Argentina XV on a baking hot day in Chicago. I scored a try, dropped a goal and kicked well. The Sky commentators made me man of the match. I still have the bottle of champagne.

Happily, I now had more space for trophies. I became a property owner that year. I was now a man of means, half-way through a much improved two-year contract for €85K a season. I'd been desperate to move out of home. Here was my chance.

This was 2008, just as the Irish property market was about to crash. I thought I was getting a great deal – a two-bed apartment in Goatstown for €500K. Sure, there was no such thing as a bad property purchase in Dublin.

Two years later, those apartments were on the market for €270K and weren't budging. Mercifully, Dad had made sure I got a tracker mortgage. Still, I wonder if that apartment will ever be worth what I paid for it.

It didn't take very long before I asked Laura to move in with me. I was slightly uncomfortable with the idea, at first. Not uncomfortable with the actual living together, more with how it would look. I was still only twenty-two, twenty-three. None of my friends lived with their girlfriends. I remember one night having some of the lads in for a game of poker and never mentioning that Laura was in bed asleep.

There was an in-betweeny phase when she was half with her folks, half with me. But it was awkward moving her stuff in and out. Besides, I noticed that the place was tidier when she stayed! I also ate better. It just made sense. Why delay the inevitable?

She insisted on paying rent at first. At this stage she'd got a job as a primary teacher and wanted to pay her way. After a while, I refused. I was on good money for someone my age. She had looked after me when I was a poor, pudgy Leaving Cert student. Now it was my turn. Besides, this wasn't what you'd call a business relationship.

8

I should recall 2009 as the happiest of times. It was the year when I was air-dropped into a Heineken Cup semi-final at Croke Park, the year Leinster conquered Europe for the first time, the year I made my international debut.

But it was also the year when I made up my mind to leave Leinster.

Psychologists talk about 'negativity bias' – the idea that negative experiences are more affecting than positive ones because they are more intensely felt, and therefore more likely to lodge themselves in your memory. I was suffering from negativity bias at the start of 2009, feeling very low. In January I decided that there was no way I would make it in Leinster. I asked my agent, John Baker, to see what clubs might be interested in me. There was some brief interest from Worcester, but it never went anywhere.

John also offered my services to Connacht and to Munster. Both provinces turned me down.

I looked around me at Leinster and saw Rob Kearney – a year younger than me but with ten international caps already. Or Luke Fitzgerald – two years younger than me, eight Ireland caps.

Meanwhile, four months before that famous Heineken Cup semi in Croker, the only rugby I was getting was with Mary's in the AIL.

Ironically, one of the reasons given for Leinster's success that 2008/09 season was that we had a happier workspace.

Leo and Cheiks had pushed hard to get us our own dedicated changing room at David Lloyd Riverview. The previous season, we'd been mixing in with Riverview members. You had to mind what you said. There was hardly any of the banter that warms up a dressing room.

Our new home was basically Cheiks's old office. It was a bit cramped but it was ours. More intimate, you could say. Established internationals were encouraged to sit beside academy members and to engage with them. Cheiks actually stuck names on the wall above where he wanted people to sit. Younger players were plonked in between senior internationals. It helped us to build relationships. The dressing room became the place to be. Where all the craic and banter was had.

There were new faces, too. Jono Gibbes came in for Mike Brewer. Knoxy had been replaced by Alan Gaffney, also known as Riff – from Australia and a lovely bloke – who divided his time between Leinster and Ireland over the next couple of seasons. Kurt McQuilkin was still in charge of defence and doing a great job.

Cheiks had convinced the Leinster board to buy in some quality players, too. In came Rocky Elsom, CJ van der Linde and Isa Nacewa.

I wasn't going out of my way to be best mates with Isa. I couldn't pretend that I was happy to see him because I'm no good at pretending. He's a lovely bloke who became a great friend, but back then he was a threat. Graham Henry had wanted him for the All Blacks, but he was ineligible, having played a couple of minutes of Test rugby for Fiji in his teens. He'd been signed as a utility back, but Cheiks made it clear that he saw him as an out-half. In two of our three pre-season games, he moved Isa to 10 at half-time.

You can imagine how jumpy I was. I'd just helped Leinster win the Magners. We'd done the double on Munster in the league and I'd played in both games. Declan Kidney, the new Ireland coach, had included me in his training squad. But the message I was getting loud and clear from Cheiks was that he didn't trust me to get the job done for him.

Years later, I came to understand his point of view. Munster had just won Europe, again. If Leinster didn't emulate them soon, he'd be out of a job. He didn't need an inexperienced player in the pivotal postion. I was only twenty-three, still learning.

At the time, I just felt threatened. Confused, too. We now think of Isa as Leinster's greatest import. One of our greatest ever players full stop, someone who had a profound impact on the whole organization, who changed our entire way of thinking. But at first, I was insecure. I understood why they signed him but I didn't see him as a 10. He was tough, all right. Ultra-competitive, ultra-professional. He ran outrageous lines, had good hands. But an out-half?

Typically, I overthought things. I decided that if I was going to get picked ahead of Isa, I would have to play like Isa: run hard, take the ball flat to the line, challenge defences. It wasn't much good for me. I was trying to be something I wasn't. It also wasn't good for my body when I suffered an early concussion against Edinburgh. My first-ever concussion and probably my worst.

This was in Round 2 of the Magners. I don't remember how I got a bang to the head, but then I remember virtually nothing about that whole day – and the tiny bit I do recall came to me the next day, in the form of a flashback.

It is after the game and Laura is driving me out of the RDS. Brian pulls up alongside to ask how I am. He smiles at my attempts to communicate. It seems both of them are amused by my confusion – none of us had a clue about the seriousness of concussion at the time. Brian then tells Laura to make sure I'm OK.

Apart from this snippet, I'm relying on other people's accounts of what happened. Brian and Felipe told me that I was speaking gibberish out on the pitch, coming up with calls that they'd never heard before.

It was Brian who flagged the problem to the touchline doc. Newspaper reports said that I looked furious when I was called ashore after thirty minutes, shaking my head, cursing in the general direction of the coaches' box. I have no recollection of this.

All I know is that I woke up in the apartment with a saucepan beside my bed and a towel on the ground, thinking that it was the morning of the game.

Laura was there, which completely threw me – back then, she used to stay with her parents the night before a game. She tried to explain what had happened the night before. Apparently I took some convincing.

If a player suffers a concussion like this now, he is kept in hospital overnight for observation. Back then, guidelines were a bit looser. Laura had come down to the dressing-room area to collect me. She was told to keep an eye on me, not to let me drive, to contact the team doctor if I was feeling unwell.

She says that I was a tricky patient. Once we got home, I went for a shower and locked the bathroom door behind me. It was a long shower – about thirty minutes, apparently. Laura was banging on the door but getting no response. When she eventually picked the lock, I was still standing under the shower in my Leinster gear, the water now freezing.

While she was drying me off, I kept asking the same three questions.

Johnny: What happened?

Laura: You got taken off. You had a bad concussion.

Johnny: Who came on?

Laura: Isa.

Johnny: How did he do?

Laura: He got man of the match.

Johnny: Ah, fuck.

Five minutes later, the same conversation repeated itself.

What happened?

You got taken off. You had a bad concussion.

Who came on?

Et cetera.

She says I asked the same three questions, in the same order, maybe a dozen times. Laura said the worst thing about it all was having to tell me Isa got man of the match repeatedly and seeing the devastation on my face each time. She was worried about me, naturally. Eventually I slept.

If you had an injury, the deal was that you reported for a medical examination the day after the game. But you wouldn't be highlighting a concussion back then. It probably meant that you'd be stood down for two weeks – and I definitely didn't want to give Cheiks an excuse to do that.

When Cheiks was asked by reporters why I had been replaced so early, he said that I'd got a 'bump', and that wasn't questioned. He stood me down for the following week anyway, starting Isa against the Dragons.

We had another blazing row after training on the Tuesday after the concussion. Cheiks obviously sensed that I was unhappy and asked, amicably enough, if everything was OK.

I would have been on the defensive, as I invariably was at the time, hearing criticism in every word. It didn't take long before conversation turned to confrontation.

His basic message, as I recall, was to stay positive, not to get the hump as I'd done when I was replaced in those pre-season games.

Don't get down about it, mate. Get better.

He said he wanted me to stay in the fight with Isa and Felipe for the 10 jersey. Fair enough.

I don't remember the exact back-and-forth of the conversation. I just know that voices were raised, that there was no happy resolution and that I carried a sense of grievance around with me for the next couple of days.

It wasn't always confrontation between myself and Cheiks. He put a lot of time into coaching me. He used to show me grainy old clips of the Ella brothers and other guys he'd played with at Randwick, how they used to follow the pass, look for a second or third touch. On one hand I loved the information he was giving me and I listened intently. On the other hand, I took it as criticism. The things he was showing me were things I wasn't doing. I look back and wish I knew then what I know now. Having worked with some great coaches and sports psychologists later in my career, I now realize I wasted a lot of time and energy being hypersensitive and insecure, rather than having a growth mindset and ambition just to get better day in day out.

Was I being ultra-defensive? Undoubtedly. But then Cheiks could have that effect on people. He could needle you. He wanted to change Leinster's casual, cosy culture, so he was always on people's cases. But ultimately it was me who needed to change.

I remember telling him once that I needed an afternoon

off, as I had a commerce exam coming up. His response was typical.

'Commerce exam? Mate, you better decide if you wanna be an accountant or a footy player.'

Isa broke his arm against Ospreys, putting him out for a couple of months and handing me an opportunity. But I wasn't in the best place psychologically, certainly not where I needed to be against Munster, who returned to the RDS the following week intent on revenge. The sight of Rocky and CJ making their first starts for Leinster only fired them up more.

It finished Leinster 0, Munster 18 – our first defeat at the RDS in twelve months, the first time I heard 'The Fields of Athenry' being sung there. Not a pleasant experience.

The newspapers didn't make for easy reading, either. Gerry Thornley in the *Irish Times* praised O'Gara's performance warmly and wrote that I had been 'pedestrian by comparison'. In the *Sunday Tribune*, Neil Francis said that my performance was 'below AIL standard'. Nice.

I read everything that was written about me back then. Not only would I scour the papers, I'd type my name into search engines, go digging in fans' online forums, hoping for positive mentions, dreading the negative ones. I knew no better. I wasn't the only one doing it. It's natural to want to know what's being said and written about you. But it can fry your brain.

I took it as a positive sign when John O'Brien in the *Sunday Independent* asked for an interview. I was honest with him, especially in what I said about O'Gara. I said that I had to stop 'looking at him in awe'. And I admitted that I was desperate to put some heat on him.

'People write about the difference in class,' I said. 'They

talk about how good he played and how far away you are. That gets to me at the moment a little bit. People saying if O'Gara gets injured we're in big trouble. That'd get to you.'

O'Brien seemed to understand me. He described me as 'something of a brooder, haunted for days by defeat and the question of his own hand in it'. And I agreed with him. 'I probably need to give myself a break sometimes,' I said.

I could show a level of self-awareness to a journo, but could I follow it through and actually give myself a break? Not when results were going against me. The week after Munster, I started against Connacht in Galway and we lost – a result that dredged up all the old doubts about our fragility. Then Felipe came in for the first Heineken game, away to Edinburgh, and everything clicked. The following week, we had another bonus-point win, at home to Wasps – again, with Felipe starting at 10.

At least I had a positive input off the bench against Wasps. With my first touch, I put Luke over in the left corner with a lovely pass. I watched it back on tape that night, replaying that moment a few times.

Will Greenwood on Sky Sports described it as 'magical, an absolutely brilliant piece of skill by the replacement, Kearney'.

The following week, I started away to Glasgow. We lost. I took solace from the fact that Deccie had included me in the training squad for the November internationals – valuable experience for me. What's more, Felipe was now out of action with a nasty hand infection. With Isa still recovering, I had a good chance of making my first start in the Heineken when we played Castres back-to-back in December.

I was still haunted by doubts, though, convinced that Cheiks didn't really believe in me. This was only made worse when he flew David Holwell in from New Zealand as short-term out-half cover. Holwell had been a Leinster fan favourite. Was he a threat? Of course he was.

Cheiks put him on the bench for the first Castres game, at the RDS, and he replaced me in the final quarter. It seemed like the crowd was applauding Holwell on to the pitch a lot louder than they were applauding me off it.

We won that game by 30 points but failed to secure a four-try bonus point, so it was reported almost as a failure. The media abuse was only starting, though. When we lost in Castres the following Friday night, the flak really flew. Leinster 'ladyboys' – all that stuff.

I'm tempted to absolve myself of guilt here, seeing as we were leading 12–9 when Cheiks gave me the hook. At half-time! I'd just scored a try and I'd played pretty well in general, barring one sloppy missed conversion. But this was Felipe's first game back after the hand infection and I'm guessing Cheiks had decided he was going to give him the second forty, regardless. He just came into the dressing room and said: 'Phil, you're on. Johnny, you're off.'

He started talking about where we needed to improve. I heard none of it. I felt like I'd been winded. Devastated.

That was probably the night I decided that I was leaving Leinster. This might sound like me being unreasonable, over-emotional. I was still not established, whereas Felipe had been nominated for World Player of the Year only twelve months previously. It still felt unfair. I'd never been replaced at half-time, in any team. And it had been done so casually.

Phil, you're on. Johnny, you're off. The humiliation.

As I sat frozen in the stand for the second half, I was wondering where I would go play my rugby next year, and half-rooting for Castres. They'd already lost at home five times that season, but they had some decent players and they sniffed an opportunity to win back some respect from their supporters. Meanwhile, we were awful, off the pace. Castres 18, Leinster 15.

Two nights later, when the Ireland squad assembled in Enfield for a two-day camp, I was at rock bottom mentally, in need of some love. Deccie provided it. I'd barely walked into the hotel reception when Ireland's new coach was over to me for a quiet and comforting word.

He told me to keep my head up. He felt that I'd been treated harshly by Cheiks, that I had been playing well and it was ridiculous to take me off. He reassured me that I was one of three out-halves in the Ireland squad and that I'd a good chance of getting a run with Ireland A, who were due to play England Saxons and Scotland A in February. This gave me a huge lift. I soon received another.

In the histories that have been written about Ireland's 2009 Grand Slam, that weekend in Enfield is seen as being pivotal – the time when Rob Kearney raised questions about the Munster contingent and where their real priorities lay. I remember it for the determination of the senior players to win a Grand Slam. But mainly I remember it for Pádraig Harrington.

Deccie had invited him to speak to us that Sunday night. I was blown away by Harrington's openness, his honesty. He seemed so normal, so vulnerable to the doubts that go through every sportsperson's head at some stage. Harrington had just won three majors in the space of thirteen months. He was a superstar. And yet he seemed so humble, so human.

He told us about how he'd choked on the final hole of the British Open the previous year only to be rescued by his caddy, Ronan Flood. Standing on the seventy-second tee at Carnoustie, he led Sergio García by a shot. But he drove his tee shot into the Barry Burn and then knocked his third into the water at the front of the green.

'When I hit the second ball in the water, I just died there,' he told us. 'I just felt embarrassed. I felt I'd thrown away the Open.'

As he walked down towards the drop-zone, he allowed himself to imagine his father's disappointment, to imagine the disappointment of Irish people watching in pubs and golf clubs all over the country.

Flood had kept at him, though, bombarding him with positive thoughts. Screw your head on, Pádraig. You've a pitch from forty-five metres. Get up and down for a 6 and you've a good chance of being in the play-off. And of course, Harrington won that play-off with García.

You assume that these superstars are bulletproof mentally, but this made me realize that they aren't. They've won majors and yet they're fragile. They're human. I'd had those doubts on the pitch, especially as a place-kicker. And I'd allowed them to affect me. It felt like he was speaking directly to me.

Pádraig also warned us of the dangers of paying too much attention to media comment. He recalled how a journalist had labelled him as a choker after he had lost a tournament by a stroke. He felt he'd played brilliantly but had just been beaten on the day. The following year he returned to the same tournament and was unbelievably lucky to win – fortunate lies, lucky bounces, everything. The same journalist celebrated him for his resilience, when in fact he'd bottled it more the year that he won.

From that point on, he'd decided to pay no attention to

the media. He told his wife he didn't want to hear what was being said about him.

Again, this chimed with me. I wasn't good at dealing with criticism, whether it was from Cheiks or from the media. When it was criticism with no basis in fact, it infuriated me.

You've no idea how uplifting it was to discover that one of my sporting heroes had suffered from such doubts and insecurities. It felt like a real turning point – my first insight into the thinking of an elite sportsman. It sparked an interest in sports psychology. The following week, I went out and bought *Golf is not a Game of Perfect* by Harrington's sports psychologist, Bob Rotella.

I was half-jealous of O'Gara, who went and spoke to Pádraig one-on-one after his talk in Enfield. Their tête-à-tête provided much amusement for the other Munster players, who got stuck into O'Gara at the earliest opportunity.

I went straight to my hotel room and rang Enda McNulty, the performance coach who'd been doing some work with Mary's, helping me with my place-kicking in particular.

Pádraig Harrington has exactly the same thoughts as me, I told him. *I will never read media ever again. I need to get my routine better than ever. I need to improve my mental strength.*

For all the encouragement I was getting in Camp Ireland, January 2009 found me in a strange place. Essentially I was one injury away from featuring in the Six Nations – a scary state of affairs when you consider the only rugby I was getting was in the AIL. Deccie was blessed that O'Gara stayed fit for the entirety of that season.

Here's another way of looking at it. Between 12 December and 21 February, I didn't play a single second for Leinster, despite being fully fit. No wonder I was looking to leave. The club had offered me a new two-year deal at €100K, so clearly they saw me as part of their future. I just couldn't see a future for me in Leinster.

Cheiks now had everybody on board. Isa, Felipe and Darce were all fit again. Cheiks started Isa at 10 for five straight games before realizing he had more to offer in the back three. I trained with the squad all week, running with the bibs, or I was in Ireland camp, again running with the bibs. The weekends I spent with Mary's.

The day Leinster played Wasps at Twickenham, their second-last pool game, I was up in Templeville, slogging it out against Garryowen in appalling conditions – so bad that the game was abandoned at half-time.

I was properly pissed off that the ref had called a halt. We trailed just 0–3, despite having played into the storm, and I'd enjoyed getting stuck in. I suspected that someone influential from Garryowen had got in the ref's ear.

At least the early finish meant I'd definitely get back to the apartment in time to watch the game at Twickenham. Kev McLaughlin and Ross McCarron came over. We ordered pizzas and settled in to watch the demise of Cheiks.

That's how this game was being viewed. If Leinster lost, their chances of qualifying were effectively gone. And if they didn't qualify, Cheiks was gone.

Myself, Kev and Ross were all in the same boat: disaffected, feeling victimized and hoping that Wasps won. We still have a laugh about it among ourselves and exaggerate the details – how we were sitting there with Wasps flags, wearing yellow and black face-paint. Complete traitors, sworn conspirators. But part of me did want Leinster to fail.

Instead, Leinster won with a bonus point, and secured

qualification to the knockout stages by beating Edinburgh the next week.

The day before that Edinburgh game, I'd been playing for Mary's in Belvo. There were so few people watching that I had no difficulty spotting Cheiks leaning on the railing behind the posts at one end. When I kicked a touchline conversion in front of him, to seal a Mary's win, I resisted the urge to say something at him.

My plan was to make my point against the England Saxons at Donnybrook – Deccie had picked me in the A team, even though a few people had been calling for Ian Humphreys to get a run. I felt cheated when the game was abandoned due to a frozen pitch. Deccie came into the dressing room to commiserate with me, which I appreciated.

The following week – Friday 13 February – felt like a turning point. Ireland A 35, Scotland A 10. The RDS was almost empty but the game was televised and I did well, scoring 20 points, including an extremely dodgy try.

Running towards the left corner, I was convinced that someone was closing on me from behind. I could hear footsteps – my own footsteps, probably. I dived a good five metres short of the try-line, intending to slide over, but lost control of the ball. Fortunately the ref was miles behind, and he didn't think to check upstairs. Try. Relief.

Cheiks had called the night before, saying he wanted to wish me all the best. He also asked me why I hadn't signed the contract I'd been offered a couple of months previously.

At this stage it was out there that I had itchy feet. The *Irish Sun* even ran a story linking me to Perpignan, which was news to me! I'd received supportive phone calls from team-mates.

Leo and Jenno urged me to be patient. They said we were a good team with me at 10, that my chance would come.

I spent hours on the phone with Bernard Jackman, who suggested that I email Cheiks to let him know my frustrations. I didn't feel comfortable about doing that, though. I really appreciated the gestures of support from my teammates, but the paranoid me suspected that Cheiks had put them up to it.

When he called, I basically told him that I loved Leinster but that I didn't want to hold tackle-bags for the rest of my life. He told me he wanted me to stay and reassured me that there would be opportunities. This was good to hear but I committed to nothing just yet.

When I did eventually sign, it was partly because my options were limited. John Baker informed me that Connacht had committed to Ian Keatley, while Ulster were happy to stand by Humphreys and Niall O'Connor. I was encouraged by the rumours that Felipe was leaving for Toulon, but they were only rumours at that stage.

Deep down, I never wanted to leave. I had this fear that my native province would win the Heineken Cup and that they would do it without me. I told Bakes to ask for more than the figure they were offering, as I'd heard Keatley was on more than this and I was supposedly ahead of him in the rankings. But eventually I accepted what I'd been offered.

Cheiks warmed to me a little around that time, started to give me more minutes off the bench. It was probably in Llanelli, mid-Six Nations, when he started to see me as a genuine contender for the 21 jersey. I made a difference in the final thirty, getting a nice second touch in the move that set Jenno up for the winning try. Cheiks was waiting for me in the dressing room, beaming: 'THAT'S what I'm looking for, Sexto!'

Or maybe the turning point was in Thomond Park, when we had most of our Ireland players back. Again, I made an impact off the bench. In fact, I stirred up a massive fuss.

This was when it all kicked off with O'Gara.

I replaced Girve with thirty minutes to go, at which stage we trailed 9–0. In other words, we still hadn't scored a point against Munster that season, in two hours of trying. I was desperate to shake things up. Within minutes of arriving, I was stuck into a shouting match with Shaggy. No idea what it was about.

The real flare-up started when I went to clear out Lifeimi Mafi after he'd tip-tackled Chris Whitaker. I caught him above the eye with a stud by accident and he retaliated. A few fists were thrown.

Paul O'Connell was quick on the scene, asking Mafi who'd caused the gash above his eye. Suddenly I have Paulie pointing the finger at me and giving me a mouthful. A scary sight. I squared my shoulders at him, but from a safe distance.

With Paulie there for protection, O'Gara was also in my face: 'What the fuck are you doing?'

I responded by shaping to punch him, just drawing my fist back. When he winced, I called him a coward. That really set him off.

'Call me a coward? You're nothing! You're useless! A nobody!'

It soon broke up, but I stored his words in a place where they could fester.

O'Gara and I avoided each other on the final whistle. When people saw Paulie coming over to me, they assumed it was to warn me that they'd get me the next time! But he came in peace. 'You caught him a good one,' he said, smiling. I think he was under the impression that I'd punched Mafi rather than kicked him by accident. I did leave the boot in, but I would never kick someone in the head intentionally.

I suspect that Cheiks was impressed, too. I was given a two-week suspension for reckless use of my studs, but he still brought me to the Stoop for the infamous 'Bloodgate' Heineken quarter-final against Harlequins, where I acted as water-boy and message-carrier. Johnny O'Hagan's assistant, basically.

Even with another strong impression off the bench against Glasgow the week before Croker, I wasn't confident of making the twenty-two. With Isa in the back three, Cheiks had cover for out-half and Rob had been flying at full-back – already an established international, and he'd been selected for the Lions tour to South Africa that summer. But he'd been flattened by mumps after the quarter-final and wasn't ready for the semi. His misfortune was my first big break.

Smythie had said it to me a few times: *Your chance will come. When it does, make sure you're ready.* After Harrington's talk I had a new mindset. I had started to meet regularly with Enda McNulty. We worked together for hours on my routine. He would throw in all sorts of distractions and scenarios. We spoke about visualizing big moments in a European final. Still, you never think that it will be twenty-five minutes into the biggest club game in Irish rugby history, at Croke Park in front of a crowd of 82,300, in a Heineken Cup semi-final, against the reigning champions, with the entire country tuned in.

You definitely don't imagine that your first act will be to kick at goal. Or that you'll be kept waiting about two minutes to take that kick, with your knees shaking. Literally.

Felipe was coming off, having slipped awkwardly on his knee. My second big break. As I'm waiting for the nod to replace him, I'm wondering: Do the laws allow a replacement to take a shot at goal as his first act? I'm half-hoping they don't. Then Isa will have to take it. But no. It's me. OK. Where's my tee?

Usually, having Johnny O'Hagan on tee-duty was a blessing. A familiar face. A kind face. A face from my childhood. This time, it's a half-apologetic face. He has three tees in his hand – orange, red, green. I think the match-day organizers used the green one to perch a Heineken-branded ball near the entry to the tunnel and Hago had just grabbed it. However, he doesn't have MY green tee. He's mixed them up. This is a problem.

For the love of Christ, Hago. I gave it to you earlier!

Just use one of these, Johnny. It'll be grand.

No, Hago. Fuck sake!

Mercifully, referee Nigel Owens was patient with us. He stopped the clock while Hago hobbled off with his gammy ankle, back to the far side of the pitch for a rummage in his bag. It seemed to take him an eternity.

Suddenly I'm standing there like Pádraig Harrington, trying to block all negativity.

Don't think about missing what is a regulation kick – on the 22 and just inside the 15, left of the posts.

Don't think about letting Dad down. Funnily enough, I'd seen Dad and Billy Keane when we were on the bus ride to the stadium, the two of them standing outside a pub on Jones's Road, both in deliberately neutral colours.

Don't think about the fact that on this beautifully warm Saturday afternoon, the entire country is tuned into this sporting civil war, and Croker is jammed, with rival fans corralled into massive blocks of blue and red. Don't think about the fact that all of them are looking at me.

Luckily, it never occurred to me at the time that this was my first 'live' place-kick in nearly three months, since that game against Scotland A.

I hadn't place-kicked for Leinster because that was Felipe's gig. At Mary's, it was usually Barry Lynn. I had been practising, though. Hago had told my old man on the QT that he'd heard the coaching staff saying that I wasn't reliable enough off the tee. So I'd done lots of sessions with Enda and with Richie Murphy. I'd even done the occasional session with Dave Alred, the kicking guru then best known at that time for his work with Jonny Wilkinson. Paul Moloney in Adidas Ireland had set it up for me.

All three – Richie, Enda and Dave – had shown me the importance of formulating a routine that I would stick to, rigidly, for every kick. It's amazing to think that I was only getting around to this at the age of twenty-three. These days, kids have got this nailed before they're playing Junior Cup. I'd spent hours honing the process. Sometimes I worked with Enda on GAA pitches in the back end of nowhere. Or I'd work with Richie down in Belvo, concentrating on a process that I could rely on, a process that would allow me to block out any match situation. Then they'd test my ability to block out external pressure.

Right, Johnny, we're 2 points behind, so this is an absolute must-get.
Or:
We're in overtime and this is to nail the win . . .

Neither of them had ever come up with a scenario where I'm kept waiting for Hago to come back with the right bloody tee. In times gone past I would have experienced all these thoughts as a huge distraction. A reason that I was going to miss the kick. But Harrington's words had taught me that this is all normal. I was ready.

Thank God Hago found the tee. I set up, picked my spot in the stand, stuck to my routine, drilled the ball between the posts.

Leinster 6, Munster 3.

The final scoreline was 25–6. This was a massive upset. Munster had already thumped us twice that season, and had crushed Ospreys in the quarters. Eight of their players had been selected to tour South Africa with the Lions, compared to four of ours: Rob, Luke, Brian and Jamie. Munster had been almost unbackable favourites to retain the Heineken.

But that was the day when we finally delivered on our potential, the day our pack really stepped forward, the day when Rocky Elsom became a cult hero – although he had been exceptional at the Stoop also, and would be brilliant again in the final. Sometimes you wonder if the reason he's such a legend with Leinster supporters is because he was only here for one memorable season. Then you look at some of his clips and you realize he was freakishly good. He barely trained, as he was managing his body through consecutive northern and southern hemisphere seasons. He only spoke when he needed to. But when it mattered, he delivered. Put it this way: I don't think we'd have won the Heineken Cup without him.

I was delighted with how I played at Croker that day, but my performance is remembered for two things only: that first penalty kick and the famous flashpoint, in the left corner just after Darce's try, when I got into O'Gara's face.

I've spent a lot of time apologizing for that moment over the years – how I regretted being disrespectful towards him, how I may have caused embarrassment to my Munster relations. I remember that I received a letter from a Munster fan, telling me how unsportsmanlike I'd been.

At this stage, I'm actually glad that I did it. I was just being me.

I know it wasn't setting a great example to the thousands of kids who were watching. I'm not sure how I'd feel about my kids seeing it, or how I'll explain it to them when the time comes. But stuff like this happens in competitive sport. And was it really that bad? His words had played over and over in my head for weeks building up to this game. 'You're useless, a nobody.'

During the lockdown, I watched some old GAA re-runs on TV and what I did was nothing compared to some of the stuff that went on in hurling and football. And those lads were celebrated for their passion.

Besides, I went over to O'Gara on the final whistle and offered my hand. He told me to fuck off. He had the hump, big-time. Maybe it had something to do with the fact that Brian had intercepted him for our final try.

He must have cooled down a bit by the time he came into our dressing room to congratulate his Leinster buddies, Brian and Shaggy. He still made sure to give me the death-stare on his way out. I was sitting in one of the subs' spots, near the door, and he paused just long enough to let me know I was in his bad books.

We went on the town that night with girlfriends, wives and partners. Almost everyone we met asked me what I'd said to O'Gara. I have no idea what words came out of my mouth or whether they were remotely coherent. I'm sure it was just a roar.

At one point we bumped into Les Kiss, who was coaching

both of us in the Ireland set-up. Even he said he'd been delighted to see me 'put it up to Rog'. But I cringed a bit when I saw the papers the next morning. I had managed to take Pádraig Harrington's advice on board and would not read a word, but the picture was everywhere. I knew it was going to cause me grief.

I had distractions, thankfully. By then, I knew that Felipe had played his final game for Leinster, having ruptured his ACL the previous day. Cheiks would have to pick me for the final, against Leicester at Murrayfield, in three weeks' time.

Wouldn't he?

We were on the pitch in Murrayfield, maybe an hour before kick-off, when Cheiks approached me, calm as you like. Shaking my hand, he told me: 'Sexto, I'm really glad that you're playing today.'

I thanked him, but as we went our separate ways, the grump in me thought: *Yeah, right. You wouldn't have had me near the starting line-up if Felipe had been available.*

It was only a flicker of negativity, though, and I didn't let it in. I was ready for this. We were ready.

Felipe had actually helped get me into a positive frame of mind. He told me to concentrate on what I could do to help the team, rather than agonize over personal performance. Simple? A lot of the best advice is. And I appreciated Felipe taking the time to talk to me. Our relationship was always excellent, but for him it must have been devastating to miss this game. He had got us here and now he was missing out.

I was feeling pretty confident, anyway. The week after Munster, we'd smashed the Scarlets at the RDS, 45–8. I'd place-kicked well and scored a try from forty metres out.

In Edinburgh, we stayed at the Dalmahoy, a palatial country

club. In eve-of-match meetings, there's usually not much pressure on younger guys to contribute. But the 10 is a leader by definition, so I said my piece in the dressing room:

We have to believe that this is our year. We have to believe that it's scripted for us. Look at the way we were written off post-Castres, the way we defended for our lives in Harlequins, the way we beat the reigning champions at Croker. This is our year – but we have to start believing it.

I was probably fortunate that Kev McLaughlin wasn't there to remind me that only a few months previously, we'd been rooting for Wasps to knock Leinster out of the tournament, or that I'd been trying to leave the club. I'd forgotten all that.

I had plenty to occupy my mind. The days leading up to the final were stressful, to say the least. I'd struggled to sleep all week. My mind was working overtime, as it still tends to do in the countdown to a big game. Negative thoughts chipped away at me. This was a career-defining game. What if it went badly for me? I was the only non-international in our backline. We were playing our first Heineken final and this was Leicester's fifth. Didn't they say you had to lose one to win one? Lying there up in my apartment, I kept visualizing Leicester's giant backs, Ayoola Erinle and Alesana Tuilagi, thundering down my channel. This might have been the Wednesday or Thursday night – wasted nervous energy, doing me no good. The only positive was that I was knackered by the eve of the game so I did get some sleep eventually, when my roomie Luke Fitzgerald eventually stopped yapping. He was full of beans, as usual, not a nerve in sight.

I was grand once I got to the stadium. It helped that I'd played there before. It also helped that Murrayfield was mostly coloured blue. We'd read all the interviews with

Munster players who'd gone on about their supporters taking ownership of Cardiff when they'd played finals at the Millennium Stadium. Well, now it was our turn.

When we were walking the pitch, Stan Wright gave me a pat on the back and muttered something about me having nothing to worry about. Given that Stan rarely said anything to anyone who wasn't a front rower, I reckoned he must have been worried on my behalf. This was only my third start in a Heineken Cup match, after all. The lads were used to having Felipe there but Felipe was in his suit, hobbling around on crutches.

But I was fine. I usually am, once I get to the ground. Time to get on with it.

I had a good first touch, which helped. It was the first touch of the match, in fact – a kick-off aimed at Geordan Murphy that hung in the air long enough for our chasers to wrap him up. Geordan was their go-to man for clearances so it had been the plan to deny him that chance. A positive start.

Young players thrown into a sporting cauldron often go out with the intention to 'keep things simple' in order to reduce the chances of making an error. Battling with this is an impulse to announce yourself, to make an impression. That day in Edinburgh, around eighteen minutes into the contest, the impulse took over.

The idea of trying a long-range drop-goal had implanted itself well before kick-off. I had been practising all week, after hitting a bad one against Munster in the semi. During the warm-up I'd noticed Tom Varndell banging long-range drops. Tom wasn't even a kicker, wasn't even in the Tigers' twenty-two that day. But his drop-kicks were flying miles, right into the crowd behind the sticks. That's where I got the idea. The first anyone else knew about my plan was when Darce took a quick throw to me on halfway, and I loaded up to have a shot. Up in the stands, Dad, Laura and little Jerry all winced.

No, Jono.

Mum and Mark were both watching at home, one on a work break from the salon, the other on a study break – he had exams the following Monday. They both shouted at the TV.

No, Jonathan!

It was the same in the coaches' box, where Cheiks let rip, as only he can.

'NO, SEXTO!'

It was a high-risk play. All fourteen of my team-mates were ahead of me. If I'd scuffed it, we were severely compromised. But I caught it sweetly and trusted the breeze to do its work.

As I was running back, allowing myself a celebratory fist-pump, Stuart Barnes was gushing on Sky: 'That is a wonderful kick from the twenty-three-year-old. He's made such a composed start. That's a pure strike.'

Confidence surged through me. I found other ways to assert myself. Because Leicester were using a rush defence on Brian, passing to him was rarely an option, so I was effectively forced into attacking the 12 channel. I was fine with that. I had a dart, offloaded to Darce with my left hand. He didn't get over but it was only a matter of inches.

We were all over them. And yet the Tigers led 13–9 at the break. Having defended like dogs, they made the most of their period of dominance at the end of the half, at which stage we were down to fourteen men after Stan had taken Sam Vesty out off the ball. Soon Vesty's offload put Ben

Woods over and we were trailing for the first time. Leicester's lead became 16–9 when Julien Dupuy landed a penalty early in the second half.

Just as we looked in trouble, Brian stepped forward – as he usually did in big games. He finally found space and shimmied into it. Off that momentum, Jamie was soon being driven over the try-line by Jenno. My conversion made it 16–all.

We always looked likely to finish stronger, given that we'd all had the previous weekend off, when the Tigers had been on Premiership duty. They had English and French internationals to bring off the bench, but our scrum held up brilliantly. At the lineout, we had the advantage of Leo and Jenno's insider knowledge. We made it count.

It still came down to a penalty shot, ten minutes from the end, thirty-five metres out on the left-hand side. Out came Hago with the tee, and some advice from Richie: Stay tall and strike through the target. It wasn't the purest strike. In fact it was pretty ugly, starting off well right of the posts but then hooking back on the breeze. I knew from the warm-up and Dupuy's penalty in the first half that it would move right to left. It had just enough on it. Watch the tape and you see me giving Richie a knowing smile as I run back. It almost looks like I'm enjoying myself.

Ten minutes later, I'm distraught. Nigel Owens has blown for a breakdown penalty against us and it's just about in kickable range. I'm forty metres away with my head in my hands. Then I realize it's a peno for us. I run over and Chris Whitaker tosses me the ball to bog into the stands. It's over.

I was engulfed by some of the younger squad members, guys like Paulie O'Donohoe and Eoin O'Malley, then Richie. Little Jerry tried to get me, too, and got in a bit of bother with the stewards. He was only sixteen at the time and with a few beers inside him, he decided he couldn't wait to congratulate me. I had a word with one of the high-vizzers and so we got to have a boozy, brotherly hug.

This had been a long journey and I'd played a relatively small part in it. For some of the senior players it was their tenth Heineken Cup campaign. Brian paid tribute to the Denis Hickies, Victor Costellos, Reggie Corrigans, guys who'd given so much to the Leinster cause, who'd put up with the abuse during the dark days. Leo forced Chris Whitaker to accept the cup with him. Typically, Whits didn't want to take centre stage but we knew this was his final appearance for the club so Leo wouldn't take no for an answer.

After we'd received our medals, Jamie and I were asked to do some TV. I remembered to thank all my coaches. I made sure to give Richie Hughes a mention.

'I probably had the most nervous week of my life,' I said. 'It was a struggle all week but I'm just happy we won it and that I played my part.'

As we did our lap of honour, draped in Leinster scarves and hats and flags, with U2 blaring and so many familiar faces in the stands, it occurred to me how mad this outcome was – how low I'd been in the dressing room in Castres only a few months previously, how ecstatic I was now. And then I just stopped thinking and let happiness wash over me.

9

The day we beat Leicester in Edinburgh, I was supposed to have been in Vancouver, making my international debut. I had it down in the diary from months back: Ireland Tests in Canada and the US, with no Lions involved. O'Gara was always going to South Africa. This was my opportunity.

OK, so playing in a Heineken Cup final wasn't the worst trade-off. The only thing making me uncomfortable was that while I was busy in Edinburgh, Ian Keatley would be leapfrogging me for an Ireland cap. And he'd get a second against the US – unless I could get to Santa Clara in time to play.

A week or two before the Heineken final, I called Paul McNaughton, the Ireland team manager, and put it to him: If I flew out of Dublin on the Sunday evening, I could be at training in California by the Tuesday. Why not?

He knocked me back. Edinburgh would be the biggest game of my life, he said. I'd be exhausted afterwards. It would be silly to put me on a transatlantic flight the next day. Besides, I'd already been selected for the Churchill Cup, to be held in Colorado directly after the USA Test, and Deccie and the rest of his coaching team would be staying on to prepare us for those games. Deccie was viewing it as one extended tour, Paul told me.

I'm thinking: Yes, but you're not giving caps for the Churchill games. I'd happily hop on a flight if it means playing for Ireland.

I felt cheated.

It was the right decision, of course. I was exhausted after Edinburgh – from the tension of the build-up, from the final itself, from the celebrations. Just getting through the mill at Edinburgh Airport was draining. There was a reception back at the Burlington Hotel for family and friends and then it was into Krystle nightclub on Harcourt Street. I surfaced just in time for the fans' reception at the RDS on Sunday afternoon, held in brilliant sunshine. Then we went for a few more celebratory beers. Some of the guys were only warming up.

I took it handy. It was an enjoyable few days but also a busy few days. There was suddenly lots of media interest in me. I did three interviews with Sunday newspapers that week, telling the story of my topsy-turvy season. A few of us brought the cup in to show it to children in the Temple Street and Crumlin hospitals. I also had to get ready to fly to Colorado.

I heard a rumour that I was on a standby list for the Lions. Supposedly I was second reserve out-half behind Cardiff's Nicky Robinson. A wind-up? Probably. That didn't stop me giving it consideration. Plenty of consideration. I started to see some logic in it. I was in form. I was going to the Churchill Cup so I'd still be 'in season'.

I imagined a scenario – Stephen Jones getting injured in South Africa, me flying in first class from Colorado.

Bottom line, it was no harm that the idea had popped into someone's head. And it was no harm that I'd be staying sharp in Colorado. As it turned out, Deccie didn't overwork me. He put me on the bench for the games against Canada and Georgia, before starting me in the final, against the Saxons. We smashed them 49–22 – another trophy in what was already an exceptional year for Irish rugby.

I enjoyed Colorado – training in beautiful weather, getting to work closely with Deccie and Kissy and Riff. Their coaching was excellent and their feedback was all positive. I flew home feeling good about my chances of getting a cap that November, when Ireland were due to play Australia, Fiji and South Africa.

The only thing eating away at me was O'Gara. Deccie's next camp was scheduled for September. I couldn't think of it without feeling jittery.

I was still slightly in awe of O'Gara. Yes, I reckoned I was closing the gap on him. Even though Ireland had just won a slam, I didn't think he had been at his best during the campaign. He was now thirty-two and back then, I thought thirty-two was middle-aged. But he was still Ronan O'Gara, the out-half I'd admired most as a kid, the guy who'd been playing for Ireland when I was playing Junior Cup for Mary's.

He had an aura about him, a natural authority and a quick wit. All the banter in camp seemed to go through him. Most of the Munster guys seemed happier sticking with their own, but O'Gara had his Leinster mates in Brian and Shaggy. He was the man. Me? I could be lippy on the training pitch when the adrenaline was pumping. Around the hotel, I'd have kept myself to myself.

Deccie had already tried to build a relationship between us, before any of the trouble. He roomed me with O'Gara in one of the early camps, when I was a complete newbie. That had been a head-wrecker for me. The camp was in Dublin, so there was zero pressure on me to overnight in the hotel. But what would people think if I went home? That I was too scared to room with him?

I stayed, even though I was petrified by the prospect of

trying to make conversation. It was grand, of course. O'Gara was friendly. I remember him asking me about my relatives in Listowel and Limerick. I didn't expect much small talk out of him this time, though.

It would have been easier to stay out of each other's way had we not been place-kickers. Sometimes it was just the two of us with Mark Tainton, Deccie's kicking coach, who'd been working with O'Gara for years. Say we were being driven to and from a stadium for kicking practice, there was this bizarre situation where O'Gara would be looking out one window in silence, me looking out the other. Two stubborn kids.

We provided great entertainment for the other lads, of course. You could be sitting having dinner in the hotel when Ronan would walk into the dining room and Donncha O'Callaghan would pipe up.

'Rog, Rog! Look, there's a free spot here beside Johnny!' It's hard not to smile in that situation.

I wasn't about to make the first move in patching things up, though. Not after what he'd said to me in Thomond Park. He was probably waiting for an apology for what I did in Croker. But we couldn't avoid each other for ever. Neither of us really apologized but we shook hands. The temperature moved from Arctic to chilly.

Leinster felt different that autumn. No Felipe, for starters. He'd moved to Toulon, to be replaced by Shaun Berne — another Randwicker, a great bloke and a handy footballer. Normally I would have felt massively threatened, but I sensed that Cheiks's attitude towards me had changed. He asked for my opinions on stuff. He talked me up in meetings. I was actually disappointed when he announced that he'd be leaving the club at the end of that season.

Rocky and Whits were already gone but we had a new Aussie voice in Nathan Hines, who turned out to be a brilliant signing. We also had Eoin Reddan, a Heineken Cup winner with Wasps. We'd first played together in that A international against Scotland and hit it off immediately. I picked his brains about Wasps, about Shaun Edwards and Warren Gatland and Lawrence Dallaglio, about their attack shape, about their defensive system. We talked about all sorts of stuff. We became close friends.

Having left Munster a few years previously because he couldn't get a look-in, Reddser loved what happened when they turned up at the RDS that October. Leinster 30, Munster 0 is still a scoreline that's hard to believe.

Coming five months after Croke Park, it was billed as Munster's revenge mission and as a final trial for the November Tests. And, of course, it was about O'Gara v. Sexton.

I went in confident. My place-kicking had been good through September, and the week before Munster I dropped a late goal to nick a win in Edinburgh. I was determined to remain composed, not to get drawn into any trouble. I needn't have worried. Munster barely threw a punch.

It's worth mentioning that Paulie and David Wallace didn't appear until the third quarter and almost as soon as they did, John Hayes was sent off for stamping on Cian Healy. The contest was already over. We were sharp in attack, with Brian, Darce and Shaggy all scoring tries. And we were really chuffed to nil them, twelve months after they'd done it to us on the same pitch.

I didn't need to read the newspaper reports to know that I'd won my 'duel' with O'Gara. I kicked six from six, linked well with Reddser, kicked well from the hand and distributed nicely.

People speculated that this was a big moment but I didn't buy it. O'Gara had been first choice for the previous six years. He'd just won a Slam, just been on the Lions tour. He had credit in the bank. He and Deccie went way back.

Realistically, I pretty much knew that I would get a run against Fiji, at the RDS. Deccie had to find an alternative to O'Gara so it made sense. And I was hoping to make the twenty-two for the Wallabies. I reckoned it probably depended on whether Deccie went with Paddy Wallace ahead of Darce at 12.

I went through the permutations with Dad. He liked to think that he could read Deccie's mind. Early in the week of an Ireland Test, he'd be on the websites of photographic agencies like Inpho and Sportsfile, spying on the pictures that had been taken during training, seeing who'd been wearing which coloured bibs and piecing the team together days before it was due to be announced. Whenever I called him early in the week, he'd be quick off the mark: 'I see you're in,' or 'I see you're on the bench.' In fairness to him, he was usually on the ball. He wasn't the only one who was using this system. I'm pretty sure Deccie eventually figured out what was going on and started to mix things up just to throw people off the scent.

Deccie went with Paddy at 12 for Australia so I was on the bench. I didn't make any assumptions about getting on, but let's just say I was keen. It was a massive weekend for Irish sport with two sell-out crowds at Croker, one day after the other – football on the Saturday, with the first World Cup play-off against France, then Ireland's first home game since winning the Slam, against a team that would be in our pool at the World Cup in New Zealand. They had guys like Matt

Giteau and Quade Cooper in their midfield. Rocky was their skipper. I visualized coming on and laying down a marker. Maybe myself and Reddser replacing O'Gara and Tomás O'Leary for the last twenty minutes?

It never happened. At one stage, it looked like Paddy was coming off with a blood injury. You've never seen someone get out of a tracksuit quicker. But he was grand. That was the closest I came. We were chasing the game in the final quarter so Deccie clearly wanted his most experienced soldiers out there. I guess he was vindicated, as Brian scored a try at the death under the posts to get the draw. The team was still undefeated in 2009.

I was jealous of Cian Healy. He'd made an amazing debut – standing ovation as he came off. Laura kept reassuring me. Next week. You'll get your chance next week.

Deccie clearly wanted to ease me into Test rugby. The Fiji game was at the RDS so that would allow me to make my debut in familiar surroundings, with plenty of familiar faces – I was one of six Leinster players in the backline, with Reddser at 9. Leo would be starting. Seánie O'Brien and Seán Cronin – two of my closest rugby pals – were on the bench and in line to make their debuts too.

It felt like Deccie had built the team around me. Brian said plenty of complimentary things about me in the build-up. O'Gara had congratulated me and wished me well. It was all set up.

My nerves were in shreds, though. I was rooming with Darce – the messiest man in the squad. He kept telling me I'd be fine but the night before, I lay awake trying, and failing, to block negative thoughts. Fiji were a decent team. They'd made the quarter-finals at the 2007 World Cup. They'd given Scotland a game the previous week. Mike Brewer, their forwards coach, had been talking them up. What had he been telling them about me? The forecast was crap – wind and rain. Jesus.

Around 1 a.m., I texted the doc and asked him for a sleeping tablet. I know people say you don't get the benefits of REM sleep with a tablet, but it's definitely better than just lying there expending nervous energy. You get six or seven hours with your eyes shut and your brain switched off. You might be a bit groggy at first, but at least it was an evening kick-off.

The weather was still OK the following afternoon so I slipped down St Theresa's on Clarendon Street – an oasis of calm only fifty metres away from Grafton Street, which is mobbed on Saturday afternoons. Some of us went for a stroll in St Stephen's Green. We watched the All Blacks beat England on TV.

The Shelbourne was filling up with rugby fans in for a pre-match pint, and to cheer us on to the bus waiting outside. It's kind of a taster for what's coming later on. You come out of the team room on the first floor and it's relatively quiet but as you reach the top of the stairs, you suddenly sense the swell down below in the foyer. This was when Brian turned and made way for me.

What?

Just go, Johnny.

Normally the captain would lead the team down but Brian offered me the chance to do it on my first cap. A special gesture.

Once they see you coming down the first few steps, the roar is unbelievable. I had tears in my eyes getting on the bus. Good tears, though: I was up for it.

By kick-off at the RDS, the conditions were atrocious so

all the advice was to keep it simple, ease myself into the game. I had my first touch after thirty seconds, when my opposite number Nicky Little banged the ball into our 22. I had a wind behind me, and plenty of time to launch the ball down the left touchline. But just as in Edinburgh, six months previously, there was an urge to announce myself. I shaped to kick, but dummied, then stepped a Fijian. I made thirty metres before being hauled down. I was into the game.

It couldn't have gone much better for me. The gods arranged for me to have my first kick from short range, just to the left of the posts, ten minutes in. My first 3 points in international rugby. When I cross-kicked for Earlsy, I got the distance right and the ball stuck. When I punted for distance, I got great length and kind bounces. With familiar targets outside me, my handling was assured.

It shouldn't necessarily be this way, but the first measure of the performance of a place-kicking out-half is his success rate off the tee. I kicked seven from seven for 16 points, including three from the touchline. All the work I'd been doing with Richie and Dave Alred was paying off.

We won 41–6. I was chosen as man of the match by RTÉ's co-commentator, Ralph Keyes – a Cork Con clubmate of O'Gara, funnily enough. The post-match analysis was pretty much the same across the board: O'Gara now had a competitor at out-half. The fact that Deccie had paired me with Tomás, his first-choice 9, for the final thirty minutes, was presented as evidence that Deccie had a decision to make.

But everyone seemed to agree: there was no way he would start me the following week – not against South Africa, not while there was still the chance of going unbeaten for the calendar year.

And everyone was wrong, including Dad, including me.

It was typical Deccie, really – determined not to follow the consensus. When asked to explain his selection, he said he needed 'to find things out', as we were less than two years from a World Cup.

I didn't expect O'Gara to be the person to give me the good news. He approached me at breakfast on the Tuesday morning. Deccie had spoken to him the previous night. O'Gara congratulated me, told me to make sure I got in as many reps as possible at training.

It was classy of him. It must have been hard – the first time he had been dropped from the team since 2003. It's not like I had done a huge amount to deserve it, either. I'd only started in five Heineken Cup games at that point. But he was man enough to shake my hand and wish me all the best.

I guess what might have tipped things in my favour was my physicality. So much of what Ireland were about in 2009 was Kissy's defence system and the choke-tackle tactic in particular. South Africa were the most physical side in rugby and the most direct. If you could provide resistance in the channel, it gave them something to think about.

Looking back, I kind of see that day as my proper Test debut. The RDS had been a dry run, albeit in the rain. This was a real challenge. The Springboks had won the Tri Nations and Ireland had won the Slam so it was a final of sorts, played on the final Test weekend of 2009. It may not have been part of any official tournament, but there was an edge. We had a record in our sights.

The Boks had lost on their last two trips to Dublin so they were keen to make a point. The crowd, meanwhile, was keen to let Schalk Burger know what they thought of him – he'd served an eight-week ban for gouging Luke Fitzgerald during the first Test against the Lions. Burger didn't help himself by booting the ball into the Davin Stand after he scored the game's only try, fifteen minutes in.

Things weren't looking great when Morne Steyn dropped a goal ten minutes later. They led 10–3 and had established superiority in the scrums. There were chinks of hope for us, though. We had insider info on their lineout, thanks to our forwards coach, Gert Smal, who'd been part of their set-up only two years previously, so were able to disrupt their possession. We matched them at the breakdown, and then began to dominate them there. Also, for some reason, they kept bombing Rob Kearney, despite the fact that he was gobbling up everything and running it back brilliantly.

A freezing fog descended in the second half and the Boks lost their way. Their discipline was poor and they offered up penalty opportunities. I was in that happy place where I felt I couldn't miss, despite the fact that by the final quarter, the posts were only just about visible through the fog. At one stage I saw they'd put my picture up on the big screen and a statistic underneath saying, '100 per cent goal-kicking success rate in international rugby'. I liked the look of that.

The TV director did manage to pick out O'Gara, just after I kicked my fifth penalty, putting us 15–10 ahead fourteen minutes from the end. He was in a well-padded tracksuit and a beanie, and he was smiling, having just seen himself on one of the giant video screens.

We were in full-on survival mode towards the end, right down to the Springboks' final attack when Brian drove Zane Kirchner back with a great hit. That brought the final whistle. Croker erupted.

The only thing restricting my celebrations was the throbbing in my left hand. I'd broken it in the midst of a choke-tackle five minutes from the end – when you try and tag the ball, you can stub your fingers. If I'd been in my right mind, I would have come off to limit the damage. No chance.

My recovery time was set at six weeks, so naturally I aimed to get back in five. Leinster v. Connacht on 2 January 2010 was my target. The nature of the injury meant that I could keep in reasonable shape until the cast came off my hand. The fact that it was my left hand made it easier to deliver a couple of my commerce assignments.

The other thing I could do that December was see how O'Gara responded to being dropped. No surprise there. It brought out the best in him.

Munster were in trouble at home to Perpignan and he dug them out of a hole, kicking seven penalties and a left-footed drop-goal to squeeze a 24–23 win.

The following week was the return match in Perpignan. A classic Heineken Cup scenario for Munster. They'd already lost on the road. Perpignan had pushed them close in Thomond. Lose, and there was the danger that they wouldn't make the quarters for the first time since whenever. Some people wrote them off. Not only did they win, they won with a bonus point. In fairness, it was a great performance.

Leinster's European form had been patchy. We'd lost at home to London Irish first up but recovered by taking maximum points against the Scarlets, with Shaun Berne slotting in well at 10. With two rounds to come in January, people were already talking about the possibility of an all-Irish quarter-final: Leinster v. Munster, Sexton v. O'Gara, all over again.

I had the cast off before Christmas, was ready to go for Connacht. It was to be my fiftieth game for Leinster. But we had heavy snow and then a big freeze. First the Connacht game was postponed, then the one against Glasgow the following weekend. I was bulling.

Mercifully, we did go ahead against Brive at the RDS mid-January. I played the full eighty – not ideal on my first game in seven weeks, but we had to push till the end to nail the four-try bonus. I picked up a dead leg but generally felt OK. That left us on top of the pool but still pushing for a home quarter.

I made things difficult for myself by hurting my quad during the week of the London Irish game. Stupid stuff. I went to do some place-kicking after training, but after we had cooled down. Later I learned to ease my way into it, starting off with some short punting, drop-kicking, then short place-kicks and so on. I felt a twinge but tried to kick through it, stopped, then tried again. Not clever.

I still played at Twickenham. Munster had edged Northampton the previous evening. O'Gara was man of the match and got all his kicks. I needed to deliver – not just because of selection for the Six Nations but because London Irish put it up to us, again. If they'd taken their opportunities, they would have beaten us.

It was sweaty at the end. When Chris Malone kicked them 11–8 in front, the clock read 77:25. By 78:10, we were back level. Once we'd reclaimed the re-start, it took one surge by John Fogarty to take us into drop-goal range. Redser hit me in the pocket, thirty-eight metres out. I stood tall and my quad took the strain, just. It was never missing.

Running back, I allowed myself a double fist-pump but there were no celebratory huddles. There was still time for Malone to have two shots at drop-goaling Irish to victory. He missed them both.

These were big moments for both clubs. Had Irish won,

they were through to the quarters. We'd have still topped the pool but we'd have been in Clermont for the quarters.

My only frustration was that niggly quad. I went for a scan and it showed a small tear. I had only two weeks to get ready for the first Six Nations game, at home to Italy.

The press built up the out-half selection as Deccie's Big Decision, but he never had to make a decision as I lost the race for fitness. When Deccie announced the side, he was asked which way he'd have gone if I'd been fit. Naturally, he gave nothing away. Why would you?

O'Gara went well against Italy and held his place for Paris, even though I was fit enough to sit on the bench. From a purely selfish point of view, it mightn't have been the worst thing. France had their tails up and won 33–10 – the end of a twelve-game unbeaten streak. Tomás and Ronan both struggled behind a beaten pack.

Reddser and I did OK in our ten minutes off the bench at the end, and I gave Deccie a solid nudge during a down weekend for the Six Nations, scoring 22 points as Leinster beat Scarlets convincingly in the RDS. I got the nod to start at Twickenham.

I saw a re-run of the game during the Covid lockdown. It's something of a Six Nations classic, at least from an Irish point of view – Tommy Bowe scoring a brilliant try five minutes from the end for Ireland to come from behind and win 20–16.

Re-watching the game a decade later was a pleasant surprise. I played better than I remembered. I set up for Tommy's first try with a nicely weighted grubber, just five minutes into the game, and I was central to Earlsy's try, too – setting up an attacking lineout with a decent line-kick, then sending him into the left corner with an accurate pass under pressure. But my memory had been clouded by my place-kicking numbers that day – one from five.

Kicking stats. They can melt your head.

I guess I'd set the bar pretty high the previous November, landing my first twelve shots at goal, before missing one at the end of the Springboks game. So this was a bit of a come-down.

Watching the game back, I wondered what the hell I was doing taking on a long-range peno in the first half, with a slightly dodgy quad? I remembered how the injury was on my mind. I didn't get through any of the kicks properly and as a result, I missed a couple to the right.

But I'd forgotten how muddy and windy it was at Twickenham that day, also how all my misses had been tough kicks. Jonny Wilkinson had struggled off the tee, too.

Just to be playing opposite Wilkinson was a massive buzz. There was a moment during the game, one of those rare awakenings where mentally you step away from the turmoil just for a second and say to yourself: That's Jonny Wilkinson. My opposite number is Jonny Wilkinson.

Swapping jerseys with him afterwards was a special moment. I had so many reasons to be happy. It was my first Six Nations start and we'd won at Twickenham – I couldn't get over how happy Paul O'Connell was in the dressing room. With two home games to come, our Six Nations had been reignited. Deccie told me: I thought you were outstanding today.

But his words washed over me. Those missed kicks were nibbling away at my mind. Most of the squad went into London that night to celebrate, safe in the knowledge that we had a two-week gap before Wales and they could let their hair down. I should have been with them. Instead I was in my hotel room, icing my quad and playing things over in my head.

I was still hypersensitive to any possible slight from O'Gara back then. There was one night in camp where we went out as a group and I overheard someone ask him why he was only drinking Coke. He said he was taking it easy because he had a kicking session the next morning. I felt stung. Normally, the kickers always worked together. It made sense just on a practical level. The more participants, the less time you spent herding balls. You could compare notes, coach each other. But that level of trust clearly wasn't there yet. Or at least that's the way I read it.

I could have done with some help on place-kicking, too. Mark Tainton was there as kicking coach but he'd been part of the set-up for years and it seemed to me that he was firmly in the O'Gara camp. I felt stressed coming into the Wales game and all the stress was related to place-kicking. I had just missed four shots against England. My quad was still an issue – though not to the extent that I was willing to make a big deal of it and run the risk of losing my place. Finally, I knew that every time I lined up a shot at goal at Croke Park, O'Gara's face would appear on the screens in the stadium, staring down at me.

We beat Wales 27–12 and everything went well for me – except place-kicking. Three from seven: not good enough.

All around me were calming voices – Deccie, Laura, Mum – telling me not to be so hard on myself. Ollie Campbell sent me a lovely text, complimenting me on my general out-half play. It meant a lot to hear that from one of the all-time greats, who has been a great support to me over the years.

It didn't stop me from beating myself up. I did my best to heed Padraig Harrington's advice and stay away from the papers. But I was exposed to social media for the first time, through some Facebook page where the players had to 'create content' for IRFU sponsors. A few Munster supporters took it as their opportunity to get stuck into me in the comments section.

Why should I give a damn about some keyboard warrior? Why did I even look? I didn't know any better. Worse still, I assumed what they were saying was representative of how people felt, and of what was being said about me among the wider public.

France were heading towards a Grand Slam, but Deccie reminded us that we still had a Triple Crown to play for against Scotland. This caused a few sniggers. This group of senior players had won plenty of Triple Crowns and, just off the back of a Grand Slam, I don't think this was their goal. They wanted Championships and Grand Slams. Looking back, Deccie was right, considering how few Triple Crowns we have won.

Scotland beat us 23–20 – their first win in Dublin in twelve years – with Dan Parks kicking a great penalty at the death. I gave him my jersey afterwards and let him keep his own, as a souvenir of a great win. I knew Dan had gone through tough times in his career but this was his day. (Maybe I do have some empathy in me after all. Eh, Laura? ☺)

In a game as tight as that, place-kicking was always likely to be the difference. I landed just two from four. After fifty-two minutes, Deccie gave me the hook.

I understood his decision. What annoyed me was that he ballsed up the timing of the substitution. We'd just been awarded a penalty – fifteen metres right of posts, twenty-five metres out – and I'd indicated I was going for goal. Suddenly, I heard this big cheer. O'Gara is up on the screen and his tracksuit is off. He's coming on. He's itching to get out there and take the kick.

But he can't come on just yet. If he or Deccie had known the laws, they'd have realized that he could only take the kick if he was replacing an injured player. I tried to explain but I don't know if they could hear. It was awkward. Then I had to wait for my tee to appear, with O'Gara still standing there, looking on. It was a head-wreck and Deccie later apologized for putting me in that situation.

But I nailed it.

Maybe I was helped by the experience of having to wait for Hago against Munster the previous year. Either way, it was an important kick for me. A turning point. And that's because of a conversation I had with Dave Alred soon afterwards.

Dave asked me how I'd felt standing over the kick. This was the first time I'd been asked a question like that by a coach. I told him that I'd felt angry – angry at being replaced, angry at the way it had been done, angry that every time I took a kick at goal, I had O'Gara glaring down at me from the big screen. Dave reckoned that the anger had worked for me. I'd put some of that anger into the kick and blasted it between the posts, rather than trying to hope the ball over, as I had been doing for a lot of kicks.

So he came up with the idea of using O'Gara's face to my advantage. Pick your target in the crowd and then transpose his face so that the target is right between his eyes. It was a brilliant bit of coaching – an example of taking negative energy and flipping it into a positive way of thinking.

My place-kicking percentages improved gradually. They were only so-so against Connacht the following week. The week after that, we were in Limerick, of all places. I missed a couple but got the one that counted near the end, the one that ensured a 1-point victory – Leinster's first win in Limerick in fifteen years.

Little did Munster realize that I'd used their number 10's mug as my motivation.

My own mug took a battering soon after that. Twenty minutes from the end of our quarter-final against Clermont at the RDS, it felt the full force of Morgan Parra's shoulder. He was supposedly cleaning me out of a ruck. He broke my jaw.

I knew it wasn't good. Everything in my mouth felt off-kilter. My bite was totally off. I couldn't get my gumshield back into my mouth. My jaw was basically displaced.

The problem was we were in a proper scrap. We'd led 20–10 at half-time but Clermont were coming back at us. As I was being examined by the doc, the message coming loud and clear from Cheiks was that I had to stay on. It looked like going down to the wire so he wanted his best place-kicker on the pitch. I wanted to stay on as well. I gave the doc my gumshield to mind and got on with it.

It was reckless behaviour. A couple of years later I broke my jaw playing for Racing against Toulon and walked off the pitch immediately because I knew the severity of the injury. But this was a Heineken quarter-final, at the RDS. The fact that Joe Schmidt was there with Clermont may have been in the back of my mind. He'd already been confirmed as Cheiks's replacement and I wanted to impress him. I also had a fear about coming off and the X-ray showing no damage – and my team-mates thinking badly of me.

But I knew I wasn't right. I pretended to tackle Julien Malzieu as he ran in for his third try, knowing instinctively that

I couldn't take another belt to my jaw. Even place-kicking was painful. Luckily we only needed one more penalty to keep us ahead of Clermont. I finished with seven from eight. Leinster 29, Clermont 28.

I was taken for an X-ray and had an operation that night, with braces and a plate implanted to hold everything in place, with just enough of a gap to allow me to suck liquidized food through a straw. Lovely.

My recovery time was set at six weeks, which meant I could aim for the semis of the Magners and the Tests in New Zealand and Australia that June. But Cheiks was holding out hope that I could somehow be ready for the Heineken semi. It was just three weeks away.

These days, the coach wouldn't have a say. It's doctor's orders and that's it. But protocols were looser back then. Cheiks said he'd read some article about a bloke in Australia with a similar injury who'd played after having a plate inserted. The week before the game I went back to the surgeon and asked his opinion. He was amazed that I'd even ask. Play while the jaw was still healing?

I was upset delivering the news to Cheiks but he said he understood. I didn't attend any of the meetings leading up to the semi but from what I'm told, he talked me up, saying the reason we'd got to this stage was because I'd stayed on the pitch against Clermont with a broken jaw. That made me feel proud. Made living with the braces more tolerable.

We lost the semi, so the focus of our season became the Magners and trying to give Cheiks a decent send-off. My comeback game was at home to Munster. Our third shoot-out with Munster that season. We couldn't get enough of each other.

We won 16–6 – our fourth straight win against them, the fourth time in a row when we prevented them scoring a try. I kicked four from five and set up Rob for a peach of a try. Happy. The final was scheduled for the RDS. Happier still.

The build-up was all wrong, though. We made it too much about the fact that it was a send-off for Cheiks, also a farewell game for Mal O'Kelly and Girv, who were both retiring. Instead of focusing on our performance, the meeting on the eve of the game got too emotional. Guys getting tearful twenty-four hours before kick-off will only drain them. Maybe subconsciously we also believed we'd win because we were playing at home. The Ospreys beat us 17–12. Lesson learned.

Bodies were beginning to drop. A dozen players were unavailable for the tour. The prospect of playing opposite Dan Carter kept my juices flowing. But I picked up a mouth infection that forced me to sit out our pre-tour game against the Barbarians in Limerick. Deccie put me on the bench for the All Blacks game in New Plymouth, which made for difficult viewing.

Near the end of the first half, we trailed 38–0. Jamie had been sent off for knee-dropping Richie McCaw and O'Gara was in the bin, too. We dragged it back a little in the second half but 66–28 was a horrible scoreline. Reddser and I joked that the score was 7–7 for the ten minutes at the end when myself and him were on the pitch. We didn't say it too loudly, though.

We both started against a strong Maori side in Rotorua. The IRFU decided not to award caps, which may have given our opponents extra motivation. After twenty minutes, we trailed 18–3. We fought back really well but were edged out 31–28 in a brilliant game. I was furious with myself for missing a late penalty but my stats were eight out of nine – strong evidence that I'd sorted my place-kicking out.

I was rewarded with the 10 jersey for Brisbane a week later. I was amazed at the number of Irish supporters at Suncorp – perhaps a sign of the number of young people who'd emigrated because of the financial crash. We did our best for them. Losing 22–15 wasn't the worst result given that we had a makeshift team and given that the ref allowed a try to Luke Burgess even though he was miles offside when he intercepted Chris Henry's pass.

It was a hard defeat to take but there were consolations. Deccie had left me on for the duration and I kicked five from five, a couple of them from nasty angles. The previous time we'd played the Wallabies, he'd left me on the bench for the full eighty. Just over a year away from the World Cup I felt I was in the driving seat for the number 10 jersey.

If only life was that simple.

10

Leinster and Joe Schmidt found each other at just the right time. We were hungry, having stewed the whole summer after losing a final at home to the Ospreys and having been beaten in a European semi. And Joe was ambitious, having only worked as an assistant coach to that point. He was probably also the coach I'd subconsciously been waiting for – someone who believed in me 100 per cent, right from the start, who trusted me implicitly.

The Joe–Johnny relationship has provided plenty of entertainment for the lads over the years. They used to call me teacher's pet. They say Joe is my long-lost father, my real dad. But Joe's trust was earned. It took a little while to tune into his wavelength, to figure him out.

I reckoned I had an advantage on most of my team-mates, seeing as Leo and I had already met him. Six months before his arrival, we'd spent an hour with him in a private meeting room in the Burlington Hotel. Leo asked most of the questions. I was chuffed merely to have been sent along. Joe seemed soft-spoken, polite, unassuming. Afterwards, Leo asked me for my thoughts. 'Seems like he knows his stuff,' I said. 'But is he too nice a bloke?'

Shows how much I knew.

Isa had worked with Joe at the Blues and described him as a genius. That made me even more desperate to make a strong impression on him. I got myself into great shape over the summer – the fitness levels of the All Blacks had come as a bit of a shock. I wanted to be ahead of the pack.

I popped in to Riverview two days before we were due to arrive for pre-season, knocked on Joe's door and asked if he could show me our attack shapes. Mustard keen, I was. He said he'd put some notes together for me. We chatted for a while. Rugby stuff. I could tell he watched a lot. One addict can always spot another.

Joe did little for his popularity with the lads by announcing that our pre-season camp would be in White's Hotel, Wexford. Cheiks usually brought us to glamorous, sunny spots like Barcelona, Nice and Biarritz to name a few. Joe didn't see the value. Going to Wexford would save money for the club and allow us to spread the Leinster gospel within the province. He was never really the suntanning type.

It was down in White's that we got to see the former school principal in action. We had a meeting to set some goals for the season. His instructions to the group were clear, precise. You could see he didn't like having to repeat himself. He had an edge to him.

Under Cheiks, we'd had themes for the season. One year it was the Tour de France – a certain set of games equated to the time trials, another set to the mountain stage, and so on. Another season, we had a picture of Everest on the wall of our team room. Joe was more about setting values than setting goals. He got us to focus on what we were about as people as well as players.

He split us into three groups. We all had to answer the same three questions: how we saw ourselves at the moment; how our fiercest rivals would describe us; and what we wanted people to say about us at the end of the season.

All that information was distilled into a list of positive

qualities. Then he asked us all to list the six players among us who most embodied those qualities. When the 'scores' were tallied, Joe effectively had his leadership group. I was included. We met with him that evening to take the distillation process a step further. After a couple of hours, we had boiled everything down to three words: Humble, Disciplined, Ruthless. These were the values to which we could hold ourselves accountable.

I was uneasy about the humility thing. Someone had suggested that there might be a negative perception about us out there, that maybe we rated ourselves too highly just because we'd won one Heineken Cup. And Joe had jumped on this. Maybe he was wary of us being a team with a star culture.

But I was used to Cheiks, and humility had never been a focal point for him. His attitude had been black and white: work hard, win on the weekend. I argued with Joe about it. How does 'humble' matter? We are here to win. And if we work hard, we'll win.

He said: Don't worry, Johnny. I will make sure you work hard. But I'll make sure you work smart, too.

He opened my eyes to the value of rest, to the danger of overwork. He showed all of us the importance of doing the simple things to a very high standard. Initially I was a bit frustrated by the simplicity of everything we did in training. I'd been excited by the idea of having a head coach who'd been a back. I came armed with loads of fancy plays.

Joe's shapes were all basic but he insisted they must be executed to perfection. Take a simple switch play where the 13 runs under the 12. He was incredibly fussy on detail here. It was essential that the transfer happened at the moment when the two players were precisely aligned, thus creating maximum uncertainty in the defence. If we were an inch off, it was: Go again, guys.

We played loads of training games but hardly any contact in July or August. We'd been given a brute of a pool in the Heineken – Racing, Saracens and Clermont – and Joe obviously knew all about the two French sides. He wanted us to peak for heavy collisions in October and December and instructed our strength and conditioning, or S&C, coach Jason Cowman to tailor our gym work accordingly.

Partly because of this and partly because the internationals were drip-fed back into the team, we had an awful start to the league, losing three of our first four games. We even lost to Treviso, becoming the first Irish side to do so. Joe took a rinsing in the media. I remember calling up to him to reassure him that we were behind him. What he was doing was going to come good. We just needed everyone to get fit and on the pitch.

We noticed that he was quite happy to put a senior player in his box, if he saw fit. In a team meeting before we played Edinburgh, Shaggy announced that Edinburgh always came hard in defence. 'You obviously haven't done your homework, Shane,' Joe said. 'Edinburgh have changed the way they defend this season.' All you could hear was the sound of throats gulping.

Cheiks had nearly always deferred to the rock stars. In the video review of the Edinburgh game, Joe clicked the pause button after Brian had spilled a low pass.

'Good players take those, Brian.'

More gulps.

He was polite to people. He liked us to be well-mannered, to shake hands with each other every morning – a habit he had seen and liked in Clermont. But we also saw Joe's ruthless side early in the season when he told Stephen Keogh he'd be letting him go. Stephen had been a popular member of the squad, an important presence in the dressing room. People were annoyed to hear he was getting the chop, but it also made everyone sit up and take notice. It didn't matter how popular you were.

We were encouraged to contribute in meetings, but if Joe didn't agree with you, he cut you dead with one syllable: Nah.

It was devastating.

Joe, I reckon we should have a runner coming short here . . .

Nah. We don't need to do that.

Joe, last season we used to do X.

Nah.

The good thing was that he'd explain why X wouldn't work. I loved the clarity he was giving us, loved his certainty. You suggest stuff to some coaches and even though they disagree with you, they won't say it straight. They'll give you some wishy-washy answer to keep you onside. With Joe, there was a right way of doing something and a wrong way, and you were left in no doubt which was which. As an outhalf, this is what you want. You want every single player in the whole squad to be on the same page.

He educated us and also entertained us – whether he knew it or not. Anyone who'd got the Joe treatment in a meeting got a proper going over in the dressing room, too. Someone got one of those Leinster baseball caps and taped a sticker with the word 'NAH' over the logo. Anyone who got burned by Joe in a meeting had to wear the cap in training.

Joe did have a great sense of humour and was really quick-witted. One day he asked why Darce was always wearing 'that cap' – and it nearly always was Darce, in fairness – and Ferg or Eoin O'Malley explained everything to him. He thought this was hilarious.

But if you wanted to take him on, you needed to have your argument watertight. Ian Madigan learned the hard way. It might have been Joe's second or third season at Leinster. Mads had been coming up with lots of flashy plays and getting plenty of positive press. But there was one game where he'd been part of a bench that failed to make an impact. Having led by maybe 20 points when the subs arrived, we'd ended up winning by eight. Joe was highlighting this shortcoming, asking what we needed to do to solve it. That's when Mads raised his hand.

Yes, Ian?

Joe, you may disagree with me but I think it would help if the guys on the bench got more reps in training . . .

He went on a while and when he was done, Joe says: Are you finished?

Yes, says Mads.

Well, you're right, Ian. I do disagree with you. One hundred per cent. It's your responsibility to know your shit. If you're not happy with the number of reps you're getting in training, then keep the team out there at the end and do the reps that you need and everyone needs.

The message was clear: Take ownership. Set standards and live up to them.

We went through our attack plays at the start of the week – no handouts, you took notes if necessary. You didn't turn up for field sessions unless you knew your shit. Say we were running plays off a lineout and someone was thrown into the backline for a rep but ballsed it up, they were subbed out. Gone. For the rest of the session. Someone else would just take their place. And it worked. People did their homework. We became sharper.

The values we set out were also policed by Joe and his leadership team. How you turned up on a Monday morning was as important as how you turned up on Saturday for a game. Performing in a walk-through before training was as important as the game itself. When we were on we were on. High standards and live up to what we said we were going to do. The culture in the club went to another level.

People slagged me. Teacher's pet never gets burned by Joe, they said. That was because I knew my detail. I'd done my homework.

Joe's only problem with me that autumn was that I'd strained my kicking quad again. I'd asked Dave Alred over for a session in early season and probably overdid things. I didn't play until the Munster game in early October and that was only for twenty minutes off the bench, without place-kicking. At least I got a feel for the Aviva, which had only just been opened. We won, too. That made it five in a row.

I wasn't ready to kick against Racing the following week, but Joe still wanted me to play – which pleased me no end. We saw the quality of his prep that week. He created profiles of the Racing players and stuck them on the wall of our meeting room. He showed us how Andrea Masi was a man-watcher in defence and how vulnerable he was to a wraparound between myself and Brian. We tried it just before the break and it worked a treat, with Rob finishing in the left corner. We carved them open a few times and ended up outscoring them by five tries to one.

Saracens at Wembley was more of a battle – they were on the cusp of their period of dominance in England and put it up to us. We won 25–23. I relieved Isa of the place-kicking duties and was delighted with how it went. I kicked seven out of seven and felt all of the benefits of the one-on-one strength sessions I'd been doing with Ireland's S&C man, Brian Green. I scored our only try, too, and converted it from the touchline. The November Tests couldn't come quickly enough.

You'd need to have played at the old Lansdowne Road to appreciate just how excited we were about being part of the first Test at the Aviva. The spacious, comfortable dressing rooms, the warm-up area, the medical rooms, the playing surface – everything was state of the art. Granted, it took some getting used to for place-kickers, given that the two ends are completely different in terms of visuals and wind currents. But here was a stadium to make you feel proud.

Until we turned up to play the Springboks and the place was only two-thirds full. The IRFU later admitted they'd over-priced their tickets that autumn. This was 2010. People were broke. The place felt dead. To make matters worse, our special commemorative jerseys were soon ripped to shreds and we had to change them at half-time. Plus we lost – 21–23.

It was no disgrace losing to the world champions, especially given we were missing Paulie. But we hadn't played well. The ambition was to move on from the limited game-plan that had won a Slam, to expand our attacking options. On a wet evening, our execution wasn't up to it.

I didn't play badly, but with fifteen minutes left we were trailing 9–23, and Deccie had to make changes. Typically, on the occasion of his hundredth cap, O'Gara grabbed his opportunity. We scored two tries before the end and he had a hand in both. He had a conversion to tie the scores but it rebounded off the upright.

I probably wasn't in the mood to do a Q&A in one of the sparkly new corporate boxes after the match, but it's part of the gig. At least I knew the guy asking the questions – Fred Cogley, the former TV commentator who'd done some media training with us in the academy, and a Mary's man. He'd previously told us that we had to be prepared to answer the hard questions, but I wasn't ready for his:

Well, Jonathan, what about that masterclass from Ronan O'Gara?

Maybe it was supposed to be a gag but I don't remember anyone laughing. I presented a straight bat and said nice things about Ronan, as you do. And got out of there as quickly as I could.

I was relieved when Deccie started me against the All Blacks. And nervous, given what had happened in New Plymouth. This time we lost 18–38 but didn't feel too bad about ourselves. That's just a reflection of where we were at in 2010, and where they were at.

The first forty was the best I'd experienced in ten appearances for Ireland. We took the game to them, played with old-fashioned aggro but also with width and variety. The Aviva responded, too – it was heaving on this occasion. But then the All Blacks responded. Approaching the break, we led 13–12 but then they brought the speed and relentlessness of their recycling game to another level, until eventually they broke us. We staggered back to the dressing room and I threw up in the jacks. I had never experienced intensity like that before.

I doubt Dan Carter was puking. While I felt beaten up from tackling Richie McCaw and Ma'a Nonu, Carter looked like he barely broke sweat all day. He also place-kicked beautifully, missing just one kick in nine. I'd studied him closely, courtesy of some video clips that Mervyn Murphy had sent.

I'd seen how he floated, played people early and then supported on the inside, how he knew when to break – bang, and he was gone.

I fluffed my one opportunity to get hold of him, midway through the second half. We were numbers up in defence. I should have nailed him but I wasn't decisive and he managed to get his hand under my chin and shove me up and back. I was surprised by his strength. I was now an easy target for his cleaners, who gave me a good going over.

They scored at the end of the second half, just as they had scored at the end of the first, to prove the superiority of their fitness. That was a gap that could be bridged, though. What about the gap between me and Carter? Enda McNulty was now doing more performance analysis with Leinster. He sat me down the following week and we went through Carter's game and mine, category by category – place-kicking, tactical kicking, restarts, distribution, defence. He showed me that Carter essentially did the basics incredibly well and consistently. And he was exceptionally fit. He also showed me that I'd compared pretty well with the best in the business. Playing opposite him could only help my development. I watched that game so many times. Playing against arguably the best 10 to ever play the game was something I'd dreamed of.

You didn't tend to hear much sniggering in Joe Schmidt's team meetings, but we struggled to keep a straight face when he started gushing about some of the Clermont players ahead of the Heineken back-to-backs. It was the nicknames that got us going. Aurélien Rougerie was 'Ro-ro' and Julien Malzieu was 'Ju-ju'. I could tell the admiration he had for their out-half, 'Brocky' James, too. When he was finished, Shaggy said: Jesus, we've no chance against this lot!

Sure enough, Ro-ro put Ju-ju over for one of the Clermont tries, but we came away with a losing bonus point, despite being without Brian, who was injured. The Stade Michelin was hopping so it was a decent effort.

I was back in my apartment the following morning, a Monday, when Dad called with sad news. Daddy John had died. It wasn't really a surprise. He was eighty-three and had had cancer for a few years. I'd seen him a few months previously and he was struggling. We'd watched TV together, with him in bed, attached to a drip. He never complained.

Dad was already in Listowel with his four brothers. He said the coffin would be kept open for me if I could make it down by Tuesday night – it was a typical country funeral with a wake that lasted a couple of days. I headed off with Laura after training. It was only when we arrived in town that the emotion hit me.

By that stage, Daddy John's coffin had been on the counter in the shop on William Street for two days – the passageway into the sitting room had been too narrow to carry it in there. A lot of people had passed through to pay their respects. There were tears and storytelling and laughter and joking. My uncles were having a great laugh winding up this man who was at the coffin paying his respects. They kept calling Daddy John's mobile, which was in the coffin with him, just to watch the man's reaction. Would he answer the phone? This had them in stitches. Then all of a sudden, the emotion would take over again.

They buried Daddy John with his phone and a deck of cards. He used to call you whenever it was quiet in the shop. He chatted to my mum a lot, and to Laura. Loved keeping in touch with people. And now here we were the next day, walking behind his hearse all the way from the church to the graveyard on the Ballybunion Road, stopping outside the shop where he had lived all his life, the whole town at a stand-still. This was the week before Christmas and it was freezing. I remember because I was only wearing a suit. I picked up a cold but was determined to play the return game against Clermont at the Aviva that Saturday. We won well but I was overcome with emotion in the dressing room afterwards. Grief can show itself at strange times.

I missed Leinster's Christmas party a few nights later. I was on a secret, pre-arranged mission to Paris, where Cheiks was giving me a tour of his new club, Stade Français. He had made offers to myself and Seánie.

I'm joking when I say the mission was secret. I wanted to be discovered. I left my phone on so that when team-mates called to ask why I wasn't at the party, they'd hear the foreign dial tone and the rumours could begin circulating. It might sound childish but when it came to contract negotiations with the IRFU, there was often a game to be played.

I had hired Fintan Drury as my agent around the start of that 2010/11 season, on the recommendation of Lukey, Darce and Shaggy. Fintan was shocked when he heard that I was still on a salary of €100K. As the holder of the Ireland number 10 jersey, he reckoned I should be earning at least three times that amount. He said the same thing to the IRFU, knowing that I was out of contract at the end of that season. They eventually agreed a two-year contract extension at €280K, but Fintan argued that I should start earning at that level for the remainder of the existing contract. Negotiations dragged on a while, as they tended to do.

I therefore had to give the impression that I was willing to leave Leinster. This explains the trip to Paris, which became a bit of a nightmare when my return flight was cancelled because of heavy snow. I spent twenty-four hours at Charles de Gaulle, with only *The Sopranos* for company. I got through an entire series. I just about made it home in time for Christmas.

We were almost into February when Deccie asked me where it was at. I told him that I didn't expect to be on the same deal as O'Gara, given his experience and achievements, but I did expect my salary to reflect where I was in the pecking order. He didn't give me any reason to think that I was being unreasonable.

It was eventually agreed that I'd be paid significant bonuses for every Six Nations appearance that year. I was happy to get it sorted. I had zero desire to leave Leinster, of course. Joe Schmidt was helping me to enjoy my job like never before. We swept Saracens aside in Round 5 and then hammered Racing in Paris, where I scored a couple of tries and 21 points altogether – good timing, with the Six Nations approaching. We topped our pool and earned ourselves a home quarter-final against Leicester after the Six Nations.

Probably for the first time in my career, I felt completely comfortable playing for Leinster, because I knew that the coach trusted my judgement. I loved the way he thought about the game. He would encourage us to attack space from anywhere on the pitch. 'If it's on, you backs better be ready to go.' If I ran from my own try-line and threw a pass to the edge and the guy dropped it, it was his fault, not mine. Joe coached with such clarity that I had his voice in my head going through games. *Chase the space, no matter where you are on the field.* He was going to back me, every time.

Out-half is probably the position where you most need to feel that you have the coach's trust. You're his quarterback.

You have a different relationship with him. Maybe other guys need to feel some heat to operate at their best, but if the out-half is looking over his shoulder, wondering if he's going to play each week, it's impossible to drive the team effectively. That was my biggest problem with Ireland at that time.

Deccie had great technical coaches in Les, Gert Smal and Riff, while Merv's analysis was always top-class. But while we talked about expanding our attacking game, I always felt that Deccie was a bit uncomfortable with the idea of moving the ball from deep. We clearly needed to develop our attacking game if we were going to challenge at the World Cup, however. We had so much attacking talent. But it didn't help our confidence that we made such a shaky start to the Six Nations.

First, we had a narrow escape in Rome, where O'Gara came off the bench to steal the result with a late drop-goal. You had to hand it to him. It was a great moment for him and put the pressure back on me.

Suddenly I was racked with doubt again. It didn't help that Brian had a pop at me in the video review. At one point in the game, he had dropped my pass – an 'unsympathetic' pass, according to him. I'd taken too much out of the ball, apparently. I needed to give it earlier. From where I was sitting, it looked like he was blaming me for him dropping the ball. I didn't feel confident enough to come back at the skipper in that environment. Instead I bottled up the grievance and let it ferment.

The following week, we lost 22–25 to France, in Dublin. We put even more ball on the floor and our discipline was poor but I thought I'd played pretty well. Riff told the media he was pretty happy with me. So did Deccie. He still dropped me for the trip to Edinburgh.

'I thought Jonathan had a very good game but Ronan

has been playing very well then too,' he told the media. 'Not everybody that you'd like to get a game, gets a game, but I think Ronan deserves a game and that's why he's getting a start.'

I didn't get much more out of him when we spoke face to face. In that situation, the player craves guidance about where they can improve, but Deccie said he was happy with me. There was one situation against France where he'd have preferred me to kick rather than run from deep, as we had turned the ball over near halfway. I thought it was on to run, and getting turned over wasn't my issue. I was thinking that Joe would have analysed why we turned the ball over. Looking back, I shouldn't have been so sensitive to negative feedback, but when you know you are going to get left out of the team because of it it's hard to accept it as constructive.

Deccie said he wasn't blaming me. Still, he must have thought that Ronan was a safer pair of hands for a game he had to win. Or maybe Deccie just wanted to keep things competitive at 10. Competition can keep you sharp. But what you don't want is to feel that you're going to be dropped for bad outcomes on decisions that may have been good. That way, you don't know if you're coming or going. The message I took was that he didn't trust me to get the job done in Murrayfield.

We very nearly didn't. O'Gara was man of the match, scoring one of our three tries, but we had only a six-point lead when I replaced him with twelve minutes to go. That had been reduced to 3 points by the end, when we were defending for our lives. When I hoofed the ball into the stand to end the agony, O'Gara raced on to the field to celebrate and we had an awkward hug.

I had mixed feelings – happy to have got the win, of course, but annoyed that I hadn't been able to steer us to safety with more authority. My mood only darkened when I switched on my phone. It was hopping, mainly with messages giving out about RTÉ pundit George Hook. Apparently he'd been on a rant, saying that Deccie shouldn't start me again until the game against Russia at the World Cup. Great.

I came on against Wales in Cardiff with half an hour to go. We led 13–9 at that stage, but I started like a man unsure of himself. It was my mistake that led directly to a highly controversial Welsh try.

When I gathered the ball near my own 22, my instinct was to run. It was on. But I had a million different things going on in my head. In two minds, I ended up kicking. Badly. I sliced it into touch. But the trouble was only beginning.

Matthew Rees, the Wales hooker, took a quick throw to Mike Phillips, who nipped in at the corner. Rees threw the wrong ball from the wrong place, so there was no way the try should have been allowed. But between them the referee and touch judge decided it was fine. James Hook converted the try to make it a seven-pointer. We ended up losing by six. Sickener.

To make matters worse, I missed a very kickable penalty before the end. For all that, I took some comfort. As we chased the game in the final quarter, I felt a spark, a positive charge. It might have been an exchange with Paulie. At one stage we opted to kick to the corner, but my line-kick barely made it into the Welsh 22 and he let me know what he thought of my effort. Next time we tried it, I spiralled it right into the corner. Getting his seal of approval made me feel a million dollars.

We didn't score. I don't know how the Welsh held us out, but they did. With England coming to Dublin on course for a Slam, we were in danger of finishing in the bottom half of the table.

No doubt I took plenty of media flak for two big errors, but in fairness to Deccie, he'd spotted all the good stuff and picked me to start against England. I felt I had a point to prove and I was narky all week. It felt like everyone was on my back, everyone had an opinion. No matter how hard you try, you can't avoid everything that's been said in the media. In the team room, I saw a headline over a piece on the back page of the paper, which said something about me being the 'wrong' out-half for the Irish back row. It was bullshit but it was more scrutiny. I'd never experienced anything like it.

It all came to boiling point in a training run at the RDS. Brian had a go at me for another of my 'unsympathetic' passes and I exploded at him, telling him maybe it would help if he just caught the fucking ball. He wasn't impressed.

'You know you *can* be wrong!' he said. 'It *is* possible. You don't *always* have to have the last word!'

'Last word,' I snapped back, just to needle him. It worked. He was fuming. So was I.

I hadn't forgotten the meeting after the Italy game. I had let it fester. It wasn't only Brian. It was everything. The press. The scrutiny. My own frustration that I couldn't play for Ireland with the same freedom as I did for Leinster.

'You just threw me under the bus after the Italy game! Yeah, thanks for that.'

'Shut up or I'm going hit you!' he shouted.

'Let's go, then,' I barked back, squaring up. 'I've been waiting for you to throw a punch!'

I was ready to go. So was he. Red mist on both sides. Darce had to step in and separate us. We were within inches of a full-scale punch-up. Even when things died down a bit and we got back to running plays, it felt like it could have kicked off again any minute. When we were finished, we went our separate ways.

I'd been out of line and I knew it. I sent Brian a text that night to explain and to apologize for being disrespectful. He said he appreciated the text and said that he should have called me. We hugged it out the next morning.

Our little outburst set the tone for the week, for the match. England were coming to win a Grand Slam? On our patch? Deccie stirred things up nicely in the build-up. So did Brian and Paulie.

I didn't need any further stirring. I was so pissed off with all the crap about me that I actually felt no pressure at all. I just wanted to get out there. I made a conscious decision that week that I didn't care how the game went. I was just going to play what I saw, trust myself and go for it. When we got an early penalty on our own 22, I tapped and ran. We made seventy metres and the crowd was buzzing.

I was buzzing. Focused enough to land three first-half penalties as our pack got on top, but aggressive in everything I did. Soon I was presented with the option of a fourth but I could tell England had switched off, so I tapped again, and sent Tommy in for a try.

Nine minutes after the break, Brian scooped for his twenty-fifth championship try, breaking the record in the process. I was first in for the hug. When I landed the conversion from the left touchline, we were 24–3 ahead. It was my best all-round performance for Ireland to date.

The crowd gave me a good send-off ten minutes from the end. Someone in TV-land had decided that I had been man of the match. When I was interviewed pitch-side by RTÉ's Tracy Piggott, I smiled, and resisted the urge to ram it into

everyone that had been on my case. In the mixed zone, journalists asked about my relationship with O'Gara. Naturally.

'What happens on the pitch between Munster and Leinster goes out the window when we come into the Irish camp,'
I said. 'I'm sure in a couple weeks' time we'll be back killing
each other, down in Thomond, but we are great friends today
and as we build towards the World Cup.'

Ever the diplomat.

As it turned out, we did have a good workout in Limerick,
with Munster finally ending their losing run against us. It finished 24–23. Our heads may already have been in Europe.
We knew we were playing Leicester in the Heineken quarters
the following week, at the Aviva.

Of our Heineken wins, 2011 remains my favourite, for a
couple of reasons. First, you couldn't really pick a more
difficult collection of opponents. Racing, Saracens and Clermont all had designs on the Cup that year and would all go
on to play in Heineken finals. Leicester were still a force back
then and had the motivation of seeking revenge for what
had happened in Edinburgh two years previously. They gave
us a game of Test match intensity, which we won 17–10. So
did Toulouse in the semi – not surprising, given that their
side was made up almost entirely of French internationals,
along with a couple of physical freaks like Patricio Albacete
and Census Johnston.

Again, we had the advantage of playing the semi at the
Aviva, but that was justifiable reward for our pool performance. We were battered, but had three weeks to get ready for
the final. Northampton, meanwhile, had to play a Premiership semi just seven days before meeting us in Cardiff.

The second reason that I treasure 2011 above the other

Leinster wins, of course, is the drama of the final. A lot of neutrals still pick it as their favourite European rugby final, so you can imagine how special it was for us.

The bare facts are pretty incredible – how we trailed 6–22 at the break and then scored 27 points unanswered. A freakish turnaround. It can also be remembered as the day when we lived by the values that we'd set ourselves in Wexford, ten months previously.

We were disciplined, for example, in the way that we took care of possession in the second half, compared to the way that we didn't in the first. And we were relentless in the way we used that possession, pounding Northampton until they crumbled.

Where was the humility, though? This was an issue for me, especially. Once Brian got in front of a microphone after the final whistle, he created a narrative where I had cast a magic spell, simply with what I'd said in the dressing room at half-time. 'Some inspirational words,' he told Will Greenwood. 'Sexto was just phenomenal.'

It sounds a nice idea. And people needed an explanation as to how such a remarkable transformation could have taken place. You think back to how devastated the Leinster supporters must have been feeling as we headed up the tunnel to face Joe. Once again, they had travelled in their tens of thousands and easily outnumbered Northampton's fans. Then there were all the supporters back at home whose weekend was in the process of being ruined.

Poor Richie Hughes couldn't watch any more. At half-time, he went out for a walk, turned off his phone. Later, he told me of how he'd walked down to the Church of the Annunciation in Rathfarnham to light a few candles, as we clearly needed inspiration from somewhere. Luckily he turned his phone back on when he got outside the church and received a flurry of texts telling him to rush home. Leinster were on the comeback!

It didn't feel like I was saying anything particularly magical in the dressing room, just what was in my head.

I was fuming, because I knew the scoreboard was misleading. Yes, we had slipped off a few tackles and yes, we needed to sort out the scrum. No better men than Greg Feek and Mike Ross to come up with a solution. But everything had bounced Northampton's way up to that point. I think back to the spiral I kicked from my 22 in the first five minutes – maybe the best-struck punt of my career. One second it's nose-diving beautifully into the right corner, the next it takes a wicked bounce left, and runs dead. Scrum back, and Northampton score off the scrum.

I had it all clear in my head:

If we make a break, take the simple option rather than the risky pass.

We have scored points in big clumps before. Think back to the semi against Toulouse. Toulouse are twice the side that Northampton are.

We are fitter than they are. They played a big semi last week. Funny things can happen in finals. If we win this one, it will be remembered for ever. We all set out on our individual journeys wanting to be remembered at the end of it. This is our chance.

That was pretty much it.

I ended up getting the headlines because I scored 28 points. That's the nature of the gig when you're the out-half and the place-kicker and when your pack gets on top. The good days are great.

People might forget that it was Brian – playing on one leg, practically – who lit the fuse, by darting through the middle of a breakdown and running into Northampton's 22 before finding Jamie in support. People might forget the way Isa darted through another gap off the recycle, or the intelligence of Reddser's pass which took me outside of Soane Tonga'uiha less than four minutes after the restart.

I gestured to the Leinster fans after sliding over, jabbing at the air. As if they weren't making enough noise already. It's pretty noisy in the Principality whenever the roof is shut. This felt like someone had turned the volume up full. They never turned it back down.

People might also forget Reddser's general urgency, how he set the pace. They will remember Seánie's power on the ball, of course. He was outstanding. Jenno made a big impact off the bench. Jamie was brilliant, too, but in more subtle ways. Take his running off the ball for our second try. Joe always stressed the importance of 'staying big past the ball' – in other words, continuing to run forward after you have passed, to stay in the game or, as in this case, to block defenders on the inside. Dowson was pissed off that he was prevented from getting at me as I looped around. On another day, the ref might have called us back. Not that day.

That score brought us to within 2 points. The deal was more or less done in the fifty-seventh minute when our scrum walked them backwards in the middle of the park – the perfect symbol of how the game had been tipped on its head. I rammed the penalty home from thirty-five metres and we're ahead 23–22. With all that time remaining, you'd think maybe we should have won by more than 11 points. But the third quarter probably took a lot out of us. We had emptied the tank.

Someone said that at half-time I had mentioned Liverpool's Miracle of Istanbul from 2005. I don't remember doing that. I'd have been more likely to mention Manchester United's Champions League semi in 1999 – Roy Keane's

I was first introduced to Dave Alred when I was twenty-two. He became a great mentor to me – and not just for my kicking. He helped me develop the mindset to try to get better every day, and he was a neutral sounding board through the tough times.

Down 22–6 at half-time of the 2011 Heineken Cup final, we kept it simple and backed our fitness and skill. Eoin Reddan gave me a great pass for a try early in the second half, the first of 27 unanswered points. (Inpho/Ryan Byrne)

As we defended our line towards the end of the 2012 Heineken Cup semi-final away to Clermont, we were surprised to hear Joe Schmidt standing behind the dead-ball line, shouting instructions. At the final whistle, he and I celebrated a great win. (Inpho/Dan Sheridan)

Brad Thorn made a huge impression when he joined Leinster for the last months of the 2011–12 season, helping us to our third European Cup in four years. In the dressing room after the final, he handed me a beer and said: 'Don't change, mate. You're a champion. Don't change.' It meant the world to me. (Inpho/Dan Sheridan)

For me, the Lions is the pinnacle. I was thrilled to go on the 2013 tour to Australia, and to score the try that finally broke the Wallabies' resistance in the decisive third Test. (Inpho/Dan Sheridan)

Laura and I got married after I came back from Australia in 2013. She and I first met when I was ten years old. We have been best friends ever since.

We went to Paris for the last round of the 2014 Six Nations knowing that a win would secure us the championship. We were down 6–0 when I scored this try; my second gave us a lead we would never surrender. (Inpho/James Crombie)

In keeping with a new concussion policy in France, where I was playing my club rugby in 2014–15, I took a twelve-week break – from which I returned to face France in round two of the 2015 Six Nations. There was much talk of the danger I faced from their big centre Mathieu Bastareaud, and sure enough he and I had a clash of heads; but after passing my HIA I nailed a penalty – one of the most satisfying kicks of my career – and was named man of the match. (Inpho/Dan Sheridan)

After beating Scotland by 30 points to put ourselves top of the table on the last day of the 2015 Six Nations, we had to wait for the result of France v. England. Thousands of Irish fans hung around in Murrayfield to celebrate our second consecutive championship. (Inpho/Dan Sheridan)

During our great win over France in the 2015 World Cup group stage, I injured my groin, and it was hard to watch the quarter-final from the stands. We were also missing Paul O'Connell, the best captain I've ever played under; Seán O'Brien, of his day the best loose forward in the world; and Peter O'Mahony, already a great lineout operator and leader. (Inpho/Billy Stickland)

The Leinster I returned to at the end of 2015 was a mess. Leo Cullen – an absolute legend at Leinster – had been thrust into the hot seat after the sacking of Matt O'Connor. Our relationship came under strain for a time but we had huge mutual respect and after a tough season things got better. (Inpho/Dan Sheridan)

The arrival of Stuart Lancaster was a game-changer for Leinster, and for me personally. He and I spoke at length once a week and he helped me to become a better leader. (Inpho/Oisín Keniry)

This conversion of our first try against the All Blacks in Chicago in 2016 put us ahead for the first time – and unlike in 2013, we would never lose the lead. Our first win ever over New Zealand was special, as was the pre-match tribute to the late Anthony Foley.
(Inpho/Dan Sheridan)

Playing with Owen Farrell – me at 10, him at 12 – in the second and third Tests for the 2017 Lions in New Zealand was a special experience. Owen is one of my all-time favourite team-mates, and having a second playmaker in midfield made my job easier.
(Inpho/Dan Sheridan)

As soon as I struck my drop-goal attempt in Paris in 2018 – with us a point down and the clock deep in the red – I was confident it was going over. The Grand Slam we had dared to target was still on. Bundee Aki got to me first, with Fergus McFadden, Robbie Henshaw, Conor Murray and Rob Kearney close behind. (Getty Images/Thomas Samson)

We completed the Slam with a brilliant performance at Twickenham. We gave that celebration a proper lash, first in London and then back in Dublin. (Inpho/Dan Sheridan)

match – or the final in the Camp Nou against Bayern. Whatever. Turnarounds of that nature are rare enough in top-level rugby. In a tournament, you might learn big lessons in the post-match review and then get to implement them on the pitch the following week. The magic of Cardiff 2011 was that we figured things out on the run, made the necessary adjustments and achieved something heroic. That's what made it so special.

Watch our post-match celebrations and you can see how giddy we were – jumping around, spraying each other with champagne. And the celebrations carried on for another forty-eight hours.

It was suggested that we still hadn't dried out by the time we got to Limerick the following Saturday for the Magners final. I reckon we were mainly psychologically drained post-Cardiff.

I watched the game back during lockdown. Nigel Owens didn't do us any favours, but we still didn't play well. We desperately wanted to complete a double, but then there were probably bigger things at play for Munster that day. They were desperate to win for their strength and conditioning coach, Paul Darbyshire, who died from motor neurone disease a few weeks later, aged just forty-one, with a wife and four young children. They had Paul up on stage with them after the game, along with the trophy. Sometimes you realize that you have to play a part in someone else's story.

When I think back to 2011, I remember how tight we were as a group. I think of the sponsors' gig in the Guinness Storehouse the night after that Magners final when the entire squad was there with partners, all dolled up but feeling a little bruised after losing in Limerick. But sometimes the best parties are the ones that aren't planned.

Once the formalities were concluded and the other guests began to drift away, the players congregated in the famous Gravity Bar, with its panoramic view of Dublin city. In the middle is a circular bar, so naturally we formed a circle around it and took turns to down pints of stout. We sang, we laughed, we drank. From there, we took taxis to Darce's bar in town, the Exchequer, and the party carried on into the night. We ended up in Copper's, where the Heineken Cup made an appearance on the dance floor.

Kings of Europe.

We had some craic.

11

It's hard to imagine that Ireland will ever have a more manageable route to the World Cup final than we had in 2011. By beating Australia in Auckland in our second pool game, we lined ourselves up on the 'European' side of the draw for the knockout stages: Wales in the quarters, France in the semis.

Very doable. But we blew it.

Everything was teed up nicely for me. I was just past my twenty-sixth birthday and in the shape of my life. I had just helped Leinster win our second Heineken Cup. This was my chance to announce myself on a world stage.

New Zealand should have been fun. And it was fun, in parts. Unlike 2007, when the lads told me they spent their tournament in an industrial estate outside Bordeaux, we got to see New Zealand in all its beauty. We got to see it at a nice time of year, too, in September and October – normally, we tend to tour there in the depths of their winter, in June and July. The days were longer, the temperatures a bit milder.

The welcome from the locals was warmer, too, especially after we beat the Aussies on the second weekend of the tournament. With thousands of Irish fans following us around in their campervans, we didn't lack support.

Deccie played a blinder by arranging our pre-tournament training camp for Queenstown, a stunningly beautiful corner of the South Island. That got us off to the ideal start. Then it all went downhill. For me, anyway.

If I could go back and change one thing, I'd probably play less golf in the build-up to the tournament. Seriously. I'd go back and spend more time on my place-kicking. For it was my place-kicking that let me down in New Zealand, my place-kicking that put doubt in Deccie's head. I only have myself to blame for allowing that to happen.

My golf was good, actually. We were playing so much that I was going round the Montgomerie Course at Carton House in one or two over par. It was a lovely summer that year and some nights we were still out there at 10.30. We'd work hard during the mornings and afternoons, get some food into us and then it was almost a race to get into the buggies and down to the first tee. Reddan, O'Connell, McFadden, Trimble, O'Driscoll – these were the most regular participants in our four-balls. It got very competitive. Great craic.

Enda McNulty had convinced me that I needed to build some fun into my schedule, to enjoy the World Cup journey rather than fret too much over performance. When things went pear-shaped for me out in New Zealand, I started to agonize over my preparation.

I still wasn't feeling fully confident in the Ireland set-up. Brian used to urge me to act with the same authority as I did with Leinster, to drive things, to impose myself. But this wasn't as easy as it sounded. How could I be authoritative in training on a Monday if I was unsure about whether I was going to be selected on the Tuesday?

Given the way I'd finished the previous season, I should have backed myself more. But Deccie put a screw in my head by picking me to start the first World Cup warm-up, against Scotland in Edinburgh, as part of what felt like a mostly second-string team. It was explained to me that Ronan was carrying a niggle that week, and that's why I was starting.

But then O'Gara got to start in Bordeaux the following week with the first-choice team, so immediately I was overthinking things. Was this a bad sign? It wasn't, but it took surprisingly little to make me doubt myself in the Ireland set-up back then. I was verging on paranoid.

Things were better between me and Ronan. We were finding a way to get on. Say we'd have kicking practice in the Aviva in the week of a Test, then the pair of us would go for a soup and sandwich afterwards and swap gossip. We'd both figured it out that it was bad for everyone if there was tension between us.

I should have reassured myself that the important thing was to start the opening game, against USA in New Plymouth, because that was our dress rehearsal for the pivotal pool fixture – against Australia in Eden Park. The third game, against Russia in Rotorua, had always looked like Deccie's opportunity to mix things up, to make sure everyone in the squad got a run, before we wrapped up the pool in Dunedin against Italy.

Sure enough, I was selected at 10 for New Plymouth. We won but it didn't go well. It was a filthy night, wind and rain, and the Eagles were tough – not surprisingly, given that they were coached by Eddie O'Sullivan. It finished Ireland 22, USA 10. My place-kicking hadn't helped. Two out of six didn't look good, even in difficult conditions. The rest of my game was fine, but those stats followed me around like a bad smell. When I was replaced near the end, I took my place on the bench, stared at the floor and muttered to whoever was sitting beside me:

Well, there goes my fucking World Cup.

Paul McNaughton might have overheard me. The following Monday I was rooming with Reddser in Auckland when

I got a call from Deccie asking me to come and see him in twenty minutes. Immediately, I started catastrophizing.

I told Reddser: That's it. I'm not starting against Australia.

He tried to reassure me but I wasn't convinced. Then, when I got to Deccie's room, he asked: Well, why do you think I want to speak to you?

This was classic Deccie. You wanted him to come out and say what he was thinking. I said that he'd obviously decided not to start me against Australia. No, it wasn't that, he said. He just wanted to have a chat. I needed to start believing in myself more. I needed to stop worrying about O'Gara, he said. Then he told me I'd be starting against the Wallabies.

I'm thinking: *Why couldn't he have told me that in the team room? Why have me spend half an hour thinking that I'm dropped?*

Auckland saw probably Ireland's best one-off performance at a World Cup to that point: Ireland 15, Australia 6. A great result and an incredible occasion, too, with Ireland winning in the stands as well as on the pitch. It seemed like all those emigrants we'd seen in Brisbane the previous summer turned up again, in even greater numbers. They made Eden Park feel like a home venue for a night.

I was swept along by the dressing-room euphoria, but by the time we were on the bus back to our hotel, I knew I'd be awake all night agonizing over missed kicks. It doesn't matter how well you have played in all other aspects of your game – and I was happy with how I'd gone. I had missed three shots out of five and that, in my mind, was all that counted.

That, and the fact that I'd allowed O'Gara to become the story again. He'd come off the bench in the third quarter, nudging me into the centre, taking over the place-kicking, steering us to victory.

I thought back to the two shots I'd missed before the break, how I'd been tentative, rather than drilling the kicks. Conditions weren't easy but these were shots I needed to be getting. I recalled the dressing room at half-time and the conversation I'd overhead between Deccie and Mark Tainton – they didn't know I was listening because I had my head buried in a towel. Deccie asked if he needed to change place-kicker. Taints said I should be allowed one more.

No pressure, then!

That opportunity came within five minutes of the restart. I committed to it and the ball flew between the posts to put us 9–6 ahead. I felt good. The pressure I had on me for that kick was massive. I knew if I missed I was off. Now I was back on track. O'Gara soon came on but as an injury replacement for Darce, meaning that I relocated to 12. In the fifty-second minute, the Aussie scrum collapsed, presenting me with another shot, thirty-five metres out, ten metres in from touch to the left of the posts. Again, I drilled it, but it rebounded off the left upright. To this day I don't know how that kick missed. I nailed it on the line I wanted. But it drifted ever so slightly on the breeze. And that was that. O'Gara took over the place-kicking. You couldn't complain.

He kicked two penalties to seal the win. Both kicks were relatively easy. I was thinking: *I'd have got those.* You think: *If my last kick had been an inch to the right, I'd have kept the place-kicking duties. I'd have kicked five from seven plus a drop-goal and been one of the heroes of a famous Irish victory.* Yeah, and if my granny had balls . . .

I was fortunate to be rooming with Reddser for most of the tournament, as he is one of the more positive people I know. He knows when to reassure you, when to take the piss.

He said he was going to blame me if he was dropped for the next game, against Russia in Rotorua. The two of us came as a package deal back then – both in or both out. Therefore, if I missed kicks, I was putting his starting place in jeopardy as well as my own.

It was funny, but true. Against Russia, O'Gara started and he went well. I worked hard on my place-kicking between games. I phoned Richie Murphy and Dave Alred for feedback. Richie sent me a video with a few pointers. Dave suggested some drills to give me more momentum into the strike. He suggested being more on my toes as I was struggling to get my weight through the ball. But all the while I was wondering if my chance had gone.

The low point came in Dunedin, a few days before we played Italy. The team hadn't been announced but I'd already figured that I was on the bench. That was when my frustrations boiled over. Leo got the brunt of it.

I was in the bibs when it all flared up, and he was in the first team. He grabbed me at a ruck and I slapped his arm away aggressively. It happened again and I swung again. He slapped me in the face and that's when the red mist descended. I grabbed him by the collar and started swinging like mad. People tried to drag me back but I lost the rag altogether. I split him open, just above the eye.

I'm sure I took him by surprise. We were very close, after all. He was my club captain and I had massive respect for him. I'm sure it took everyone by surprise. Not my finest hour.

On top of all that, I had to go and practise my bloody place-kicking afterwards and it was a daft-looking drill that Dave had suggested, one that probably made people wonder if I'd lost my marbles altogether. Basically you tee up under the posts, fifteen metres out, aiming to drill the ball against the crossbar or under the crossbar as hard as possible. It's actually a great drill, designed to improve your foot position and point of contact on the ball. But I'm sure people were looking at me thinking: *Look at your man. He's blown a fuse and now he can't even get a kick from in front of the posts.*

This might sound funny now, but no one was laughing at the time. Normally after a training-ground scrap, you have a kiss-and-make-up session in front of everyone the following day and the slagging is relentless. There was none of that. It was never mentioned. Well, not in front of me. It was bad. I apologized to Leo, and of course he was good about it. I still felt shit.

As expected, Deccie took me aside and told me he didn't have a start for me. They were going with Ronan for this one. I just needed to keep doing what I was doing.

We stuffed Italy 36–6 at the Forsyth Barr stadium and O'Gara kicked six out of six. I got thirteen minutes off the bench. At least my place-kicking work paid off as I landed two great kicks, one from the touchline. I gave a small fist-pump after that one. I felt that these were important kicks.

Maybe I'd still get the nod to start the quarter-final in Wellington? Surely Kissy would prefer me to defend against Jamie Roberts? Maybe Deccie might remember how well we'd attacked against Wales in Croke Park the year before – the last time I'd started against them? Maybe he'd play me at 12? That's how we'd finished the game against Australia – O'Gara at 10 and me at 12.

He put me on the bench. I didn't react well. I was snappy with him. It was mainly out of annoyance at myself, for allowing this to happen. Eventually I knuckled down and did my best to help the team prepare.

But Wales did a number on us. They took their chances and defended brilliantly, with Dan Lydiate and Sam Warburton chop-tackling Seánie and Stephen Ferris out of the game. We ignored shots at goal and went to the corner.

By the time I got on the pitch with twenty to go, we were chasing the game. Almost immediately, we conceded an unbelievably soft try to Jonathan Davies. That was a 12-point gap. We never looked like bridging it.

I look back on that trip with huge regret. By the end, I was happy to be going home. At departures in Auckland Airport, Deccie asked me for my thoughts. I didn't know if he was looking for advice but I gave it anyway.

I suggested that in future, if he was going to drop me, to give me reasons, not to say: 'Keep doing what you're doing – but we're not picking you.' I wanted feedback. In my own mind, though, I knew the answer: that my kicking wasn't as bulletproof as it needed to be and I had to improve.

Cheiks would tell you straight: I'll pick you when you start running on to the scrum-half's pass. Or he'd tell you he was picking Felipe because Felipe was a world-class goal-kicker and I wasn't, so I needed to do something about it. Joe was very precise in what he prescribed, too. I wanted Deccie to be more upfront with me, more direct.

I think he respected me for my honesty. I hope he did. I've lots of time for Deccie. He gave me an opportunity when lots of other people wouldn't have. He's a good man – compassionate, empathetic. It's part of the reason he was successful as a coach. He was shrewd and knew how to push the players' buttons. I felt sometimes he wouldn't say things out straight because he didn't want to hurt your feelings. But players need clarity above all else.

Players need to be honest with themselves, too. The reason that World Cup didn't go as I wanted it to go was mainly down to me. I knew my kicking was good enough as I kicked over 90 per cent in the previous year's Heineken Cup, but I got my prep wrong and paid the price. The experience thickened my hide. It forced me to turn myself into a better place-kicker, too. I came back from that World Cup more determined than ever.

I'd reached a turning point in my relationship with O'Gara. We were still rivals, because I played for Leinster and he played for Munster, so we were virtually guaranteed to go head-to-head twice a season. But by the time we came home from the 2011 World Cup, he was heading towards his thirty-fifth birthday. I knew that he wasn't going to feature at the next World Cup. Barring injury or a loss of form, it made sense for Deccie to pick me as his starting 10.

That awareness should have been reassuring, empowering. But for the next while, I kept hearing the same question: How come Sexton can't play for Ireland like he plays for Leinster? At the time it was a question I used to ask myself. It frustrated me. The England game showed that I could do it, but the consistency I had with Leinster wasn't there yet.

Deccie was in charge for fifteen more Tests after the World Cup and won only four of them. I felt sorry for him because he didn't have much luck. A lot of critical reffing decisions seemed to go against us. I'm thinking of the way the ref blew us off the park in Paris, or the bad scrum call Nigel Owens made in Christchurch, when we were on the verge of causing an upset.

He had no luck with injuries, either. Brian and Paulie, his two most important leaders, missed chunks of 2012 and

2013. Mike Ross got injured in Twickenham in 2012 and we paid a heavy price. I missed most of the 2013 Six Nations. By the time we lost to Italy in Rome, in the final match, bodies were dropping left, right and centre. In the space of twelve months, Deccie had gone from being in the mix to lead the Lions to being out of a job. Being a professional coach is a ridiculously fickle gig.

As a player, though, you expect that the standard of preparation will go up when you go from provincial to international. Les Kiss and Gert Smal are quality coaches. I learned a lot from them and from Anthony Foley, who was part of the Ireland set-up for a while. But the job descriptions kept changing. Les was in charge of defence, then he was in charge of defence and attack, then just attack. With Leinster, there was zero doubt about who was in control.

Joe did have more time with us, which was to his advantage. But the clarity of his messages and the certainty with which he delivered them was so impressive. Take the way he coached the breakdown. What happens post-tackle can look messy, with bodies all over the place. Joe turned it into a scientific process for us, letting everyone know precisely what was required of them – the tackled player, the first man in support, and so on. He broke it down into basic physics and geometry – how essential it was that the ball-carrier squared up pre-contact, allowing the cleaners a route that was perpendicular to the try-line, forcing any would-be poacher to come through the gate.

Like any good teacher, Joe used images and cues to clarify the idea – the ball-carrier was the barrel of the gun, the cleaners were bullets. I won't give any more of his imagery away, though. I know he was annoyed at certain players revealing his 'intellectual property' when they went into the media!

We became true believers in the way Joe coached the breakdown, to such an extent that when the Leinster players went into Ireland camp, we were impatient at the lack of detail in this area. The guys from other provinces would look at us and shake their heads. What's your problem? Why do you keep going on about this? We're grand as we are. But grand wasn't good enough.

The quality of our preparation at Leinster was just on a different level. The other area where it really showed was in attack. Joe was brilliant at spotting a weakness and devising a play that would expose it. Take the try against Cardiff in the 2012 Heineken quarter-final, when there were seven of us involved from the time that Richardt Strauss threw the line-out until Brian's touchdown, and not one Cardiff hand laid on any of us. We practised that play countless times, to get the timing absolutely on the money – and not just the guys who touched the ball. Everyone had their role. It was a thing of beauty.

Joe still found fault with it, though. I had stepped to the right a millisecond too early, or whatever. A better opponent would have defended it, he'd say. This was the type of perfectionism you were dealing with.

The 2011/12 season was the peak for that Leinster team. We'd got huge confidence from winning the Heineken Cup for a second time and we didn't want to take our foot off the gas. Our pool was easier than the previous year's but still, we played some unbelievable rugby. We ripped teams apart. My own form was good, too. It helped that I had sorted out any place-kicking niggles. I was operating at around 90 per cent all that season. I had Dave Alred over nearly every month.

I structured my Adidas contract so that Dave got paid through that. It was the best investment I ever made.

Then we went up another level when Brad Thorn arrived on a short-term contract for March, April and May. We were lacking a little depth in the second row and somehow, Joe managed to get approval to hire a thirty-seven-year-old All Black to see us through the knockout stages of Europe. It was probably the best bit of business he did at Leinster. Brad gave us oomph in the scrum and in the maul but he also opened our eyes to the real meaning of professionalism – the way he looked after his body, the emphasis he put on mental preparation. I really hit it off with him.

As a player, Brad probably made his biggest contribution in Bordeaux, in the semi against Clermont. That's where he was needed, too. In other years, our pool performance would have earned us a home semi but back then, the location for last-four games was down to the luck of the draw. You couldn't have got much tougher than Clermont in France, on a Sunday. It was a day for warriors and Brad is one of those.

No disrespect to Ulster, our opponents in the final, but we knew before the semi that Clermont would be our toughest game. We'd watched Ulster's semi against Edinburgh on the Saturday, seen them walk a lap of honour at the Aviva afterwards. They looked a bit like a team who had just reached the summit of their ambitions.

I spoke privately with Joe that evening in our hotel. We both knew that the Clermont game was the one. Clermont would have their revenge theme, having lost a quarter-final by a point in Dublin two seasons previously. And they had insider info, courtesy of Nathan Hines. But we had Joe. Games against Clermont were special for him. Joe generally didn't show much emotion, but he did on those weeks. Automatically, that raised the stakes for me. I was on a mission to out-play Brock James.

My best moment that day may have come in the dressing room at half-time, by which stage we were trailing 6–12. I suggested a play that wasn't on the sheet for that day but which I knew would work. I can't recall the name but it involved having Straussy as pivot off a midfield ruck, passing inside to Rob, running on a concealed line. Joe gave it the OK.

Ninety seconds after the restart, Kearns was slicing through and sending Cian over. The only try of the match, and my conversion put us in front.

We needed something a bit special to overcome that Clermont side. Rob's monster drop-goal gave us a four-point cushion but they threw everything at us. It was a proper goal-line siege. Joe even broke protocol and left the coaches' box to stand behind the dead-ball line, roaring instructions at us. I had to double-take at one stage while the ball was in play. What's *he* doing there?!

Most of the lads didn't over-celebrate when the ref finally blew up. It might have been an inbuilt awareness that we hadn't won anything yet. Maybe it was just that people were too knackered. But I couldn't help myself. I sprinted straight over to Joe and leaped into his arms, hugging hard. It was the first time I'd done that since Templeville Road in 1999 when I'd squeezed the life out of poor Richie Hughes. Pure joy.

Funnily enough, I'd been up in Templeville only a few weeks previously – hugging people again, as it happens. Mary's had won their second AIL title by beating Young Munster and

Mark had been one of the stars, coming off the bench to score two tries. The RTÉ TV cameras were there, and a big crowd of around 3,000 people. We still have the tape. You can see me hopping over an advertising hoarding and sprinting out to embrace my kid brother. I was delighted for him, for Smythie and Steve Hennessy, for everyone involved. I owe Mary's so much.

A lot of Mary's people were in Twickenham a few weeks later to see Leinster win their third Heineken title. It's still the best-attended European rugby final, with a crowd of just under 82,000. They may not have watched the most spellbinding final, but none of us were complaining. My lasting memory is of the special and unexpected few hours that the players got to spend together in a function room at the stadium while we waited for poor Dave Kearney to complete his drugs test.

Normally it would have been a rush to Heathrow, where you'd get to mingle with the supporters, which is fun, but a different kind of buzz. Occasionally it's nice to have just the team together, enjoying a few beers and a few songs. Basically, the longer it took for Dave to produce a urine sample, the longer we got to spend toasting our victory! I remember enjoying a few beers and a chat with Brad, who was delighted to have won his second major trophy in the space of a few months. We both had our hearts set on picking up another pot the following week, when we were playing the Ospreys in the Pro12 final.

We lost. Again. At the RDS. Again. This one was even harder to take, given the way it finished. With ten minutes left, we led by 9 points but right at the death, Shane Williams slipped through a couple of tackles (including mine) in the right corner, leaving Dan Biggar with a touchline conversion to win the game. He got it.

I was narky with myself for that missed tackle. I underestimated Williams's strength and slipped over him as he ducked under me. And yet, that afternoon holds one happy memory for me.

It was in the dressing room, maybe an hour after the final whistle. I'm generally not in a hurry post-match, unless there's a press conference to attend. I prefer to take my time, do whatever I need to do at a leisurely pace. You can get feedback from coaches and team-mates, if it's appropriate. It's good to get things squared away, as you know you'll be in your own head for most of that night, especially after a defeat. That time in the dressing room is almost a form of therapy.

The room was nearly empty when Brad sat down beside me, handed me a beer and thanked me for making him welcome at Leinster. And then he bowled me over.

He said: *Don't change, mate. You're a champion. Don't change anything. Not for anyone.*

I still consider it the biggest personal compliment that I've been paid from a fellow professional. Irish people generally aren't good at giving or taking compliments. We're quicker to criticize. Or if we give a compliment we do it indirectly.

But this was unconditional praise. Brad told me that I was a champion and that I needed to remain true to my standards. It was the first time anyone had said that to me and I loved him for it. Given what he'd achieved in the game and everyone he'd played alongside, it meant the world to me.

I loved Brad Thorn but I can't say the same about New Zealand. At least, I hated going there when it's summer at home and it's winter there, and when the rugby season has been going non-stop for twelve months because of the World Cup and you're knackered, and you're missing Paulie and a few other first-choicers and it's the third straight year that you've been sent down there, and the All Blacks are now world champions and really, if you don't mind, I'd rather just lay my aching bones on a sunlounger in Portugal.

We actually gave the ABs a proper fright in the second Test, in Christchurch. We were definitely worth a draw, if not a win, but a few critical moments went against us. I'm thinking of a scrum penalty awarded against us by Nigel Owens in the second half: Mike Ross, who knows about these things, is still convinced that the penalty should have gone the other way. I'm thinking about a long-range penalty I tried with the scores tied on 19–19, with seven minutes to go and Israel Dagg in the bin. Should we have gone up the line and tried to make our extra man count? And I'm thinking about how lucky the Kiwis got at the death when Seánie got a fingertip to a Dan Carter drop-goal attempt that was wide of the posts anyway. That gave them another attacking scrum and Carter was never going to miss twice. Sickener.

The wheels came off the following week. Scheduling a few days in Queenstown before the final Test in Hamilton might have seemed like a good idea at one point but inevitably, it felt a bit like the start of our summer holidays. Darce was out injured, so too Jamie. Meanwhile the All Blacks had been copping flak for nearly losing to us. They took it out on us. New Zealand 60, Ireland 0. I'd never been on the end of a tonking like it – not in school, AIL, anywhere. I was devastated. I sat in the dressing room with my head in my hands, in tears. *Why is it like this with Ireland?* I was desperate to be successful in green, but it was one disappointment after another.

Luckily I had a distraction that summer. I was going to propose to Laura. Now, I'll admit, us getting married wasn't exactly shocking news. We'd been a pair for half of our respective lives by that stage – or rather, we were two halves of one whole. But still, I wanted the proposal to be a surprise for Laura, to be something different. She still says that I haven't a romantic bone in my body. For once, I wanted to prove her wrong.

That's not as easy as it might sound, not when your lives are as entwined as ours were, and still are. I had the location sorted, having booked a holiday in Cancún – not our normal midsummer destination in Portugal, but I could say I just fancied something a bit different. I'd managed to source an engagement ring, too. Reddser had put me in touch with a jeweller he knew in London. I popped over soon after we got back from New Zealand, telling Laura I had an appointment at an Adidas shop – which wasn't a lie.

She probably knew something was up. If she'd looked up the hotel online, she'd have seen it was a real couples' resort. Even at reception, when we got there, they were asking us if we had just got engaged. No, no, just the room key, please. But she wouldn't have expected me to actually source a ring, buy it and bring it. She probably expected me to ask the question with any old piece of crap and leave it to her to choose something appropriate when we got home.

The difficult bit was hiding the ring for a few days. I wanted to enjoy the break together. If I proposed on our first night there, the rest of the holiday wouldn't have been a holiday. It would have been Laura on the phone, making wedding arrangements. I was worried about security standards in

Mexico but also worried that if I put it in the safe in our hotel room, she would be nosing around. I put it in a case for my headphones, threw that in the safe and hoped for the best.

I think I got away with it in the end. I booked dinner in a restaurant that had a table for two at the end of a pier, out under the stars, well away from the other guests – you could hear the waiter rattling his trolley all the way out to us. It was lovely. It was, well, romantic.

I have my moments.

12

We set a date for the following summer: just a message into the Leinster WhatsApp group and another to close family and friends. We had a few drinks with my brothers and uncles down in Listowel the weekend after we returned from Cancún. Our big celebration would be the wedding itself.

We planned a reception in Adare Manor for Saturday 13 July. We only told those closest to us. I didn't want people knowing we'd chosen the weekend after the Lions Test series in Australia, just in case they thought I was getting ahead of myself.

The Lions tour was on my mind, though. In 2009, I'd watched as two of my contemporaries, Rob Kearney and Luke Fitzgerald, played in an unforgettable Test in Pretoria. Envious? You could say that.

For me, the Lions is the pinnacle. It probably has something to do with the memory of watching the 1997 Tests with my dad in Kiely's of Donnybrook. Keith Wood and Scott Gibbs became instant heroes. Dad subsequently bought the *Living With Lions* documentary on video cassette. I probably still know every line of all the pre-match speeches by heart.

I backed myself to make the 2013 tour. A sign of my confidence was that I accepted an offer from Michael McLoughlin at Penguin to do a ghostwritten diary of my season, with my involvement in the tour as a central theme.

Like our wedding, the book had to remain top secret, at

least until after the tour. Imagine Warren Gatland, the Lions coach, discovering that I was inking myself in as a Lion before the season had begun.

The diary wasn't to be entirely about the Lions. It was to provide an insight into Leinster, and Joe, and Deccie and the Six Nations, and so on. I wasn't to know that so much of my head space that season would be taken up by contractual wrangling with the IRFU and secret trips to Paris. But we'll get to that.

To flick through the pages of *Becoming a Lion* is to be reminded how much my life has changed. My twenty-seven-year-old self actually had time on his hands – for the first half of the season, anyway. I spent a lot of time going for coffee with team-mates. Laura was still working at that stage and I had finished my degree. When I wasn't training or playing or drinking coffee, there was still time to fill.

I kept myself busy in various ways. Omar Hassanein, CEO of the Irish Rugby Union Players' Association (IRUPA), asked me to take over as chairman from Brian, who had been in the role for a while. Omar said he was looking for someone a bit younger and he'd noticed that I'd had an opinion at various meetings.

I also accepted an offer to be on the board of Headstrong, a charity for young people suffering from mental health problems. They were the charity of choice for O2, which was then the IRFU's shirt-sponsor, and I'd been chosen as a brand ambassador, so that's how the connection came about. Board members brought expertise from finance, marketing and IT. I found it interesting.

The other thing I notice from my diary entries for September and October 2012 is how tight that Leinster squad was. We had been successful together, which obviously helps. That season we were aiming to become the first club to win the Heineken Cup three years in a row, and the final was scheduled for Dublin. We had a huge support base and top-quality facilities, having just moved the whole operation to our amazing new base in Clonskeagh – gym, video analysis, medical, training pitches all together on one site, all state-of-the-art. We also felt that we had the best coach in the game. Our only collective worry was about whether Mick Dawson, the Leinster CEO, could convince him to extend his contract for a few more seasons.

As players we worked together and we socialized together. There were no longer any cliques. There were niggles on the training pitch, of course, and I was probably involved in some of that. Creative tension, you could call it. I'd bark at people if they didn't have their detail spot-on when we were going through plays in training. Very occasionally, Joe told me to go a bit easier, but I sensed he wanted me to keep driving standards.

Most of my team-mates were able to take it, and give it back. I remember Jenno putting me in my place during one session, probably during the Cheika era. We were on opposing sides and as he was running back to get onside, he shoved me from behind, full force, into a ruck. I was livid. For the next few minutes, as play carried on, my only objective was to get even with him. When I finally got close to him, he just squared up and smacked me in the mouth. That shut me up. For a while.

Reddser was another who could take it, and give it. During one session where I'd been moaning about the quality of service or about his decision-making, he waited until I made a mistake and then shoved me in the back on his way to the next ruck and snapped at me out of the side of his mouth:

'Sort your own shit out.' Imagine the look on Joe's face when I ran after Reddser and tripped up my own team-mate to get him back. We still laugh about it.

Jenno and Reddser knew how to handle me but not everyone did. On occasion some senior players had to sit me down. Some felt it was counter-productive if I was putting everyone on edge, constantly having a cut at people. I argued my corner. I was just driving standards. I eventually told them I'd make an effort to be more selective in when to voice my frustrations.

Brian, as Ireland captain, would have been part of that group. Looking back, I understand that he wanted to improve my leadership, but at the time I would never have viewed it like that. Our relationship had developed to the point where I considered him a friend. I had always been a little mistrustful of the fact that he seemed such good mates with O'Gara. We had a conversation on that subject, during a bus trip to what was probably the first game of that 2012/13 season for both of us, in Treviso. He was telling me how he was in the process of writing his autobiography and how difficult it was to write about me and Ronan.

So I listened to him rabbiting on about Rog having such great bottle, being able to land last-minute penalties and drop-goals.

Only an hour or two later, he was giving me another of his 'disappointed parent' looks. We'd been playing poorly – typical early season Leinster – and I'd been having an ongoing bitch-fest with Reddser.

This was just the sort of carry-on Brian had asked me to stop. But it was a hot evening in the Stadio Monigo and we were not playing well. I only just managed to stop myself from telling Brian to fuck off.

Weirdly, the memory of that bus conversation popped into my head in the final moments of the game, just as I was lining up a drop-goal – a drop-goal that I needed to get, as we were 2 points behind. As I was in the pocket, waiting for Reddser's pass, the thought occured to me: Christ, myself and Brian were only talking about this type of situation a few hours ago.

I nailed the drop-goal, from all of forty-five metres, and as I was running back, I'm thinking: *Stick that in your book.*

That game in Treviso was in mid-September, more than six months before Gatland was due to announce his Lions squad, but already the hype around the tour was building. It was all put into perspective when we received the news about Nevin Spence, a talented young Ulster player who had trained with the senior Ireland squad. We were in the airport after the game discussing other results when news started to filter through. Nevin, his father and brother had all died in a tragic farming accident. We were numb.

The Lions tour was many months away, but the media were already talking about who should be in the squad, and who in the Test XV. I was trying to stay away from it all, but I happened to see a TV discussion in which one of the commentators picked Leigh Halfpenny at 15 on the grounds that the Lions needed a world-class goal-kicker. What the fuck? What was wrong with my goal-kicking? OK, so I'd had issues at the World Cup, but that was ancient history. I'd been hitting around 85 per cent for Ireland since then.

That comment got to me. Proved why I can't watch the media. They might say five good things about me, but I would always find something to annoy me. A week later I was standing over a conversion against Munster at the Aviva when

I allowed a stray thought into my head: Is Gatland watching this? Right now?

I actually kicked well that night, but still decided to book a session with Dave Alred, just to be sure. My brothers told me not to stress about whether or not I'd be taking the place-kicks on a tour that was months away. But they should have known me better. I feed off stress.

Some of the stress was having a negative effect. The uncertainty over my contract was gnawing at me. Before the season even started, I let the IRFU know, via Fintan Drury, that I was hoping to have a deal done and dusted early so I could concentrate on my rugby. But Maurice Dowling, the Union's man, wasn't biting. That wasn't how they did business, he said. The irony is if the Union had offered me in September 2012 what they finally offered me five months later, I would have taken it.

The Union refused to negotiate until after the November internationals. Their tactics were obvious: leave it as late as possible and in the vacuum, the wealthy French clubs will recruit elsewhere. The vacuum forced me to consider my options. It would have been naive of me to do anything else. So Fintan opened dialogue with agents and club presidents in France. A process was started.

There was interest. Fintan mentioned some very flattering figures, but I did my own research. Bernard Jackman was coaching in Grenoble at the time and he was well-informed on market forces in the Top 14. We chatted about who was going where and for how much. It was just chat, though. None of it felt real – until the Union came up with its offer. That's when moving to France became a real possibility.

I'd reckoned that I was in a strong position coming out of the November Tests, that I'd proved my value. I was now one of the team leaders. When Paulie and Brian were injured, the captaincy had gone to Jamie, but Deccie told me that he had considered me for the role, which was encouraging. We lost narrowly enough to the Springboks but thrashed Argentina – a game we needed to win to make sure we stayed in the top eight, for World Cup seeding purposes.

Would any of this be reflected in the IRFU's contract offer? I wasn't confident on that score. I even had a €20 bet with Fintan. He said they wouldn't dare offer me a basic salary below what a particular team-mate of mine was making. He knew this because he represented the player in question!

I won the bet.

Dowling had come back with two options – an increase of five grand a year with the same match bonuses, or a twenty-five grand increase with no bonuses. To make matters worse, it was only a two-year deal, when I'd let it be known that I was hoping for three or four years, in the interests of security.

Was I annoyed? Yes. They were taking the piss. But was I surprised? Not really. The message they were sending me was: You're a home-bird, you'll never leave. Or maybe it was: Go ahead and leave. We'll gladly let someone else pay your salary for a while.

The word was that Tommy Bowe was the Union's favourite player, at least for those years when he was at the Ospreys, as he only cost them match fees. Was I to be the new Tommy?

I also heard that some people in the Union were sick of Leinster's success, were wary of them becoming more popular than Ireland. They needed to be taken down a peg, supposedly. This was what I was hearing, anyway.

The Union tried to rig the negotiation in their own favour.

Having made you wait, they low-balled you with their initial offer. According to their system, I was supposed to come back with a counter-offer, and their response to that was their final offer. You could take it or leave it.

I didn't respond directly to their initial offer. Through the Ireland team management, I let it be known that I wasn't happy, that I expected to be on a par or at least close to the best-paid players in the country.

Once I'd made that plain, there could be no backing down, no settling for less. That would mean that they had won and would set the tone for all future negotiations. So I ignored the Union's 'counter-offer' system. Besides, I needed to make sure that I had an alternative to accepting their offer.

French clubs were happy to express an interest in me, but none of them really believed that Irish players would jump ship. Guys had flirted with them before, but only as a means of getting a better deal at home. I had previously made that trip to see Cheiks in Stade Français. We had to convince French clubs that we meant business, even if my preference was still to get an acceptable deal at home.

If I had to leave, my preference was for Clermont. I loved the rugby that they were playing, but that was only a part of it. I felt an affinity for the people there, purely from all of the positive things that Joe had said about his time at the club, how well his family had been treated and so on.

I got a good view of them close up that season, as we played them in the back-to-back weeks during the Heineken pool stages, in December. It was freezing cold at the Stade Michelin, which is an intimidating venue, but we got a warm response. The place was nearly full when we first came out, forty minutes before kick-off, and they applauded us on to the pitch. You could tell they still loved Joe, too. When the stadium announcer read out the teams, he gave it an extra flourish at the end for the visitors' coach – 'Entraîneur, Joe . . . SCHMEEEEDT!!!' The locals went nuts.

And then Clermont did the double on us. We actually did brilliantly to get a losing bonus over there in that first game, especially given that we were without Brian and Isa. We walked into a post-match reception and again, the locals showed their appreciation.

The mistake we made was patting ourselves on the back, telling the media how brilliant we had been. We practically wrote Clermont's team-talk for the return match at the Aviva the following week.

Maybe subconsciously, we thought the occasion would win it for us – 45,000 at the Aviva, the week before Christmas. But Clermont meant business. And they would have been helped by having a former Leinster player in their side – Nathan Hines. Hinesy got to me that day. Just niggly stuff, off the ball, but it wears you down. I had a right pop at him on the final whistle, which I then regretted.

Everything was a bit raw around that time. That was my hundredth game for Leinster and an emotional evening – Leo had asked me to lead the side out. All the while, I knew there was an increasing chance that I would be leaving. I had conversations with a few people about the contract situation, half-hoping someone would make a really persuasive argument either way.

Dad told me I should take me whatever was on offer in France and teach the Union a lesson. My brothers were of a similar view. One minute I was with them, visualizing a French adventure; the next, I was confiding in Joe, telling him I wanted to continue working with him in Leinster, hoping he might exert pressure to find a solution. Laura was in two minds, too – both excited and scared by the idea of a new adventure.

Clermont refused to negotiate until after the Heineken Cup games, and even then they showed limited enthusiasm. They simply didn't believe that I would leave. Racing were much more aggressive. Fintan was quoting massive numbers but the club president, Jacky Lorenzetti, wouldn't commit to anything until he met me in person.

I travelled over with Fintan on a Sunday in January, the morning after we had beaten Scarlets in Round 5 of the Heineken to maintain a slim hope of qualifying for the quarters.

I wore a beanie, kept my head down at the Air France check-in at Dublin Airport. I was thinking: What if I'm spotted and Leinster lose in Exeter next Saturday? I could imagine what Leinster supporters would say. *Sure yer man Sexton was over talking to Racing Metro last Sunday. How could he have had his mind properly on the job?*

I remember thinking: *This must be what it feels like to cheat on your partner.* But I had no option. Lorenzetti wanted to meet me before he made a firm offer. He wanted to meet the coaches he had hired for the following season: Laurent Travers and Laurent Labit, who were then in the process of leading Castres to the Top 14 title. If I was taking this business seriously – which I was – I needed to meet them, too. We needed to talk, even if it was through an interpreter.

We were collected at Orly and driven to see the club's swish new training facility at Le Plessis-Robinson, a suburb ten kilometres south-west of Paris. It was seriously impressive, very high-spec, high-tech – a sprawling gym, a spa, swanky restaurants and pristine pitches.

We were shown around by the two Laurents, who had travelled up from Castres just to meet me. They were very enthusiastic about the project, and the players they had signed for the following season.We had lunch at the club president's house – a very fancy residence, as you'd expect for someone who made his billions in the property game. Jacky's English was better than my French, certainly strong enough to tell me that he wanted me to be his *numéro dix*.

He was honest enough to tell me that Dan Carter had been his first choice – Carter hadn't been available as he wanted to continue playing for the All Blacks at this point. He said he had also approached Toby Flood, though this may have been designed to nudge me into accepting his offer, the details of which he would thrash out with Fintan the following day.

Jacky left me in no doubt that he had great plans for Racing, including the building of an indoor arena in La Défense, which would also host music concerts. He expected that this would be operational by the second year of my contract. This was all very impressive. To top it off, I was flown home in Jacky's private jet the next morning, so that I could be in time for Monday training, with no one in Leinster any the wiser.

It didn't take long for the story to get out, though. At that point, I didn't realize how close the relationship is between the French clubs and the French media. The day after my return, *Midi Olympique* reported Racing's offer: €700–750K a year. When I came in to training on Tuesday, a French flag was flying from my dressing-room locker and people started humming the Marseillaise as I walked in.

I could only suck it up. What option was there? It was awkward, though. I explained to Joe that the leak had come from France, not from me. I hadn't wanted this to distract from our build-up to a critical Heineken Cup game.

Jenno must have picked up on my anxiety as he tried to put my mind at rest. 'Johnny, never feel that your loyalty has been called into question,' he said. 'You have to do what's right for you.' I appreciated his support.

It was a stressful time, though. The Six Nations opener against Wales was only a couple of weeks away and I wanted a decision either way before the tournament started.

To complicate matters, there was renewed interest from Clermont. Vern Cotter had seen the reports and soon Hinesy was on the phone. I told him that Clermont wouldn't have to match Racing's offer but they'd have to offer more than the Union. I told him I was willing to take €150K less than Racing were offering.

I was excited by this possibility. I thought: If this goes through, people will see that it's not all about the money with me. Also, I knew that Clermont were more advanced in their journey than Racing, who were virtually starting from scratch. But the Clermont deal never got off the ground. They'd already spent most of their budget for the next season. Besides, Fintan was uncomfortable about the idea, having worked so hard to get a brilliant offer from Racing.

He contacted the Union with a simple message: We have been made a generous offer. We don't expect you to match it but we know what the best-paid players in Ireland are earning and we expect you to be close to that.

I was very uncomfortable with the figures being in the public domain, and with the notion that I was holding the IRFU to ransom. I wasn't. I just wanted what, in my mind, was fair.

I was getting mixed messages from my parents. Mum didn't

want me to go because she's a massive Leinster fan who used to put blue flags outside the salon whenever we had a big game. Dad took the opposite view. That was actually one of the attractions of leaving. Mum and Dad's divorce was imminent and I didn't want to deal with all of the emotional turmoil that was going to drag up.

Laura was right behind me, as ever. She said she would support my decision absolutely. But I could tell she was conflicted by the thought of being separated from her family, especially from Cathy, her twin. They are incredibly tight. I knew she would miss her job and her friends.

It was nine days out from the Wales match when the Union made their final offer, in a letter that was couriered to my apartment, with a copy sent to my room in Carton. It was a decent offer, but not on the same level as the deals agreed with two other players in the last couple of years. I felt there was no way I could accept it.

But the urgency of the situation gave me doubts. It wasn't the worst deal in the current economic climate. Throw in the sponsorship money from O₂, plus the sportsman's tax rebate which I'd forfeit if I went to Paris, and it began to look even better. And did I really want to go to France? I found myself asking the opinion of people who would want me to stay put. Like Joe. I called him that evening, hoping for some enlightenment. I made it pretty plain that I'd stay, if only the Union would do the necessary. At the end of a long chat, he asked me to give him twenty-four hours. 'Sign nothing,' he said.

At that point, I reckoned it would get sorted, that a solution would be found – by Joe, or whoever. But I don't know if he ever got to speak to anyone. The word was out the following morning. There would be a Union statement by lunchtime. I hadn't signed anything with anyone but it seemed like the Union wanted to be first with the news, so they could get their side of the story out there.

We were training in Carton that morning. After breakfast I rang Philip Browne, the IRFU CEO, to put my case to him. He wasn't for budging. He said the match-fee incentives they had offered would bring me close to the level I'd been hoping for but they wouldn't be moved on my basic salary. And that was that.

I knew a statement would be going out because Mick Kearney, the team manager, ran it past me before training and asked if I had anything to contribute to the press release. I didn't. They were playing the poor mouth to the media, as expected.

I stayed out kicking after the team run, trying to distract myself from the knowledge that the news was out there. Sure enough, when I switched on my phone, there was a flood of messages, most of them supportive and sympathetic, some disbelieving. I guess a lot of people had believed that the newspaper stories had been a negotiating tactic.

It was really only when I saw those reactions that the finality of it registered with me: *This is really happening.*

That afternoon I hid in my room at Carton. There were people I needed to contact, out of courtesy – sponsors like Volkswagen, Adidas and O2. I also couldn't face my Leinster team-mates. I didn't answer their calls because I felt guilty, as if I was responsible for breaking up the team. Meanwhile Laura was fielding similar messages from all her friends, family and work colleagues. It was an emotional time.

I ended up communicating mostly by text, so that I wouldn't break down crying. Here is a typical message, from Ferg, one of my best friends in the squad:

> Was calling in some hope that it wasn't true. Am so shocked.
> You're a top man and a friend. Can't describe the sort of loss you
> will be to Leinster and to me off the pitch, personally. I respect
> your decision. It took balls to do it. I hope you are OK. Give me a
> shout over the weekend at any stage.

Joe also texted, and struck a sympathetic tone, which almost made things worse. I'd been one of the people badgering him to extend his stay with Leinster and now here I was, jumping ship. At that point, it felt like we only had a few months left together. I reckoned he'd be returning to New Zealand when he was finished with Leinster. My reply to his text was suitably apologetic.

> Sorry I haven't been in contact, Joe. I'll be in touch with you soon,
> when I can talk without crying like a baby. Cheers, Johnny

The start of the Six Nations was a blessing. A distraction from all the contract stress. It got a few mentions in the team room, of course, but only as a means to take the piss out of me. I reminded the lads that I was doing them a favour, especially the ones who were negotiating contracts around that time.

The spirit was good, especially after we won in Cardiff first up. That was the day that Simon Zebo famously flicked the ball up for himself off the outside of his boot, the day we raced into a 27-point lead before eventually winning 30–22. I genuinely believed that the Slam was on. We had beaten the reigning champions on their own patch. England had a young team, France were all over the place. We had both of them in Dublin. It was a brilliant opportunity.

We finished fifth.

In fairness to Deccie, who paid with his job, we were

crippled with injuries, myself included. I tore my hamstring against England in the second round – Owen Farrell shoved me just as I went to fly-hack a ball, causing me to have a painful 'fresh air'. It was a Grade 2 tear. When I realized that I was out for Scotland and France, I began to catastrophize, naturally. That was it. The Lions was gone.

Dad reassured me. So did my brothers. They told me it didn't matter if I missed the rest of the Six Nations. Gatland would be bringing at least two 10s and they said that he needed me, as my two main competitors, Farrell and Dan Biggar, were both fairly inexperienced, while Jonny Wilkinson was thirty-four and no longer playing international rugby.

Still, I became obsessed with rehabbing my hamstring. I worked with the Ireland physios, and on the weekends I saw Ger Hartmann, a physical therapist that I hired independently. I iced the hammy religiously. When Laura and I met with the hotel manager in Adare to plan for July, I excused myself mid-chat and hopped off on my crutches, supposedly to visit the loo but really back to our room where there was another bucket of ice waiting for me, as quietly arranged with one of the hotel staff.

Italy in Rome was the comeback target. The prep was going fine until the final session pre-departure, when I tore ligaments in my foot. The specialist said I'd need ten days in a boot for starters. Plus I'd need to see another specialist in London. The Lions squad announcement was six weeks away. Up the walls, I was.

I found distractions. Laura and I spent ten days in Dubai, thanks to Brian, who kindly gave us the use of his apartment. I did upper-body weights and freshened up my French with some language-learning software; I had already started taking one-on-one sessions with a tutor in the UCD French

department. We also did some house-hunting on the outskirts of Paris.

I didn't get back to action until late April, a week before
the Lions announcement. A week earlier, Adidas had asked
me to take part in the filming of a Lions promo in London,
which was a positive sign, but I was still a little jumpy on the
day of the big reveal, so I booked a kicking session with
Richie, rather than watch it with the rest of the Leinster
squad. He kept his phone on to check at the appropriate
moment, and gave me the nod. Relief.

There was more good news around that time: Joe was
taking the Ireland job. We would continue working together
after all. That May still felt like the Long Goodbye, though.
Joe, Isa and I would all be leaving Leinster at the end of that
season.

It felt like some people couldn't wait to get rid of me. One
TV pundit said that Leinster should pick Ian Madigan for
the remainder of the season, to bed him in for the following
season.

Mads was especially popular around that time. He was
chosen as the players' player of the season at Leinster's
awards night at the Mansion House. They also made a fuss
of Joe and Isa, with clips and interviews on stage. I was up
on stage briefly to receive a commemorative cap with a large
group of other guys who were leaving. As soon as the formal
part of the evening was over, I legged it.

Was I hurt? Yes. Did my contribution to three Heineken
Cups and a Magners League not count for anything? It felt
like I'd been snubbed.

I cooled down eventually, though. It had been my choice
to leave. Leinster owed me nothing. In fact, I still needed
them. I needed some rugby before the Lions tour. There

were more medals to be won, too. We beat Stade Français to capture the Amlin Cup and then beat Ulster in the final of the Rabo, also at the RDS, a week later. Not the double we'd wanted, but still a double.

There are pictures of me with a blue curly wig, shouldering Joe on a lap of honour after the Ulster game. I wanted the fans to know how much Leinster meant to me and I hated the idea that anyone would criticize me for leaving. I expressed similar sentiments to the players back in the dressing room. It was an emotional evening for Laura too, as she was loosening ties with a lot of friends. But we didn't stay long at the post-match function, just said our goodbyes and slipped away.

It was weird driving out of the gates on to Simmonscourt Road. I had the impression people thought I would be gone for a couple of years only, as if this was just something I had to get out of my system. At the time, I wasn't thinking that way. In my mind, I was leaving for good. It hurt. It was just as well that I had one major distraction. I was flying to Australia early the next morning.

Somewhere online there's a clip of me on a street in Sydney in the early hours of the morning. I am wearing my Thomas Pink Lions blazer inside out, waving an Irish tricolour and roaring 'Bread of Heaven'. I have Leigh Halfpenny and various Lions fans for company. We all look a bit tired, but deliriously happy. The Lions had just won their first Test series in sixteen years.

I loved that tour. I love Australia. Even in their midwinter, you are constantly in shorts and flip-flops, constantly outside. The non-rugby images that flood back are: dipping in the Indian Ocean after training sessions in Perth; sitting on the beach at Manly watching the lads playing beach volleyball against some Aussie girls and being in stitches at how seriously they were taking it; going along to a rugby league game in Brookvale and getting some insights from Owen Farrell, who knows a bit about league.

I like the way the Aussies are sports-mad and incredibly direct — even the bloke who was sledging me when I was on the bench in Brisbane: 'Oi, Sexton! You've got shoulders like a bloody snake!' Mostly, the Aussies I've come across have been good to me — guys like Alan Gaffney, Chris Whitaker, Les Kiss, Tony McGahan, and of course Cheiks. It's just a bit different when they're the oppo. Cheiks was coaching the Waratahs at that point and he sent a twenty-one-year-old monster called Will Skelton out to get me when we played against them. I did well to come out of the game in one piece.

I liked the competitive atmosphere in training on that tour, loved all the old-school stuff, like Ian McGeechan presenting the jerseys before the first Test. I liked the fact that all I had to worry about on tour was putting myself in the best possible position to make the Test team.

Physically, the only niggle I had was my right hamstring, which complained occasionally. In the circumstances, I should probably have been happy to be relieved of the place-kicking duties, which went to Leigh Halfpenny. But of course I wasn't happy. I sucked it up eventually, after talking it through with our kicking coach, Neil Jenkins. There was no arguing with Leigh's stats. It just feels a bit odd to be watching someone else take the kicks.

I didn't know what to make of Gats. The Welsh guys told us that he can be hard to read. I think he likes it that way, to keep people on edge. I hit it off more with Andy Farrell, who was our defence coach. Being a rugby nerd, I'd got into watching league over the years and Faz had been a bit of a hero of mine, a warrior. I found him inspiring, a strong communicator, charismatic.

I got on with his son, too. We were competitors for the 10 shirt, of course, but it's hard for kickers to maintain a cold war. You spend so much time in cars, buses and coaches together, especially on tour. Most stadiums you're playing in are new to you, so you need to spend extra time familiarizing yourself with all the sightlines and landmarks. You end up travelling separately from the main group, who return to the hotel much earlier. So myself, Owen, Leigh and Jenks got to know each other pretty well on that tour. We had our private competitions, our own playlists for the trips to and from training, our own jokes. Paul 'Bobby' Stridgeon also made sure we laughed every minute of every trip. He was firmly in the kicking crew. A great character who had such an important role on the tour. Not just in his S&C role but as a guy who gelled the squad together.

My memories of that tour are sweetened by the fact that the Lions won the series, and that I started all three Tests. The Lions badly needed a win. The first and second Tests went down to the final play, with the results hingeing on long-range kicks, both of which were missed – one by Kurtley Beale, the other by Leigh. We went to Sydney for the final Test with everything on the line.

For Irish fans, there was only one story that week: Gats leaving Brian out of the side. Jamie Roberts was fit, and he was always going to play when he was available. That made it a straight call at 13 and Jonathan Davies was picked ahead of Brian. Davies had been playing well but I don't think anyone saw it coming.

It was a massive call, huge news. Brian was such a giant of the game, and of Lions history. I'd noticed how the lads from the other countries hung on every word he said in meetings, as if they felt privileged just to be breathing the same air as him. The Aussie media made a big deal of his omission, naturally – Brian had announced himself on a world stage there, twelve years previously. And back in Ireland, it was like we'd revisited Saipan, from what I heard subsequently.

And that's what made Brian's reaction so impressive. The news broke in Noosa, a holiday resort up the coast from Sydney where we'd gone for a change of scenery before the final countdown. The lads who were out of the Test reckoning had the option of hitting the booze – and some did. But Brian didn't. He turned up to training like he was playing, even though he wasn't in the twenty-three. He kept giving positive insights. He never went into his shell.

He kept me on track, too. I was very cranky for one of the field sessions in Noosa. We were sloppy, inaccurate, unfocused. The forwards were unable to execute a simple lineout play and I could tell it was because a couple of guys were unprepared. I let rip at them, lost the head altogether. I reckoned someone needed to say something and the coaches were staying quiet. Geoff Parling and Richard Hibbard both looked like they wanted to tear my head off. Brian had a quiet word with me and told me to keep all my messages positive from that point onwards.

I ended up apologizing at the team meeting on Friday, to clear the air but also to make the point that I didn't think we'd done ourselves justice yet. Happily we did that in the second half at Stadium Australia the next day.

Typical Aussies, they gave it a go. Despite being minced in the scrum, they found a way to haul us back from our brilliant start, as 3–19 became 16–19 early in the second half. Given that I'd been at fault defensively for James O'Connor's try, I was relieved to get the touchdown that swung the game decisively towards the end of the third quarter.

I was ecstatic; then furious when I was called ashore five minutes later; and then embarrassed and apologetic (to backs coach Rob Howley) for my petulance; then ecstatic again on the final whistle, by which stage the scoreline read: Australia 16, British & Irish Lions 41. No arguing with that.

Some of the post-match memories are special: shaking hands with Daniel Craig (aka Agent 007, and a massive Lions fan) on the pitch; phoning Dad, who had been unable to travel because of a back injury, and then Mum, who'd decided against another long-haul flight after the 2011 World Cup; being dragged up to sing a song on the bus back to the hotel – what started out as Oasis quickly turned to 'Bread of Heaven' due to the boos.

With a microphone in my hand, I took the opportunity to say that it had been an honour to make my debut for Wales. That got a laugh. Ten of the starting XV were Welsh. That Lions squad was a tight group, though, and even tighter after our celebrations, which went on for days. Literally. I didn't arrive back in Dublin until the Thursday, having not slept for the entire flight.

Laura was a little twitchy by that point. We were getting married that Saturday and her husband-to-be had lost his voice from all the raucous revelling. Had it really been necessary to celebrate so long? I rationalized that the end-of-tour party had effectively been my stag do – and she couldn't deny me a stag do, right?

Fortunately, there wasn't really time to be angry with me. There were last-minute jobs to be done, although not that many of them, to be honest – Laura and Cathy had done a brilliant job in organizing everything. We were also fortunate to have Father Paul Lavelle to guide us through the ceremony at the beautiful Holy Trinity Abbey Church in Adare – Father Paul is a family friend and a former rugby referee, as it happens.

Laura and I were blessed with a beautiful summer's day, blessed also to be able to celebrate in a beautiful setting with family and friends, many of whom stayed over and continued the party the following day. Then we were off to Vegas on honeymoon. Vegas? Were we mad? Another long-haul flight?

We loved Vegas, actually. We loved having the opportunity to hang out together, see a few shows. We went for the city break option simply because we didn't have time for a longer, more relaxing break. We were due to arrive in Paris the weekend after the wedding.

13

It's not as though things settled down when we arrived in France. Laura had her wallet stolen on our first day there. We were in IKEA, buying a few bits for our apartment, when she realized what had happened. Cards, a fair bit of cash and a load of vouchers that we'd received as wedding gifts: all gone. There we were, in this industrial estate on the outskirts of Paris, frantically searching Google to see how you report a theft to the French police.

Monsieur, ma femme, son portefeuille est volé . . .

Things went from bad to worse for poor Laura. The next day, just after dropping me off at the club, she totalled our brand-new sponsored car on a roundabout. Took the front wheel right off the axle. It's like the Wild West on round-abouts over there, plus she was learning to left-hand drive. She had to ring up the team manager, Simon Raiwalui, to get someone to come and rescue her. I was in my first squad meeting at the time. Simon gave me the news as I came out. I was just relieved to know that Laura wasn't hurt.

We were blessed that we had Ronan O'Gara and Jess, his wife, to show us the ropes. Who'd have thought O'Gara would end up being my saviour?

I'd first heard that we'd be club-mates that May, only a few hours before Leinster were due to play Stade Français in the final of the Amlin Challenge Cup. Nice timing!

It was hard to get your head around at first. Was he being hired to fill in for me when I was away with Ireland? No, he said he had officially retired from playing. He was going to be Racing's kicking coach. You could not make this up.

Once word got out, that old photo from Croke Park 2009 did the rounds on social media again, but with a different speech bubble. This time, I was screaming: Stop following me around, will ya!?

I was glad, though. Myself and Ronan had turned a corner at that stage. The rivalry was over. We became pals, as did our wives. Ronan had arrived a few weeks before me, and he knew his way around Châtenay-Malabry, our corner of the Paris suburbs. Jess and the kids arrived closer to September. Jess and Laura were companions who looked out for each other. And Laura soon made friends with some of the other wives and girlfriends, especially Dan Lydiate's fiancée, Nia, who later became godmother to our daughter Amy.

With young kids, Jess was probably glad of an extra pair of hands. She could also provide Laura with plenty of maternity tips. Not long after our arrival, we discovered that Laura was pregnant. We were overjoyed.

Some people assumed that Jacky Lorenzetti had hired O'Gara specifically to help me settle, but it was more random than that. I'd been expecting to be working with Gonzalo Quesada, the former Argentinian 10 who'd been part of the previous coaching set-up. But Quesada had apparently felt undermined by the appointment of the two Laurents and left for Stade Français. Racing needed a kicking/skills coach at short notice and Ronan was available.

The time we spent kicking was only a small part of his value to me. At first he was my translator, though I was determined to become fluent in French as soon as possible. It was essential if I was going to run the show on the pitch. The non-French players had regular classes with Ian Borthwick, the media manager who doubled up as language tutor. By the end of that season, Ian said that I was *l'étudiant le plus amélioré* – the most improved student.

But no matter how quickly my French improved, I needed Ronan as my go-between with the two Laurents, and as my sounding board. There was a lot of sounding off on my part. I was desperate for things to work, to be successful, but I'd had no idea of what I would be up against. There was so much that needed fixing, so many people pulling in different directions. At times it was a complete shit-show.

The funny thing is, while I was often deeply unhappy during that first season, Racing were ultimately happy with me. Jacky had sold me this vision of what the club could become: a European super-club with its space-age stadium in La Défense. (The stadium didn't open for another four years, despite his assurances to me that it would be ready for my second season at the club.) And we were reasonably successful in that first season, reaching the semi-finals of the Top 14 for the first time and the quarter-final of Europe for the first time.

He offered a four-year contract extension – effectively a new five-year deal, given that significantly improved terms would kick in straight away. Included was a huge bonus if we won the Top 14 or the Champions Cup, an increase in rental allowance so we could get a bigger apartment, and a car for Laura. She had recovered her confidence behind the wheel by that stage!

So it wasn't quite the disaster that people tend to think. I played lots of rugby and performed well. It was a life experience, too. Laura and I did a lot of growing up. We had to fend for ourselves. When you're operating in a different language, opening up a bank account can feel like a major achievement. If the boiler breaks down, you can't just give Dad a shout and ask if he knows someone who can fix it. You have to sort it out yourself.

It felt like an adventure, living near one of the world's great cities, making new friends. We had big gangs of team-mates and their partners over for dinner. I got on well with some of the guys who'd been at Racing the previous season, like the South African, François van der Merwe, and the Argentinians, Juan Imhoff and Juan-Martín Hernández. It helped that they all had good English. But some of that existing squad could be distant at times, a little suspicious. They had been through a lot together – relegated from the Top 14, then promoted again. Guys like Henry Chavancy, Jacques Cronje, Jonathan Wisniewski, Karim Ghezal, Fabrice Estebanez. It was understandable if they felt a bit vulnerable. They'd seen team-mates cut to make way for a load of new signings. Brian Mujati, Juandré Kruger and Soane Tonga'uiha had signed from Northampton, while the two Laurents had brought Antonie Claassen and Marc Andreu with them from Castres. Then there was myself, Jamie Roberts, Dan Lydiate, Wenceslas Lauret and others – fourteen new signings that season, with over nineteen players leaving the club.

How could you expect everyone to gel suddenly? Some of the 'old Racing' guys knew that they'd be let go at the end of the season. They were already annoyed to see Quesada leave. Now all these newcomers had arrived, including this Irish guy with all his ideas about how and when we should train, who is always pissed off if training doesn't go well, who often arrives at the club with O'Gara, a member of the coaching staff, and who is regularly deep in conversation with the two Laurents after training.

I brought some of this suspicion on myself. With the

wisdom of hindsight, I wish I had gone out for a few beers with these guys at the earliest opportunity, allowed them to see that I could have a laugh, a bit of banter. But making new connections has never been easy for me. It felt a little like the difficult beginning I'd had all those years previously in Mary's.

One weekend in pre-season, we went on a week away, part training camp, part team bonding. I went to bed early, maybe because I wanted to come across as ultra-professional, maybe in part out of shyness. Looking back, I wish I'd stayed up, had a few beers, shown my more personable side.

That said, I was very conscious of the fact that I'd been hired to do a specific job. Everyone knew that I was on a huge salary – Jamie Roberts used to call me 'Johnny Cash' – and my end of the deal was to set high standards, to drive a no-excuses culture. Jacky had said that I was there as a player firstly but another reason they signed me was for leadership and to try to change the culture. I reckoned that if I gave everything I had to the cause, the players would see that I was there for the right reasons. But there are different ways to get people onside. I know that now. Everyone is a genius in hindsight.

So there was always a distance between me and the 'old Racing' guys. You'd walk into a changing room and sense from the shift in atmosphere that they'd been talking about you. Or they'd speak to each other in French at a pace that excluded you from the conversation.

Jacky got value for money from me that first season. If you include a pre-season friendly against Harlequins a week after our arrival, I played thirty games for Racing in total, plus nine games for Ireland. That thirty included twelve Top 14 appearances in my first ten weeks, with three of those squeezed into nine days – Toulouse away, Perpignan at home, Bayonne away. This wasn't ideal, coming on the back of a Lions tour, but Wisniewski and Benjamin Dambielle were injured, while Hernández was delayed by the Rugby Championship. I was pressed into service.

I didn't complain. I loved playing games. The Top 14 is a great competition – noisy, colourful, tribal, glamorous. OK, so the rugby we played was pretty basic. There was a fixation with power and size in France at the time. But we were reasonably good at implementing our pretty basic game-plan. By the time I went home for the November internationals, we were in the top half of the league table, and I had kicked a bucketload of points.

We could have been so much better, though. Our preparation did my head in. It was ridiculously old-school, with little scientific thinking behind it. Field sessions that were too long, sometimes two or even three of them in one day. Beastings after you lost, far too laid-back following a win. Totally inconsistent.

To the French way of thinking, the worst thing you could do was to lose at home. I'll never forget driving into the club with Dan Lydiate one Monday morning after we'd been turned over by Grenoble at Colombes. The training pitch was littered with tackle suits. You play at 9 o'clock on a Saturday night and by 9 o'clock on Monday morning, it's one-on-one tackling, just bashing each other, as punishment for being beaten at home. Nuts. But then the two Laurents had just won the Top 14 with Castres. They knew what they were doing, supposedly.

They seemed decent enough guys. I had more dealings with Laurent Labit as he was in charge of the backs. 'Toto' Travers was a good bloke – I appreciated the fact that he always made Laura feel very welcome at the club. But they were very hot and cold. When things were going well, they'd chat away with me while I was out kicking after training; if things were bad, they might blank you altogether. They seemed to go from one extreme to the other, often in the course of one day.

In fairness, I was too emotional in my dealings with people myself. I was forever sounding off to Simon Raiwalui about the way we were doing things. Like the mad system we had for home matches, where we'd spend virtually the whole day together prepping for an evening kick-off. Colombes, a crumbling old stadium that was badly in need of a lick of paint, is a thirty-five-minute drive away from the club's training base, and the Laurents were petrified that if we left it until the afternoon to bus over there, we'd get caught in Paris traffic.

So we'd head over at around 10 a.m., dump our bags in the changing rooms, maybe walk the pitch, have a meeting and then hole up in a crappy Ibis Hotel beside the stadium for the whole day. We'd have meetings and a bite to eat, but mostly it was sitting up in your room waiting for the hours to pass. I almost preferred away games.

Traffic was a major consideration in everything we did. Training didn't begin until 10 a.m. – because of the traffic. I couldn't understand why we couldn't all just come in earlier and use our time more wisely. I kept asking for shorter, more intense sessions that would replicate match intensity, not the long slogs that would leave you fatigued come match-day. They went with it for a while and the lads loved it, as it meant an earlier finish to the day. Once we lost a game, though, the Laurents went back to what they were used to.

I'd go in early anyway, usually arriving at around 8 o'clock.

I'd get my first coffee of the day from Hadji, Racing's groundsman-cum-handyman. He only spoke French and his sole mode of communication was to abuse you. He was Racing's Johnny O'Hagan, basically. The first day I met him, he told me I was a shit player. I was only there for the money. He was hilarious. I got on really well with him.

Ronan and Hadji were always hurling friendly abuse at each other, too. Ronan would greet him with: 'All right, Hadji boy, you langer?' The three of us would sit at the counter in the kitchen at Le Plessis-Robinson, drinking coffee, shooting the breeze. It made me feel at home.

Ronan provided reassurance and companionship. We'd go out for dinner with the girls or just go to each other's places. It was usually theirs on a Friday, seeing as they had the Irish channels that allowed us to watch Munster or Leinster's league games over a cup of tea while the girls chatted away.

Watching Leinster wasn't easy. I'd always had this desire to be a one-club man, but now Leinster were my old club. It felt wrong. I hated not being there for Brian's last game and Leo's last game. I hated watching Mads or Jimmy Gopperth wearing the number 10 jersey.

And I'll admit it: I wasn't heartbroken when they were beaten by Northampton at the Aviva in the Champions Cup. It was just a human reaction. You don't want your old team to do that well without you.

I went back to Dublin full of beans for the November Tests, having left Racing on a bit of a high. We'd just beaten Stade Français in the Paris derby and I'd kicked 100 per cent. I craved Joe's approval. He knew how demanding the Top 14 can be from his time at Clermont. He was positive, but there was a catch.

'It's going really well for you,' he said. 'But Jeez, Racing are really getting their money's worth, eh?'

He told me that I looked tired. I could see what he was up to – to plant a seed of doubt about being out of the Irish system. He told me I was being rested for his first Test in charge, against Samoa. That pissed me off no end.

I knew that we'd get an immediate boost from having him in charge and that the non-Leinster guys would be blown away by the detail and rigour of Joe's preparation. And I wanted to be driving all that. But there was no budging him. He told me he was holding me back for the games against Australia and New Zealand and that was that.

There was still plenty to be done helping guys to become accustomed to Joe's way of doing things. There was no more lounging around the team room on a Sunday night. Our plays would already be up on flip-charts in the team room – launch plays off set pieces, exit options off restart receptions. You had to know your calls and know them properly. Joe would then show us clips of our next opponents to show how this or that play would work against them.

If you were unsure about one of our maps or shapes, you needed to go and ask someone who wasn't. The Leinster lads – and this ex-Leinster lad – became almost auxiliary coaches in that first camp. We stressed the importance of knowing your detail in time for the all-important walk-through.

Typically, this would take place in the team room at an appointed time, or sometimes five minutes earlier than that time – people learned pretty quickly that punctuality mattered. We would go through sequences built over three or four phases, so there was a fair bit of memory work involved: knowing which side of a ruck you needed to clean, which angle you need to run a decoy line, and so on. He got us to visualize all these sequences and everyone's precise part in the process so that the walk-through would be spot-on.

Unlike the two Laurents, Joe had figured out that our field sessions had to be short, but very intense and very accurate. We didn't spend long, fatiguing hours out on the training paddock. The walk-through was our rehearsal and you needed to know your lines.

I could name guys who missed out on Ireland caps because they weren't organized and prepared in the early part of a Test week. If someone missed their cue during the walk-through, we'd go back to the start and go again. Sometimes Joe made us stop and restart up to five or six times. You didn't want to be the guy who stuffed things up on the fifth go at it.

I didn't find the memory work difficult. I was more excited by the awareness that if we got one of Joe's strike plays right on the day, there was a better than 50 per cent chance of scoring. But it understandably took guys a while to get used to all the calls, and it wasn't ideal to be going into a Test match with a lot of new information in their heads. That showed against Australia, who beat us 32–15. Later, Paulie admitted that we hadn't brought enough emotion, which should never be an issue for Ireland.

I had other concerns. I suffered a Grade 1 tear to my right hamstring and was replaced by Mads just after half-time. I was in a race to be ready for New Zealand and by Wednesday I was losing that race. But Joe gave me every chance of playing. I was in doubt right up until an hour before kick-off when suddenly everything felt fine. Adrenaline is amazing.

That was the day when Ireland felt the Joe effect properly for the first time, the day when the Aviva was at its noisiest, despite a Sunday lunchtime kick-off. When Rob Kearney touched down in the first half, having intercepted a pass and galloped eighty metres, it was bedlam.

It was that day that I missed The Kick. To say that I am haunted by it sounds extreme, but every time I returned to that patch of grass with my kicking tee, whether it was in training or in the middle of a Test match, with over 50,000 watching, it was the first thing that popped into my head: *November 2013. Ireland 22, New Zealand 17. Seventy-four minutes on the clock.*

Looking back, I blame myself for staying on despite aggravating the hamstring making a tackle on Julian Savea around the sixty-minute mark. I tried to be the hero, decided to stay on and ended up costing us a historic win. Cost Paulie and Brian a chance to be on the first Irish team to beat NZ. They deserved that chance.

I also blame myself for allowing too many thoughts in as I was preparing to take the kick. Once Nigel Owens had penalized the New Zealanders for pulling down the maul, I pointed to the posts, placed the ball on the ground near my appointed spot – one pace to the right of the 15-metre line, just outside the 22.

When I went to pick my spot between the posts I could see hundreds of tiny white spotlights. Everyone had their phones out, taking pictures of the moment that Ireland went more than a converted try ahead of New Zealand, with only five minutes remaining. I allowed myself to think: This is the moment you have waited for. This is the moment that all the practice was for. This is the reason you have stayed on despite your injured hammy, the moment where you write your first bit of history with Ireland. I'd achieved nothing for Ireland yet and that conundrum was still out there: How come Sexton can't play for Ireland like he does for Leinster? This was my chance to shut all those people up.

These are disastrous thoughts for a place-kicker to be having. You should focus on your routine and nothing else. I eventually snapped back to the moment, to my main swing thought, whatever that was at the time: Stand tall. Head still. Or maybe I was telling myself to commit to the kick, not to go easy because of my hammy.

Just as I settled, and as the crowd were getting restless because I'd been standing over the kick for an eternity, the wind picked up. It was coming in over my left shoulder, as it tends to do in that part of the stadium. *OK, aim more left post.* Then the wind dropped. *Don't aim too far left.* Another thought. Too many thoughts, basically.

I pushed it a foot to the right of the posts.

That was my last act in the game. Mads replaced me for the final four minutes and I had to sit and watch it all unravel, culminating in Ryan Crotty's try in the left corner – four minutes that would have a defining influence on us.

Joe would drag us through those four minutes the next time we were in camp, pointing out exactly where we had gone wrong and who was at fault. It was harrowing. Being put through that made us better, but I couldn't help thinking I could have prevented the pain if I hadn't made the basic error of stepping back from that kick and seeing it in some wider context, rather than just sticking to my process. Unforgivable.

But the experience made me stronger, I'm sure of it. I learned from it. In three games during the Six Nations later that season, I had kicks from exactly that spot, when we needed the points to go two scores clear. I nailed every one of them. Things happen for a reason? Maybe.

I was in the Racing team room the following Tuesday when Jacky approached me.

'How is your head?' he asked.

I was confused. My head? I explained that the reason I was missing the game against Montpellier was my hamstring, not my head.

'No, Johnny,' he said. 'How is your head after missing the kick?'

Jamie Roberts and Mike Phillips overheard this exchange. They were pissing themselves laughing at Jacky's directness.

I didn't mind. I liked Jacky, liked his passion. You could see how much he wanted Racing to be successful. A few days after we'd beaten Clermont in the Champions Cup in that first season, I was having lunch at the club with Laura when he presented us with a magnum of his best wine to acknowledge my efforts the previous weekend.

He liked the fact that Laura and I came in for lunch on my day off – he said he wanted it to be a family club. It wasn't all smiles, though. He could lose the rag if things weren't going well. After one defeat, he stormed into the dressing room and let us have it. Kicked a table up in the air, told us we were all to come in for punishment training the next day. We were supposed to be on a week off that week, too. Guys had booked flights for getaways. They had to cancel them.

We got on well, though. I could tell that he appreciated me spending time at the club on days off, doing extras. That first year I used to come in on Wednesdays and do some yoga with Juan-Martín Hernández, then practise our kicking. Laura would join us for lunch after. I wasn't sure if she was there to see me or Juan-Martín.

I looked up to Juan-Martín. He was only three years older than me but I remember watching him at the 2007 World Cup when he was the star of the tournament. I felt like we were on the same wavelength. We wanted to play the same type of rugby. I loved playing and training with him. He played at 12 in that victory over Clermont and we worked some of the old Brumbies plays together, with Jamie running hard lines off us at 13. This was the type of rugby I'd visualized when I first considered joining Racing. Unfortunately we didn't get to play together as often as I'd liked. He left after my first year over some contractual wrangle.

I respected the fact that Juan-Martín was still looking to hone his skills relatively late in his career. Not everyone was as dedicated. Some of Racing's imports were just on the gravy train. I even heard some of them joking about it in the dressing room. It annoyed the hell out of me.

I had a right go at one of them shortly after. This was during one of the fairly pointless games of tip that we used to play, with about twenty players per team. We had a play where this guy's job was to run a short line off me. The ball usually went out the back – but not always. This time I decided to pass him the ball, which he dropped. The conversation went something like this:

The call was out the back, Johnny.

Fuck off, there's always an option to go front door. Just catch the ball.

Don't speak to me like that.

Fuck off, mate. You never do anything.

That's when he started walking towards me. He was a forward, a big guy. I was thinking: *Here we go, I'm gonna get my head kicked in here.*

Rather than wait to see what was going to happen I threw a few punches straight away. We got broken up pretty quickly, but as we were being pulled apart he broke free and smashed me in the side of the ear. Total cheap shot.

Travers called us together and sent us home, which was a

bad idea, because it meant the two of us walking off at the same time, both mouthing off at each other. It carried on in the dressing room. Now, this was the sort of thing that happened quite regularly when Michael Cheika was in charge at Leinster but it was a big deal at Racing. I was called in to the coaches' office the next morning to explain myself.

Racing could see how much I wanted to succeed, and Jacky envisaged that I could have the same influence that Jonny Wilkinson had at Toulon. But there was one obvious difference. Wilkinson's England career was almost over when he moved to France. I was part of two Six Nations championships while at Racing and I was still central to Joe's plans for the 2015 World Cup.

The friction between club and country grew steadily – and it was really my own fault. Stupidly, I'd only got a verbal agreement from Racing that I would be excused club duty during international windows. The Welsh guys had it written into their contracts, so even if they weren't selected for a Six Nations game, they would stay in camp with Warren Gatland.

When I mentioned that verbal agreement to the two Laurents, they shrugged. This was news to them. They expected me to play Top 14 during Ireland's off-weeks in the Six Nations. Madness. But they were my employers, so I needed to do as I was told.

So the weekend before Ireland opened the 2014 Six Nations campaign against Scotland in Dublin, when all my Ireland team-mates were resting up, I was playing seventy-three minutes for Racing against Toulouse. On the fallow weekend after Round 2, I came off the bench against Bayonne.

I convinced myself that I could manage all the double-shifting. We had beaten Scotland and Wales, and ran England close in Twickenham, when Kearns's beautifully constructed try was the ultimate justification of Joe's obsession with accuracy of detail. But the club–country tension came to a head the week after that.

In that second Six Nations off week, Racing expected me to return for their game against Castres, but I had badly damaged thumb ligaments in a tackle on Courtney Lawes. I rang Simon to give him the IRFU's medical read after the thumb had been scanned and assessed by a specialist: there was a possibility that I might play against Italy in Round 4 if my hand was put in a cast and the swelling reduced. It made sense that I stayed in camp with Ireland. Right?

Wrong. The word from Simon was that Racing wanted to assess the injury themselves. So I flew back to Paris and had it looked at by the club doctor, Jean-Marc Laborderie. It was still blackened and swollen but according to him, there was a chance that it might be ready for Castres. I thought he was taking the piss. There was no way that I would have been able to catch a ball by that weekend.

I understood that Racing were still chasing a spot in the play-offs. But it wasn't like I'd been minding myself up to that point. I'd played twenty games for them already, put my body on the line. Everyone could surely see that I was committed? So I was very straight with the two Laurents, and Laborderie. Jacky was in the room at the time, too.

'I'm not playing for Racing this weekend,' I said. 'But I will be playing for Ireland against Italy the week after, based on the advice of the best hand specialist in Ireland. If you don't want me to come back after that game, that's fine. I won't.'

I could see they were a bit taken aback by that. Sometimes you have to lay it on the line.

*

In some years, I might have sat out the Italy game in Round 4, but the Six Nations had developed into a four-horse race with England, France and Wales. We had all lost one match, and bonus points had not yet been introduced, so the championship would probably be decided on points difference. We put 46 on Italy at the Aviva, in Brian's final home appearance for Ireland. Quite a send-off, it was.

His last Test match was in Paris the week after that. I remember Joe using it to stoke us up – one of those rare occasions when he brought a bit of emotion to the build-up. A minor subplot was that I'd be going up against four of my Racing team-mates. I had texts from Dimitri Szarzewski and Wenceslas Lauret – *Attention à vos côtes, Johnny*. Mind your ribs.

The title was on the line. We were a little fortunate to have been scheduled for the last game of the championship. By the time we kicked off, we were tops on points difference and knew that a win by any scoreline would do it. And we deserved our win. We attacked cleverly, scoring three tries, and then we defended like dogs at the death, exorcising a few of the demons from the defeat by New Zealand.

It should have been a sweeter day for me than it turned out. I scored two of our tries and nailed that all-important kick from the same spot as the kick against NZ to put us 9 points ahead in the third quarter. In my fifth season with Ireland, we'd finally won something.

But some of the gloss was taken off by the heavy knock I took trying to tackle Mathieu Bastareaud in the final quarter. I was criticized for going high on him as he charged towards me, but I would have been flattened if I'd tried to stop someone as big and powerful and quick as him with a traditional tackle.

My plan was always to try and wrap the ball-carrier up,

off-balance him and prevent the offload. Fine in theory, except that Bastareaud's forearm caught me on the jaw. Bang.

I've seen the collision in slow motion and it's not pretty. I wasn't knocked out, though, as was reported. I didn't want to be stretchered off, as I knew this would make things look worse than they were and I didn't want my family and Laura to be frightened. I remember Dimitri had just been substituted and he walked alongside me down the tunnel to the medical room at the Stade de France, just checking I was OK. I appreciated that.

I was back out on the touchline by the final whistle, saw Fergus and Trimby and Brian hugging and jumping and screaming. I just felt a bit detached from the celebrations. I took it easy that night. Alcohol is a no-no after a head knock.

I flew back with the squad for the second day of celebrations, but I was on a 6.30 flight out of Dublin on Monday and made it to work on time. I wasn't giving Racing any excuses to complain.

Relations actually improved over the following weeks. Our chances of making the play-offs were improved by four wins in a row, including one away to Stade Français. Winning the Paris derby was always good for business. Twice, I kicked late penalties to seal victory.

We were still annoyingly inconsistent, though. In early May we went to Montpellier, safe in the knowledge that we had made the top six, and we lost 44–10. It was really sloppy. My frustration boiled over in training the following week when I had a go at Juandré Kruger and a bit of a scuffle broke out.

It wasn't as violent as the previous row but it was picked up by *l'Équipe*, who had a journalist with us for the week. For a few days, my 'dust-up' with Kruger was big news.

I couldn't get over how much power the rugby media had in France. Racing seemed far too generous with the info they gave to journalists. Sometimes the easiest way to find out Racing's selection for the weekend was to check Tuesday's paper. I complained that this was giving an unnecessary advantage to our next opponents. Simon would explain: 'But we know a reporter who will give us a steer on our opponent. It's OK, Johnny.' It was all too cosy for my liking.

I was uncomfortable about the way everyone was kissing this journalist's ass during that week. It was all, '*Bonjour, madame. Ça va bien?*' She had complete, unrestricted access – to team meetings, field sessions, even the team room, which should have been completely off-limits. I wasn't rude to her; I just didn't treat her like some visiting dignitary.

Then I saw the spread in *l'Équipe*.

She'd made me look like some kind of dark presence at Racing. She described a training session where I gave Fabrice Estebanez a dirty look for dropping a pass. She quoted Ronan saying that I had '*un très mauvais caractère*' – a very bad temper. Laurent Labit told her: 'I told Johnny that he can give out to people on Monday and Tuesday but after Thursday, stop! He must generate positive energy, he must encourage. But he is tough, Johnny. He doesn't beat around the bush. If someone messes up, he'll let them know.'

No one seemed to be complaining when we won in Toulouse the following weekend, to reach the semi-finals for the first time in the professional era. I kicked all 21 points and suddenly *l'Équipe* was full of glowing quotes from Racing about how great I had played. I remember yapping away in French in my post-match interview with Canal Plus, saying how we had turned a corner.

Our season ended the following week when we lost 16–6

in Toulon, but Racing had already initiated talks about a contract extension and soon it was on the table. It was very attractive. Laura had made loads of friends and was loving life in Paris. She was preparing to have our first baby at the end of June – in France, having dealt with a French gynaecologist throughout the pregnancy. She had settled.

I was enjoying aspects of our life, but professionally it wasn't working for me. Playing for Ireland was still number one and I dreaded another tug-of-war the following season. I was approaching my twenty-ninth birthday, coming into my prime years, but I couldn't afford to play another forty games a season.

It also dawned on me that I didn't like the idea of my son coming to watch me play for Racing. I wanted him to have memories of seeing his old man playing at the RDS.

I'd already had a call from Leinster during the Six Nations. Matt O'Connor, who'd taken over from Joe, had rung to see if I'd consider coming home early. I explained that I couldn't make the first move on anything like that, as it would put me in a weak bargaining position. He said he'd come back to me but I never heard from him again.

Because Ireland were touring Argentina that June, I had opportunities to drop the odd not-so-subtle hint in the media. In one radio interview I mentioned that Racing had offered me a new five-year deal but that I'd heard nothing from the IRFU. That did the trick. Soon Guy Easterby was on the phone, then Mick Dawson.

Mick told me that the IRFU realized that they hadn't handled my contract very well the previous year. They were worried about how me being in France might adversely affect Joe's preparation for the World Cup. They'd realized they needed to have control over players' game-time and their conditioning. He assured me that they would make the best offer they could afford. Was I willing to talk? I couldn't wait.

We set up a meeting at a hotel near Charles de Gaulle Airport – myself, Mick and Philip Browne. I couldn't meet them in Dublin, as Laura was due to give birth any day, so I appreciated them flying over.

I decided not to involve Fintan on this occasion. His nose was out of joint for a while, but it was almost a compliment to him that I kept him out of the deal. As a skilled negotiator, he would have driven a hard bargain. I wasn't going to be a pushover but I wanted things to go as smoothly as possible. I wanted to get home and didn't want anything to get in the way of it.

Philip had one big card to play. The Union would prevent Joe from picking me for Ireland unless I agreed to return home the following summer, when my second season with Racing was finished. They wanted to deter other top-level players from moving abroad and this was one way of doing it.

Philip told me that the Union's pay structures prevented them from going close to matching Racing's figure, but his plan was to supplement my salary significantly by building 'top-ups' into the deal.

Where I dug my heels in with Philip and Mick was the length of the contract. They offered two years but I insisted on four. I needed to provide Laura with some assurance of security. I couldn't face another contract negotiation in eighteen months' time. This was agreeable to Philip. We had a deal.

Joe brought the contract over a couple of weeks later with David Nucifora, who had just been hired as the Union's performance director. They popped in to Racing to meet with the two Laurents as a gesture of goodwill, designed to ease relations that had been strained by the differences in medical opinion over my fitness during the Six Nations. Racing must have been a little suspicious about their presence in Paris, though, given that I hadn't signed their contract extension offer.

I signed the IRFU deal later that day in Marcoussis with Joe and David in attendance, behind the stand while the Ireland women were scoring a famous World Cup win over New Zealand. Then I returned to my seat to watch the rest of the game with my family. Yes, we were now three: Mum, Dad and Luca, who was then six weeks old.

He'd arrived at 6.30 in the morning and I was there to witness it. I'd never experienced such a weird mix of euphoria and apprehension. You are so unprepared. We hadn't even decided on a name. We wanted something French — Louis, François and Luc had been mentioned. But Luc would just become Luke over time, so we went for Luca — Italian rather than French, but at least it was European.

Our parents had to wait a couple of weeks to see their first grandchild. Ronan and Jess came to the hospital in Paris, and we had a couple of other friends from Racing in to visit over the first couple of days. But we had to wait a fortnight before flying back to Dublin.

It was an emotional return, and the love for Luca from everyone in both families was overwhelming. It confirmed to us that coming home was the right decision. We'd make the most of our second year in Paris, but Dublin was where we belonged.

14

Three minutes from the end of our match against Australia that November, I clashed heads with Rob Kearney as we both went to tackle the same opponent. I had to go off with concussion, and it was annoying not to have been out there for the final whistle, as the team had put in a heroic defensive effort to seal the win.

My consolation was knowing that I'd had a good month personally, playing well enough to be the only European player nominated for the World Player of the Year award (which was won by Brodie Retallick). Unfortunately, this was all over-shadowed by that head injury against Australia. Just a few months earlier, in the summer of 2014, the Top 14 decided to tighten up their protocols for managing brain injury. The incident that had probably forced the issue occurred in a game in which I was playing – Racing's Top 14 quarter-final against Toulouse. Florian Fritz, their international centre, had left the pitch after suffering a suspected concussion and was then allowed to return. Now the Top 14's medical committee had imposed a mandatory twelve-week break for anyone who suffered four concussions within a year. The protocol was designed to reduce the incidence of concussion through greater awareness of its dangers, and to ensure that players had adequate time to recover from '*les commotions cérébrales*'. I never expected that I'd become the poster boy of this effort.

The campaign in France was being led by a neurologist called Jean-François Chermann. Watching the Australia match from Paris, Dr Chermann had seen the clash of heads and saw me extend my arm upwards while I was receiving attention. This was 'tonic posturing', a classic symptom of brain injury. When I returned to Racing that week, the club doctor gave me Dr Chermann's number and explained that I needed to arrange an appointment.

I found Dr Chermann good to deal with. He was very attentive, regularly sending me texts to check on my health. We met every couple of weeks and had stimulating conversations. I am interested in neuroscience and how it relates to contact sport, which is one of the reasons that I got on so well with Chermann during our regular consultations. Since the days when I'd wanted to be a doctor, I'd never lost my curiosity about how the human body works. I suspect that Dr Chermann liked practising his English on me, and I also liked practising my French on him. (In 2021, Dr Chermann came out with wildly inappropriate and inaccurate comments about me having had 'around thirty concussions' in my career. He subsequently retracted the comment, but that didn't undo all of the damage.)

When we met in 2014, I was completely upfront with him. He already knew about my collision with Mathieu Bastareaud the previous March. He knew that I'd suffered a fractured jaw after a collision with Toulon's Josua Tuisova in August. I suffered no concussion symptoms there, but Dr Chermann said a clash of heads of that magnitude could not be discounted.

I freely mentioned another clash of heads against Argentina in June; and that Eoin Reddan had hit the side of my head with a practice box-kick while we were warming up for the Australia game. I had been kneeling down on the touchline, putting a ball on the kicking tee, and straightened up just as Reddser launched. *Whack.*

The accident with Reddser hadn't caused concussion symptoms. But it had given me a migraine 'aura'. This is something that I have kept out of the public domain until now: I suffer from migraine. It's in the family. My granny Brenda in Listowel suffered from it. Mark, my brother, used to get blurred vision or headaches when he ate cheese or chocolate.

Another thing that can cause migraine is an impact to the head. I experienced it playing rugby on quite a few occasions: a relatively mild impact that triggered an aura. I would feel fine initially, but gradually my vision would become distorted: a bit like what happens when you stare into a bright light and then look away. It might last for a few minutes, and it would make certain rugby actions difficult.

There have been penalties I have taken when I've struggled to focus on the sweet spot on the ball. You're living on your wits in these situations, just waiting for your vision to return to normal – which invariably it does. You're just surviving moment by moment, afraid that if you call for assistance, your game is over. And how would you feel if your vision returns to 20/20 as you're walking off the pitch and there's nothing wrong with you any more?

Those migraine auras were sometimes followed by a migraine headache, but they had none of the side effects that might be construed as symptoms of concussion – no memory loss, no confusion, no dizziness or nausea. The bang to the head wouldn't be obvious to anyone watching. I might make a routine tackle and then out of nowhere the aura would come in. I'm not the only player I know whose game was affected by it. (I'm not going to name the others I know about, because that is their private medical information.)

I told Dr Chermann about the incident with Eoin Reddan

as an example of this: a momentary migraine aura. I soon regretted being so honest. Dr Chermann added it to a list that now had five entries for 2014. I argued that it should have been three, but he wasn't for turning. He told me I'd be out of action for twelve weeks, in keeping with the new policy in France.

Immediately I started counting back the weeks from our Six Nations opener in Rome on 7 February and realized that I wouldn't make it. The best that I could hope for was a return to action in Dublin the following week. Against France. Who else? I called Joe to deliver the bad news.

Everyone in rugby is so much better educated on concussion now than they were when I came into the game. I didn't have to look very far to see the effects of repeated brain injury. A few of my Leinster team-mates had been forced to retire early because of concussion.

There's no doubt that rugby players' awareness of concussion was heightened by developments in American football. In 2013 the NFL settled a $765 million class action taken by former players who were suffering from dementia, depression, CTE and other horrific ailments, due apparently to repeated head contacts while playing the sport. We all watched the Will Smith movie *Concussion*. We read the articles. Well, I did.

What I can say for certain is that I never knowingly put myself at risk by playing too soon after a concussion; my health was never compromised by any medic or coach; and I have never suffered any delayed symptoms after returning to play post-concussion.

One effect of the growing awareness of concussion was drastically reduced physical contact in training, to the point where there was almost zero body-on-body collision during field sessions with Leinster and Ireland. There was also an increasingly sophisticated system of identifying potential brain injuries and taking the appropriate steps – though admittedly there is still so much about this branch of science that is educated guesswork.

Dr Chermann carried out a lot of tests on me, some of them physical, some for cognitive function – my ability to recall sequences of numbers or words, for example. Every pro rugby player will do 'baseline' tests at the start of a season, the results of which can be used as reference points when the player suffers a suspected concussion. Back in the day, there were stories about guys deliberately posting mediocre baseline scores to give themselves a better chance of 'beating' concussion tests, so that they wouldn't miss any games. The competitor in me could never do this. Typically, I took pride in having the best 'cog-test' scores, whether it was at Leinster or Racing.

One of the main reasons that I became council president for the International Rugby Players, the players' representative body, was to ensure that player welfare remains top of the list of the sport's priorities. Naturally, therefore, I take an interest in everything that scientists and doctors are doing to reduce the incidence of concussion, and also to improve detection, like the 'instrumented' gumshields that were worn in the 2024 Six Nations, with inbuilt impact sensors and radio transmitters.

Later in 2014, at the behest of the IRFU, I consulted two independent neurologists in Dublin – Professor Tim Lynch and Professor Dan Healy. I have since consulted another specialist in the UK, Professor Tony Belli, who has been leading the way in the study of concussion in sport. His consultation was very reassuring.

Initially, there was some sympathy for me at Racing. They had seen the clash of heads against Australia. They knew that it wasn't my choice to be out of action. They saw that once I'd been cleared for non-contact training, I came to the gym every day during the week and worked hard.

Then there was the slagging. Jamie Roberts christened me Johnny Vacances, which was rich – I'd originally called him Jamie Vacances because of his laid-back attitude. Now he was turning it on me. At least it was out in the open and we could have a laugh.

But I sensed suspicion and some resentment, too. When you're a foreign player on the biggest salary at the club, it comes with the territory. At Leinster, I always kept a close eye on any new imports to check for any deficiencies in attitude. I always said I could judge within the first week whether the new guy had the right stuff.

Naturally, I felt that I was being judged, too. They saw me in the gym but they also saw me in the team room drinking coffee and having a laugh. I'd already missed most of August and September after breaking my jaw against Toulon. I'd already signed for Leinster the following season. I'd understand it if the 'old Racing' guys reckoned I'd already checked out.

There were benefits to my extended break, I'll admit. Laura and I got to spend Christmas in Dublin, and we got to show off Luca, now six months old, to everyone. But the build-up to the game against France was the most stressful of any in my career.

When it became clear that Joe was going to pick me as soon as possible, he was criticized. Laurent Bénézech, a French prop-turned-journalist with no medical expertise, said my selection was 'a mistake'. He predicted that Mathieu

Bastareaud would be seeking me out at the earliest opportunity. What searing insight!

When an Irish newspaper printed Bénézech's quotes, the IRFU issued a statement pointing out that I had been symptom-free for two months and also that I had been cleared to play by independent neurologists in France and Ireland, by the French Federation concussion review committee and by the Ireland and Racing medical teams.

Bernard le Roux, my Racing team-mate and friend, probably thought he was being funny when he told a journalist that I'd 'need to wear a helmet' that Saturday but it didn't help matters. I avoided the papers and stayed off my phone as much as possible that week.

Joe couldn't avoid the media, though. He had to sit in media conferences and answer questions that implied he was playing fast and loose with my health. I know the stress on Joe was huge because he called me the night before the game.

'Look, are you OK to play tomorrow, Johnny?' he said. 'I'm getting it in the ear for playing you. People are saying it's not fair on you and it's not fair on your family for me to throw you in to such a big game and that there's too much risk . . .'

I told him it was all bullshit and that I was good to go.

Myself and Bastareaud were drawn to each other, inevitably. Eight minutes in, the French got lineout ball to him as quickly as they could and I closed the space as quickly as I could. *Smash*. But I held my ground and with some help from Seánie, Robbie Henshaw and Tommy Bowe, we worked the choke tackle and won the decision from the ref. Scrum Ireland. The crowd went wild and I was into the game. All doubts and nerves gone. Major relief.

That wasn't the end of me and Bastareaud, though. Early

in the second half we were leading 12–6 and on the attack when Conor Murray fed me running towards the old Wanderers corner. Rob was free to my outside but I ducked back inside and clashed heads with Bastareaud. It was probably a red card for him in today's currency – he was upright – and I came off worse, with blood pouring from a cut above my eye.

I went off for a HIA, and returned ten minutes later all stitched and patched up. I remember the roar from the crowd when I reappeared on the side of the pitch, ready to replace Mads. And I remember giving a fist-pump after landing a penalty from wide on the right to make it 18–6 in the final quarter. One of the most satisfying kicks of my career, that one. Getting the man-of-the-match award was the cherry on top.

The next morning was the sorest I have felt after a game – there is only so much respite you can get from ice baths and rub-downs once you've gone straight into a Six Nations game after a twelve-week break. I still played the full eighty for Racing against Clermont the following week, a down week for everyone else. Not that I was complaining. With England the following Sunday, I had eight days' recovery for a game that was already being billed as a Grand Slam decider. And we were only in Round 3.

Mads replaced me after just fifty-five minutes: I had slightly strained my hamstring on a conversion to put us 19–3 ahead and cruising. It was our first victory over England in four years and one that demonstrated that Joe was way ahead of the game. He saw an area where we could dominate them – in the air – and devised a game-plan to maximize that advantage.

In time, Joe would be criticized for our reliance on kick-and-chase and on box-kicking especially. I think he was taken aback by that. He believed he was cashing in on specifically Irish skills and expected Irish rugby fans to buy into it. He saw how we now had two converted full-backs in midfield – Robbie and Jared Payne – and great aerial players in Rob, Lukey, Zeebs and Tommy. We worked hard on the accuracy of our punting and the timing and technique of our chasing. We got our reward when Robbie leaped for Conor's chip and scored the only try of the game against England.

That put us on the road towards our second Six Nations title from two attempts under Joe. My only regret is that it wasn't a Slam. Next up we lost in Cardiff, a game often remembered for the excellence of the Welsh defence. I also remember it for Wayne Barnes, who for some reason was reffing us for the second time that championship.

I rated Wayne when I watched him ref in the Premiership, but every ref has off-days, and for some reason Wayne had a few of them when Ireland or Leinster were involved. That day, he blew us off the park for the first twenty, especially at the breakdown, and we trailed 12–0. We lost 23–16.

It meant we weren't in control of our destiny on the final Saturday, as Wales and England were level with us on 6 points. It would all come down to points difference, and England had the advantage of playing last, at home to France.

That was a weird old week. From deflation post-Cardiff, we shifted to the liberation of Edinburgh, where we knew we not only needed to win but to win well. Various numbers were thrown about, all of them speculative. Joe decided to confront it head on and told us we needed to aim for a winning margin of 15 points. Just before kick-off, that number had to be revised upward: Wales had beaten Italy by 41, so we now needed a winning margin of at least 21 to get us ahead of the Welsh. (England would then need to crush

France to overtake us.) Joe came into the dressing room two minutes before we went out and told us the bad news. I remember thinking at the time that beating the Scots by 21 or more was near impossible. Winning alone in Murrayfield was hard enough.

We beat Scotland 40–10, throwing the ball about at every opportunity, leaving us with an overall points differential of +63. It meant that England would have to beat the French in Paris by 26 points or more to finish ahead of us. While most people focused on the quality of our attack, we were ultimately saved by Jamie Heaslip's brilliant try-saving tackle on Stuart Hogg in the corner. That one tackle also saved my blushes, because it took the focus off the two penalties I'd missed. I had the migraine aura for about fifteen minutes during the second half, and for the two kicks I took during that period I was half-closing one eye to try to reduce the blurring effect.

We watched the England match in a function room in Murrayfield, or at least some of us watched – Pete O'Mahony had his back to the screen for most of it. It went down to the wire, of course. Yoann Huget gave us a fright by tapping and going near his own line in the final seconds but Rory Kockott put us out of our misery by putting the ball off the pitch.

I remember feeling a bit sorry for the Scottish lads, who'd been forced to sit through another game after being beaten on their own patch, then had to watch as we were jumping around and hugging each other. We were delighted with ourselves.

OK, so it wasn't a Slam, and it felt a bit weird going back out on to the pitch to accept the trophy, witnessed by the many thousand Irish supporters who'd hung around Murrayfield to watch the last game and to see if we won the title.

But I'm sure they were glad they stayed as they watched us lift the trophy and celebrate with them for a while. We were champions of Europe for the second year running, and in a World Cup year.

We knew we had the best coach in the world. In Paulie, we had the best captain that I ever played under — strategically sharp and an inspirational talker. When Paulie was in the team we always played better. Players wanted to impress him. At least I did. Everyone raised their game. I learned so much from him. We had a nice blend of youth and experience. We were in a pretty good place.

Racing weren't in the worst place either, actually — still in the running in the Top 14 and in Europe. If we could win a trophy, I could count the venture a success. It all unravelled on a sunny Sunday in April at Colombes when we blew a European Champions Cup quarter-final against Saracens.

Sarries hadn't reached their peak at that stage and were missing Owen Farrell. I expected us to win. I could visualize a semi in Clermont — tough but not impossible. The other semi looked like Toulon and Leinster. Enticing possibilities? Not for long.

On the morning of the quarter-final I was sick as a dog. I told Ronan as much when he came to collect me. I was going to stay at home but he said I should come and report to the club doc. When I told my symptoms to Dr Labordrie, he virtually looked through me. It was like he didn't hear me. The message was clear. I'd have to be missing a limb before they'd consider pulling me from this game.

I tried and failed to eat, had a snooze in one of the medical rooms, got the team bus to Colombes, almost threw up in the dressing room before the start, then did throw up at half-time. In the circumstances, I thought I played OK, and we were leading 11–9 going down the straight. Then, for some unknown reason, the coaches decided to replace me with three minutes remaining, with the job not yet complete. I would have understood if they pulled me at half-time or at fifty minutes as I was struggling. But three minutes from the end after lasting so long?

Clearly you play the game in your opponents' half at this point, or at least as close to the touchlines as possible. But no, we worked the ball into the middle of the park so that when the penalty was inevitably awarded to Saracens it was just inside Marcelo Bosch's range. Final score: Racing 11, Saracens 12. Sickener.

There were still a couple of months in the season but that defeat felt like the beginning of the end. When the two Laurents spoke to the media after the game, they made no mention of the fact that I'd fronted up despite being ill. It almost felt like I was being blamed for the loss. That pissed me off.

We still had the Top 14 to challenge for, but I could pick up the vibes from some of the French guys in the squad and I got the odd hint from Ronan. *Sexton is heading back to Ireland. Do we need him?* The coaches put me on the bench for a game in La Rochelle. I was still professional, of course, but I no longer felt like I belonged. I was no longer a Racing man.

The irony is that our social life was great at that time. Laura had a close circle of friends and knew her way around Paris. But the rugby? Racing made it to the play-offs but were beaten by Stade Français, the eventual champions – a sore point, given that Jacky's whole mission was for the club to be kings of Paris.

It wasn't really that sore for me. I find it hard to play at anything less than 100 per cent, but part of me was detached.

There was only one thing that really mattered that summer. The World Cup.

People talk about 2011 as our great missed opportunity, but I wasn't picked to start that quarter-final in Wellington so it doesn't belong to me as such. For sure, I regret my personal failings earlier in that tournament, but I still hadn't established myself in the team. By 2015, I had a sense of ownership, which made our failure – and our misfortune – all the more frustrating.

Our pre-tournament results weren't brilliant, but this didn't concern us unduly. We knew that we had to peak for the end of the pool, when we played France in Cardiff, and for the knockouts. Our conditioning was tailored perfectly to achieving that. I played no golf in Carton House that summer; it was all about fitness. We were supremely fit. And I didn't make the same mistake I'd made in 2011 with my kicking preparation. I saw Dave Alred more that summer than I ever did before.

We were confident, too. This was as close as we could get to a home World Cup. All going to plan, we would play three games at the Millennium Stadium, which most of us knew well. There were no concerns with jet lag, with diet, with dodgy hotels. We knew our best team, had faith in our coaches, and we were used to winning. We also knew that we'd have more travelling supporters than any other team, plus a big turnout from the first-, second- and third-generation Irish living in the UK. Sure enough, just under 90,000 people turned up for the game against Romania in Wembley, almost all of them wearing green.

Without being presumptuous, we could see a very manageable route to the semi-finals. That was all dependent on winning the pool and avoiding New Zealand in the quarter-final. And winning the pool meant beating Italy (which we achieved with some difficulty) and then overcoming France, who we'd beaten two years running.

Naturally a few people had pops at me in the French media during the build-up. Laurent Labit said that I had been 'uncontrollable' at Racing. A former team-mate called me 'the Zlatan Ibrahimović of rugby'. A pity he didn't have the guts to identify himself.

I could handle all that, no bother. What I couldn't handle was a juggernaut of a tackle from Louis Picamoles, who lined me up and smashed me, shoulder into the solar plexus, just as I was taking and giving a pass in the twenty-fourth minute. I duly puked up my pre-match meal on the Millennium turf before being led ashore. My game was over. The speculation was concussion – more long-distance diagnosing by the amateur neurologists. In fact I'd hurt my groin earlier in the game and the force of Picamoles's tackle exacerbated the injury.

Mads played and kicked superbly in my absence. The entire team was inspired, in fact. The 24–9 victory went down in the record books as Ireland's biggest ever 'away' victory over France, but it felt much more like a home game. The Irish supporters must have outnumbered the French by twenty to one. When Rob scored in the third quarter, the place went nuts.

Victory came at a price, though. Paulie ripped his hamstring just before the break and never played again. Pete O'Mahony was stretchered off, too, after the game of his life. Add in Seánie, later suspended for retaliating against a cheap shot by Pascal Papé, plus Jared Payne – injured earlier that week in training, and established as our defensive leader – and there was a big hole in our first-choice XV for the quarters.

In our rush to check the seriousness of my groin problem, we probably had it scanned before the full extent of the tear could be measured. I trained too early that week, exacerbating the issue, before finally being ruled out on the eve of the game.

The Pumas are always dangerous at World Cups, but it's hard to imagine that we'd have started so badly had we been at full strength. By the end of the first quarter we trailed 3–20 – and had lost Tommy Bowe, another addition to the injury list. It was hard to watch.

I know people will say that you can't win a World Cup without depth in every position, but imagine the All Blacks of 2015 without Retallick, Kaino, McCaw, Carter and Nonu. Sometimes you need a bit of luck, and we didn't have much of it at that tournament.

15

It was a little weird being back home. Having departed Dublin as a couple, we returned as a family of three, with a fourth on the way – Amy, our second child, was due to arrive the following February. We rented in Dartry, close enough to both of our families' homes, while we searched for a house to buy.

From a financial point of view, the move to Racing had worked out well. Now just past my thirtieth birthday, I was starting into a generous four-year IRFU contract that would take me up to the 2019 World Cup. The Union's player management programme meant that my body had a decent chance of lasting the journey, as I wouldn't be flogged like I had been in my first season in France. Plus I was back at Leinster, my real club. What could be better?

Plenty, as it turned out. I was barely a couple of months into the new season when I heard myself saying to Laura: 'I wish we'd stayed in Paris.'

The Leinster I'd returned to was a mess. A complete shit-show. I couldn't believe how badly things had deteriorated in two years and, worryingly, I could see no sign of them being fixed in the short term. We had a really inexperienced coaching team. That team included some very old friends and team-mates, which made things awkward at times, stressful. My relationship with Leo would be stretched almost to breaking point.

I'd had my suspicions that things would be difficult from

as far back as the previous May, when Leinster's professional game board sacked head coach Matt O'Connor without having the faintest idea of who his replacement might be. I'd actually been in contact with Matt quite a bit while I was still in Paris, just getting his thoughts on the way forward. Then I got a call from Guy Easterby, Leinster's head of operations, to tell me that the club had given Matt the sack.

This was just an informal heads-up from Guy. I was still officially a Racing player, so he was just keeping me in the loop, which I appreciated. I asked him who they had lined up as a replacement. He couldn't tell me.

'C'mon, Guy,' I said. 'I know you've got to keep it quiet for a bit but I won't say a word. Is it between a few candidates or have you already shaken hands with someone?'

'We've no one,' he said.

I couldn't believe what I was hearing. This was May, when anyone decent was most likely tied up for the next season. Matt had just taken Leinster to the semis of the Heineken Cup, where they were beaten in extra time by the reigning champions, Toulon. The previous season, he'd won the Pro12. If you don't think he's the long-term solution, fine. Let him see out his contract and then move on.

In fairness to Guy, it wasn't his decision: he was merely letting me know. The guys on the board had been in a hurry. They obviously thought the club name alone would do the trick. They soon discovered that they were wrong.

They ended up going with Leo as head coach, with Kurt McQuilkin, Girvan Dempsey and John Fogarty as a very home-grown support staff. I wasn't surprised that Leo had interviewed well. I've huge respect for his smarts and for what he has achieved in the game. He knew Leinster and the youth systems better than anyone, and he was passionate about the club, but he was only thirty-seven years old and just starting out on his coaching journey. He needed someone with top-level coaching experience to guide him. That's what I told him when he asked me about taking the gig. Finding that person wasn't straightforward, though.

It was inevitable that there were going to be problems. Some influential personalities had moved on – Brian, Darce, Kev McLaughlin, Jenno. We did have Isa back after his two-year sabbatical, but the culture was nothing like what it had been during the Joe era. All it takes is a small slip in standards for the rot to set in: people turning up a few minutes late for meetings, or wearing the wrong gear; experienced players arriving in on Monday morning very obviously hungover.

As well as that, everything was just a bit too democratic for my liking. As part of his prep to become a coach, Leo had spent time with a couple of New Zealand franchises, where the culture is to empower players to own the game-plan. That's fine, but New Zealanders are different. They have been coached into good habits from an early age. I'm all for player input but there needs to be someone in charge. Sometimes you can have too many voices, and not enough clarity and consistency.

Our preparation was chaotic. We'd agree an attack shape in a meeting but something different would happen on the training pitch and no one would be pulled up on it. I found it very frustrating. I was used to Joe's way of doing things – inclusive of players' ideas, but only up to a point. Beyond that point, what he said went. And there was no arguing with the success of his system.

Leo was very laid-back. Sometimes I would suggest something specific about the game-plan and he'd agree with me. But then he wouldn't follow through on it and the same mistakes would happen. That would drive me crazy. It meant that I had to be the bad guy all the time.

There was a leadership vacuum. I felt the urge to step into that vacuum and take charge but I was also trying to avoid making the mistakes I had made at the start in Racing. I could imagine the response: *Ah, yer man is back from Paris thinking he's God's gift, telling us how it should be done.* So I sucked it up as best I could, until I got home, when poor Laura would get to hear all about it.

Even the most experienced head coach in the world would have struggled to cope with reintegrating twenty players after the World Cup, only a couple of weeks before the start of the Champions Cup. Even so, our performance was mortifying – losing 6–33 to Wasps at the RDS first up, shipping 50 points to them in Coventry, losing home and away to Toulon, finishing bottom of the pool for the first time since 1998. This was only four years after we'd won our third Heineken Cup. It was like we had fallen off a cliff.

I found the defeat in Toulon was the hardest to take. It was my first game back in France and I wanted us to play sharp, smart, attacking rugby, the opposite of what we had done in Racing. We had a makeshift midfield with Luke Fitz at 12 and Ben Te'o at 13 – two unbelievable athletes and play-ers, but Luke was a back-three player. And I had a shocker, with a couple of punts overcooked and passes off-target.

After that Toulon game, I got comfort from an unlikely source. When Dad came on the phone that evening, he sur-prised me by saying all the right words.

'Look, Jonathan, it will be blown out of proportion but that's always the way,' he said. 'They are easy fixes and you don't normally make those mistakes so just forget about it. Move on.'

It was exactly what I wanted to hear and all the more reassuring coming from him. I wondered if he'd been dipping into some of the books on sports psychology I had lying around at home.

With a nice sense of timing, Amy waited until the day after our Six Nations opener against Wales before announcing herself to the world. I was there for her arrival, even though I wasn't able to hold her in my arms just yet: I had taken a heavy knock to my shoulder the previous day. Poor Laura had just given birth, but one nurse who was obviously a rugby fan was more concerned about my fitness. Imagine the look I got when the nurse handed me a hot-water bottle.

We had quite the casualty list before and during that 2016 Six Nations, so to finish in the top half wasn't the worst result. I started all five games and played at least seventy minutes in all except the Italy game. I was pretty pleased with my durability, given that it seemed to be targeted a bit that year.

It's amazing to look back and see what people got away with in 2016. There was one incredible cheap shot from Yoann Maestri early on in Paris, blindsiding me long after I had passed the ball. Jaco Peyper thought it was only a penalty.

At least Alex Dunbar got a yellow card for flipping me past the horizontal and on to my back at a ruck in the Scotland game, although the media was more interested in the fact that I had 'milked' the offence afterwards. Believe me, if the officials aren't going to protect you, you have to start forcing them to take notice of what's going on, if only to protect yourself.

After the France game, Joe revealed to the media that I'd suffered a whiplash injury rather than a concussion. The following week, England's new coach Eddie Jones couldn't resist the temptation to have a pop. 'Sexton is an interesting one,' he told the media. 'They've talked about him having whiplash injury, which is not a great thing to talk about. I'm sure his mother and father would be worried about that. Hopefully, the lad's all right on Saturday to play.'

Bringing my folks into it was a new low. I won't repeat what my parents had to say about Jones.

England won the Grand Slam, which was quite a turn-around after their massive World Cup disappointment. Some saw it as a further indictment of the previous coaching team, but I wasn't so sure. As soon as those coaches were back on the market, I urged Joe to look at Andy Farrell to fill the role of defence coach that had been vacated by Les Kiss. I'd really enjoyed working under Faz with the Lions and knew he would add a lot to the Ireland set-up.

I quite fancied myself as a player on the coaching market back then. Leinster were on the lookout for an established attack specialist and I was determined to be part of the recruitment process. I was desperate for Leinster to get back to the top and I knew that getting the right person was so important. Our form after the Six Nations was reasonable – without the distraction of Europe, we could focus purely on the Pro12. But I knew we were still miles off where we needed to be.

I said it publicly, too. In April, in an interview for *Off the Ball*, I said that the club was 'culturally nowhere near where we were when we were winning trophies'. I knew that wouldn't go down well with management and players, but I felt it needed to be said. Looking back, I wish I had handled this period differently. I should have said what I had to say internally, but at that time I didn't know what I know now about leadership.

A few days later, Ulster beat us 30–6 in Belfast, with Paddy Jackson scoring a bucketload of points. We were close to full strength, too. OK, so we knew we were already through to the Pro12 knockouts, but in the Joe era, or even the Cheika era, we'd never have let that affect our performance. It was embarrassing.

Losing the Pro12 final to Connacht was a blessing, really. Winning another title might have papered over the cracks and reduced the pressure to add a heavy hitter to the coaching team. It was a painful experience in Murrayfield, for sure, especially the ease with which Connacht carved us open in the first quarter. But it demanded a radical response from the club, and that was positive.

It was a painful experience for me in a physical sense, too. Early in the game I was slammed into the turf and the impact forced my shoulder to pop out of its socket. Luckily it went straight back in and I played on, desperate to lead a fightback, and probably did further damage. Ireland were flying to South Africa for a three-Test tour the following week, but the medics told me I needed an op on my shoulder.

Could I not delay the op until after the tour? I had never been to South Africa. I reckoned the Springboks were vulnerable. I couldn't wait to see Faz having an influence – that tour was his first involvement with the squad. No matter. I was told that I'd be having the op.

The sensible thing would have been to see the positives in missing the tour. We were due to play New Zealand twice in November. We were coming into a Lions season. My body could do with a few weeks off.

But I wasn't able to switch off. The day I had the procedure on my shoulder, I went almost directly to a meeting with Guy and Isa, probably still a little high on painkillers, full of talk about how losing to Connacht was a good thing, about who we might target to coach our attack. I was on a mission.

In fairness to Guy, so was he. Finding the right person was difficult, though. I phoned various people, including Tony McGahan, formerly of Munster and my host back on that Ireland Schools trip years previously. Leo was in talks with Tabai Matson at the Crusaders. Neither was available. It was all very frustrating. I remember calling Joe to get it all off my chest.

He had other things on his mind. Soon Ireland were beating the Boks in Cape Town, our first Test win on South African soil. There was blazing sunshine in Dublin that day so we had a barbecue in the garden of our rented house and invited a few friends over. I had a couple of beers and put on a brave face watching Paddy play well. Deep down I was suffering. I hated not being in Cape Town.

Laura gently reminded me: *Jono, you're on your summer holidays. Switch off for a while. Be with us.* I couldn't have been further away. This had been a nightmare season. Leinster was a mess. Now I was watching Ireland making history without me. Was this karma for leaving to go to Paris?

I nodded to Laura. But all I could think about was: *When can I get out of this sling and start the rehab on my shoulder?*

That was the summer of the big clear-out at Leinster. About fifteen players moved on, including some influential characters like Reddser and Lukey Fitz. And some interesting ones stepped up from the academy, like Dan Leavy, Joey Carbery and James Ryan. Robbie Henshaw joined from Connacht.

We also had Graham Henry in for a couple of weeks in

pre-season, at Leo's invitation. It was interesting to get the thoughts of a World Cup-winning coach on all sorts of topics, but especially on team culture. We had some very honest meetings about how standards had slipped and what changes were needed.

The real game-changer, though, was the arrival of Stuart Lancaster. I like to think I had a hand in making it happen. The truth is it probably never would have happened but for the terrible news that Kurt received that August, when it emerged that his father and sister were seriously ill and that he'd have to return to New Zealand.

Suddenly we were down a defence coach and finding a replacement before the start of the new season became a priority. Stu's name had been mentioned briefly earlier that summer, but for whatever reason Leinster didn't think of him as a defence coach at the time. Now he was mentioned again.

I'd always had a sneaking regard for his England teams, despite what his detractors had said in the media after the 2015 World Cup. They were well organized and had good team spirit. We had always struggled against them, partly because they never showed the arrogance we loved to see in England teams. They never gave us any motivation in press conferences and always remained very humble, respectful. I reckoned that must have had something to do with their head coach.

I texted him, asking him if he'd be available, saying I thought he'd be a great fit and that we'd be mad keen to have him. He phoned back almost immediately to say that he was at a family get-together and to ask if he could call me later.

My text to Stu didn't nail the deal, but it was gratifying when he subsequently revealed it had been an important factor in his coming. After being sacked by England he'd been advised by someone that whoever he worked for next, he had to make sure that they really wanted him. We wanted Stu.

It all happened pretty quickly from there. He turned up the Monday after our first Pro12 game of the season. It took just about everyone by surprise. Only Leo, Guy and Isa had known about his appointment as defence coach. (It was a bit later that Stu's title would be changed to 'senior coach'.)

As soon as he began his first presentation, the whole mood at the club changed. He had a presence about him, as you'd expect from an international head coach. As he spoke, you could sense people mentally pulling their socks up. I just looked across at Isa and we both smiled.

In the space of one meeting, Stu fixed our defensive issues. He used the Pro12 final as his raw material and picked us apart mercilessly. He pointed out guys who were walking rather than running back into the line, guys who were slow to get off the line. He spoke about the level of detail that we needed, the honesty that we needed. It was like listening to Joe but with an English accent.

Leinster actually lost in Glasgow the following weekend, but as the Ireland players began to be reintroduced, our form took off. Under Stu's influence, our training sessions became more challenging, our standards more exacting. When we reviewed training, we were more honest with each other. The fact that we were even reviewing training was a step forward from the previous year.

I was enjoying my job again. For the first time in three years I was loving coming to work. If only I could have avoided getting injured. I'd been so keen to strengthen the area around my shoulder that my pre-season training was imbalanced, concentrating too much on my upper body. Three games into my season, I suffered a tweak in my hamstring, which meant I missed our first European game, against Castres, and then only played forty minutes in Montpellier, in keeping with a request from the IRFU. They didn't think I was fit enough to play. This was because we were only two weeks away from Ireland's meeting with New Zealand in Chicago.

It was annoying not to be in peak physical shape for the All Blacks because it was an incredible occasion. An incredible week, actually. Chicago was rocking because the Cubs, the local baseball team, had just won their first World Series in over a hundred years. The Chicago River was dyed blue to coincide with the victory parade through the city, which we watched from the rooftop of our hotel the day before our game. For some reason the IRFU had booked everyone into the Trump Hotel and this was the week before Donald Trump won the US presidential election. Mick Kearney had warned us that we weren't to be seen to be supporting Trump in any way . . . cue the lads wearing all the hotel's Trump-branded dressing gowns and slippers to dinner.

It has been well documented how we trained poorly that week but then shocked the All Blacks with the quality of our start. Part of the legend is that we were inspired by the formation that we chose to face the haka, a figure of eight to honour Anthony Foley, the legendary Munster and Ireland number 8 who had died three weeks previously.

I was shocked and saddened by Axel's sudden passing at just forty-two. I'd got to know him a bit when Deccie had brought him into the Ireland set-up to fill in as defence coach. His knowledge and passion for the game were hugely impressive and he had a cutting sense of humour that I liked.

I wrote a letter to his family a couple years later with a jersey from the France game in Paris, where he had died. In the letter I told his family three stories. The first was about the imagery that he used when he spoke about the battle, about being a warrior, about being carried back on your shield from the war, about being able to look your team-mates in the eye after the fight. I mentioned how he used always to ask me when I was coming 'back' to play for Munster; he knew about my relatives in Kerry and Limerick, of course.

Finally, I described the look on his son's face when he saw the Leinster contingent at his dad's funeral in Killaloe. We were in a line as the hearse came up the street and when Tony got out, he tapped his younger brother Dan on the shoulder and pointed at us. By the look in his eyes, he seemed to be saying: 'That's the enemy.' For Axel, Leinster were the real enemy.

When I met Olive a couple of years later, she told me that the boys had appreciated the jersey but that they especially appreciated the stories because they loved hearing and re-hearing any anecdote about their dad.

I'm not sure who came up with the idea of arranging ourselves in a figure of eight for the All Blacks match. I suggested that we put the Munster guys closest to the haka – Conor, Donnacha Ryan, CJ Stander and Zeebs. Did it give us an extra sense of togetherness? I think so, although it helped that our supporters outnumbered the Kiwis by about ten to one.

What was probably more important was the decision to chase tries rather than kick whatever penalties came our way. It helped that Mathieu Raynal was willing to penalize the ABs, who were ill-disciplined that day. We had three tries and a 25–8 lead by the break. I pleaded with the lads to keep playing. In 2013 I'd said at half-time we needed to score again and we didn't – partly down to my missed kick. I repeated the same message and Zeebs scored next. Perfect. Until the inevitable fightback began. First TJ Perenara scored a try, then Ben Smith. In the middle of all this my legs were cramping. I had been ill a few days before the game and I was really feeling it. My legs were gone. Nightmare. At the next kick-off, I felt my hamstring.

I had to watch the rest of it unfold from the sideline, with an ice bag wrapped around my thigh – Scott Barrett's try narrowing our lead to four points, then Robbie's try sealing the win. It's an incredible memory, especially the lap of honour, seeing all sorts of familiar faces in an unfamiliar context.

The celebrations were short-lived for me, though. I'd had a bug all week and was struggling with my body. My main preoccupation that evening was with icing my hamstring and keeping my weight off it. The next morning at 7 a.m., while most of the lads were sleeping off the drink, I was sitting in a café, alone, wondering when my body would sort itself out.

Looking back, my body was clearly screaming at me to take it easy, to stop putting myself under so much pressure, mentally and physically. But what was I supposed to do? The All Blacks were coming to Dublin in a fortnight's time, intent on revenge. This was no time to be heading for the health farm.

Sure enough, it was a brutal Test match that New Zealand won 19–9, and once again my body wasn't up to it. I was off the pitch in the seventeenth minute with a hamstring strain. I couldn't carry on like this. Drastic measures were required. I needed to take a six-week break mid-season, designed entirely on getting myself ready for the Six Nations and thinking ahead to the Lions tour. I would spend those weeks out in the Sports Surgery Clinic in Santry working with a rehab specialist, Enda King. I knew it would put noses out of joint in Leinster, but it was time to be selfish.

Enda is world class, the best around at what he does. He showed me how detailed I needed to be with my training. It was a real eye-opener, and it paved the way for how I would look after myself till the end of my career.

Leinster barely saw me that December. During the days I was out in Santry with Enda putting my body through the wringer. In the evenings, myself and Laura would be poking around the period house we had bought in Rathgar, keeping tabs on the builders.

It was my mum who'd spotted the house first and seen its development potential. But it was a listed building and a complex project so there was a lot of work involved. The fact that we were living five minutes' walk away meant that we probably spent too much time under the builders' feet. It was another layer of stress to deal with.

On a freezing night in Castres, two weeks before the Six Nations opener in Edinburgh and with only twenty-two minutes on the clock, I felt a pop in my calf. I was running back into position and stepped into a divot on the really poor surface.

Because of the calf, I missed the first two rounds of the Six Nations. Losing in Edinburgh put an end to our hopes of a Grand Slam, and the chance of a title went on a noisy, controversial night in Cardiff, where I had two extended spells off the pitch, one for a yellow card for not rolling away and the second for a HIA. Wayne Barnes and Cardiff. Not my favourite combo.

At least we had a great finish to the tournament at the

Aviva, beating England 13–9 to end their eighteen-game winning streak and deny them a Slam. It was funny seeing Dylan
Hartley receive the trophy in the middle of the pitch while
we were still on our lap of honour. That might sound a bit
ungracious, but I felt like we owed England one.

It's always a good idea to finish the Six Nations strongly in a
Lions year. I was feeling confident enough of selection, having
been a Test starter in 2013. But doubts creep up on you.

The squad was to be named at noon on a Wednesday, and
we had weights until 11.30. I grabbed a recovery shake and
then a coffee on the way back home. Laura had a few friends
around with their kids, and from my car I could see them
watching the announcement on TV, see them celebrating
when my name was called. That's how I found out.

From that point, all I needed was an injury-free run and a
strong finish to the season with Leinster. I got neither. That
Sunday we lost in Clermont in the Champions Cup semis – a
big improvement on the previous season and a measure of
Stu's influence, but still a disappointment. In May, we were
stuffed 27–15 by Scarlets in the league semis at the RDS. A
disastrous result, especially given that the final was scheduled
for the Aviva the following week.

My relationship with Leo was strained. He wanted me to
be a leader, but at the same time he didn't want me constantly
pulling people up on their mistakes. I found it hard to be one
without doing the other, and I resented the fact that I was the
only one who was calling people out. With Ireland, I could
leave that to Joe or Faz. With Leinster, sloppy mistakes would
be ignored unless the Big Bad Wolf piped up: me.

Midway through the first half of the Scarlets game I had a
heavy collision with Gareth Davies and took a bang to the

head. I had the migraine aura, and I convinced the medics that I was OK to carry on. But I played poorly, so I did the team no favours, plus I gave Warren Gatland, the Lions coach, reason to doubt my form.

There was a further consequence to us losing that night. Having a free weekend the following week meant that I was in line to play the Lions' tour opener in Whangārei, against the New Zealand Barbarians. And believe me, this was a game anyone in their right mind would have wanted to avoid.

We'd only touched down in New Zealand three days previously, having travelled for the guts of two days across eleven time zones. After such an arduous trip, it takes at least a week to get sleep patterns on to local time, even with the assistance of melatonin tablets. So I found myself dozing off on the five-hour drive from Auckland to Whangārei in our sponsored 4x4s. It was no way to prepare for a game and it shouldn't be allowed to happen again.

I considered flagging the head knock that I'd taken against the Scarlets as a reason for not playing, but then decided against it, because of all the concussion talk that had attached itself to me.

We knew the media would give us a hammering when we scraped home 13–7 against a team made up of fringe players. Seeing as I'd been hauled ashore after forty-eight mediocre minutes, I came in for special attention.

It's not like I was searching for what they were saying about me. It's just that when you're lying in the darkness of your hotel room, wide awake at 3 a.m., you want to know what is happening in the world of sport. One headline on the Sky Sports site jumped out at me: 'Sexton's tour already over', or something like that. Nice. I didn't click on the link but I didn't need to.

Although the 2018 European Cup final was a terrible match, it was special to lift the trophy for the fourth time after beating my former club, Racing. (Inpho/Dan Sheridan)

To beat the All Blacks, you've got to win the big moments – like this one in Dublin in 2018, when Jacob Stockdale and I tackled Ben Smith into touch. The Aviva that night was as noisy and manic as I've ever experienced it. (Inpho/Gary Carr)

At the World Rugby Awards in Monaco, November 2018, with Laura and my long-time advisor and friend Ciarán Medlar. It was special to be named World Player of the Year, though Laura and Ciarán thought it was hilarious that I had lost my voice and couldn't give my speech.

We went into the last match of the 2019 Six Nations in Cardiff with an outside chance of retaining the championship, but our form had dipped and the game was a disaster. In a moment of frustration I threw the ball towards the ref and was lucky not to hit him. (Inpho/Bryan Keane)

In the 2019 World Cup quarter-final against the All Blacks, our skills let us down and we just didn't play: you can see it on my face. Joe Schmidt took a lot of flak for our decline in his last season, but people should remember how much he accomplished. Irish rugby owes him a lot. (Inpho/Billy Stickland)

When Andy Farrell took over as Ireland coach, he dramatically changed the way we attacked, making all of us decision-makers. He also made the environment more relaxed and encouraged us to be ourselves. (Inpho/Dan Sheridan)

After I was omitted from Warren Gatland's 2021 Lions squad, I dug some jerseys out of the attic and toasted the selection with my brother Mark (England) and my friend David (Scotland) – saving the Wales jersey for myself, of course.

With Amy, Laura, Sophie (on Laura's shoulders) and Luca after winning my hundredth cap in November 2021. I'd never felt so much love on a rugby pitch, and we put in a great performance – the first of several in the Andy Farrell era.

Winning a Test series in New Zealand – something no visiting team had done in the professional era – was a huge achievement. It was brilliant to walk down the tunnel after we came from behind to win the decisive third Test and to hail the Irish supporters in Wellington. (Inpho/Billy Stickland)

Leading the team out for the 2023 Six Nations opener in Cardiff. We were in a very different place from where we'd been the last time we played there in a World Cup year. (Inpho/Dan Sheridan)

To captain Ireland to a Grand Slam was one of the goals I set myself late in my career – and we achieved it in 2023, playing brilliant rugby. (Inpho/Dan Sheridan)

I was rusty for our crucial group game against South Africa in the 2023 World Cup but the Irish support in the Stade de France was spectacular and adrenaline carried me through 72 minutes of an exceptionally intense match. You can see how elated I was at the final whistle. (Inpho/Dan Sheridan)

The end of our World Cup – following a narrow defeat to New Zealand in the quarter-final – was also the end of my rugby career. Luca, who had enjoyed some great moments around the team over the previous couple of years, was as devastated as the rest of us, but the healing process started when he looked up at me and said, 'You're still the best, Dad.'
(Inpho/Dan Sheridan)

At a dinner marking the opening of the International Rugby Experience Museum in Limerick. It was good to catch up with the two other living male Grand Slam-winning Ireland captains, Rory Best and Brian O'Driscoll.

With my siblings – Mark, Gillian and Jerry – at Mark's wedding.

With Laura and the kids in one of our favourite places, the Bold Octopus restaurant in the Algarve in Portugal.

In fairness to Gats, he told the press it would be unfair to judge anyone on that performance. I still felt judged, though, and the combination of paranoia and jet lag is not a pleasant one. It's one of my prouder achievements that I recovered from that low point to play in all three Tests, starting two of them.

In a sense I was lucky because I didn't have time to over-think my situation. The tour schedule was my friend. With midweek games, a Lions tour keeps everyone busy, and because of injuries to other players, I was busier than most. Dan Biggar failed a HIA during the second game so I got forty-four minutes off the bench against the Blues. Next it was Jonny Davies failing a HIA against the Crusaders, allow-ing myself and Owen Farrell some time together as twin playmakers. It went well and we won. My tour was back on. Gats came out with some line about me having my 'mojo' back. That pissed me off. I hadn't lost my mojo in Whangārei. I was just half-asleep due to jet lag.

The Saturday before the first Test, we played the Māori in Rotorua – the fourth Test, as it was being called. As Owen had a niggle, I got the 10 jersey and went really well. It was my best performance in a while, and we won comfortably.

I knew Owen would start the following week. He had just won a Champions Cup with Saracens and was in top form. It was just a question of whether Gats and Rob Howley wanted to go with two playmakers (me at 10, Owen at 12) or to use Ben Te'o's power to counteract Sonny Bill Williams.

It was Dad who delivered the bad news a few days later. The team hadn't been announced yet, but Gerry Thornley had had a stab at it in the *Irish Times* and we knew that he was close to Gatland: Farrell at 10, Te'o at 12, Sexton at 22.

I heard the team officially later that day when Gats read it out to the squad. I hadn't expected a heads-up from the coaching team beforehand. That's not the way it works with the Lions and I completely respect that. I did appreciate it when Rob took me aside afterwards and told me that it had been 'an incredibly tight call'.

I was gutted, of course. I'd set out with the ambition to start all three Tests on two tours. No Irish number 10 had ever done that. But I could see where they were coming from, especially with the form that Ben Te'o was in. The only thing I had an issue with was the preparation in the week of that first Test. Suddenly we were doing double sessions when I thought we should have been tapering down. I wasn't the only one thinking this.

It was actually unlike Gatland. What I liked about him was that he had a good sense of what players needed and wanted. I liked the way he talked, liked the buttons he pressed. I wouldn't rate him as highly as Joe or Faz as a technical coach, but then those two are among the best ever. As a manager and a selector, I thought Gats was quality.

He went up in my estimation, of course, when he picked me to start the second Test. I reckoned I had a good chance when we lost the first Test 30–15. The Lions had to try something different. Owen and I had already showed that we had a good understanding against the Crusaders. Just to make sure, I tried to impose my will on proceedings in training, before the side had even been picked.

Wellington was wet. We squeaked home 24–21, despite playing most of the game against fourteen men after Sonny Bill had been sent off for a high shot on Anthony Watson. Our own indiscipline didn't help, but we did enough to show that the team operated better with myself and Owen pulling the strings. Playing with Owen was a dream for any 10. His communication and decision-making take the pressure off. We spent a lot of time rooming together and talking, so playing off each other seemed easy.

My biggest regret about that tour was what happened after Wellington, when we had some mandatory 'bonding' for a couple of days down in Queenstown. This was a bad idea and I think it reduced our chances of making history.

The bonding idea took root because the 2009 Lions went on the piss in their final week in South Africa and ended up winning the final Test. Big deal. That series was already over. The Springboks picked their second-string side for the last Test.

We did it again in Australia four years later, but it wasn't like the Test match squad were on the beer down in Noosa. I was fine with having a few beers the night of the second Test, recover Sunday, organizational meeting Monday, train Tuesday, off Wednesday, light run Thursday and so on. Instead we ended up training Wednesday, Thursday and Friday because we did virtually nothing except 'bond' at the start of the week. We were supposed to be preparing for a series decider against the best team in the world at Eden Park. A shot at history. It was crazy. Unprofessional.

As a result, I don't think those Lions maxed out on their potential, not with the athletes we had at our disposal. And I'm not pointing the finger solely at Gats here. I blame the senior players for not taking control of the situation and making sure we prepped properly. I include myself in that. We had enough experience in the group to speak up. I wish I'd said something.

Sam Warburton, as captain, could have said something as well. He is a bright bloke and an impressive talker. This was also his second tour so he had more gravitas than in 2013, when Gats would often lean on the experience of Paulie and Drico. Sam's great skill as a captain was in his management of referees, in how he picked his battles and chose the moment to intervene.

The most famous example of this, of course, came right at the end of that final Test. I'm not sure if it was Sam or the TMO who convinced referee Romain Poite to award 'accidental offside' against Ken Owens and therefore a scrum to New Zealand rather than the penalty that probably would have given them the series win. Sam was certainly calm in a crisis, though, and it was no harm.

In the circumstances, a 15–15 draw and a tied series felt more like a win to the Lions and was certainly greeted as one by the management team. I don't know how you can set off on tour talking about winning in New Zealand and then celebrate a draw. But there you have it.

I was a bit beaten up physically. I'd fractured my wrist in the second Test and ruptured ankle ligaments in the third. But when I looked back at where I'd been mentally in the first week of the tour, I knew I had reason to be proud of what I'd achieved.

I came home to discover that our beautiful new home had been furnished and fitted and decorated. Laura, the project manager, had worked wonders in my absence. I could also look forward to a couple of weeks in Portugal and getting some sun on my weary bones. The cast on my wrist and boot on my ankle didn't take away from the fact that I was happy with life for the first time in a while. I had no idea of the storm that was brewing.

16

The 2017/18 season was special: a Grand Slam and a series win in Australia with Ireland, Leinster's first league and Champions Cup double – and still our only one, at the time of writing.

It was also the season when my frustration levels reached the point where I was on the verge of leaving the club for good. I remember coming home one evening to tell Laura that my relationships with Leo and Guy had broken down, that I'd had enough. I was convinced that my time at the club was over.

The trouble came to a head in September, although the cause of the tension actually went back two seasons, to Leo's first season in charge.

I could sense that Leo and Guy were pissed off that I'd missed a big chunk of the previous season when I checked myself into Santry. I'd been absent for chunks of that 2017 pre-season, too, returning home from the Lions with a broken wrist and in a protective boot for my injured ankle. I could imagine what they were saying: *Yer man is on the radio saying the culture at Leinster is nowhere where it needs to be. When was the last time he turned up to work?*

Guy called me into his office one day to ask why I hadn't come in to try the new Leinster kit on for size, as everybody was expected to do and as I'd been asked to do a few times. Then he went off on one, how I was always talking about standards yet wasn't maintaining them myself, how I was hardly ever there, how I'd missed the lads' pre-season game against Gloucester up in Templeville Road.

He was wrong on that front, actually. I had turned up, though I didn't hang around for the post-match BBQ as my stomach was at me. But there was something else he wanted to get off his chest, another 'unexplained' absence from the previous Christmas, during the Santry phase – a Champions Cup match against Northampton at the Aviva. He said he knew that I'd been at a party the previous night. So I could go to a party but I couldn't support the lads the next day?

That wasn't the full story, though. Yes, Laura and I had been invited to a party, by Paul Coulson, who was chairman of the Ardagh Group. I had driven and we only stayed a while as I was training the next morning, an extra session I had planned on the Saturday morning. As it happened, I had a back spasm during the session and sent a message through to one of the Leinster physios that it didn't make sense for me to be sitting in the Aviva in the middle of December with a bad back. The physio agreed.

Eight months on, however, this was still a sore point with Guy. And it was now a sore point with me, to have my professionalism and commitment questioned like this. I prided myself on both. Our conversation got a bit heated. In fairness, Guy apologized subsequently and said he might have gone about things in a different way.

Leo was on my case too. He wanted to know why I hadn't spoken to him about being part of the players' leadership group. His idea was that anyone who wanted to be involved should have put their case to him.

My response to this was pretty snotty, I admit. 'Listen, Leo,' I said. 'I don't need to come and promote myself to get into your leadership group. If you want me in it, grand. If you don't, that's grand too.' Or words to that effect. I can be a stubborn bollocks at times and this was probably something I shouldn't have said.

He wanted to know why I was so unhappy about the place all the time. He explained that I couldn't just keep flying off the handle with people. I was the senior pro now. People looked up to me, he said. I did understand where he was coming from. It was true that I had been miserable the previous season, before Stuart arrived. We were a mess, and I wish I could go back and change the way I led through that time. I was much happier after Stuart started, but I was injured quite a bit that season, and when you have to sit and watch matches you're never going to be in great form.

Leo reminded me that when we'd been winning Heineken Cups together, some of these guys were kids – James Ryan had been in Edinburgh in 2009 as a twelve-year-old supporter. Yes, I had to maintain standards but I had to do it in a subtler and more reasoned way. Looking back, this all made sense. I hadn't considered that the younger lads might be treading on eggshells around me.

Our little chat didn't end well. I stormed off home and gave Laura the debrief. I told her I couldn't believe what had just happened. I said I wasn't sure I wanted to go back. But that evening I received a text from Stu. Could I take a call? He'd heard about that afternoon. He wanted to chat.

We ended up having a long text conversation in which I outlined my frustrations with the way that things were being done at Leinster. I tried to explain that my frustrations were coming from a good place. I said I thought we could be so much better. Stu said that he wanted to meet, to hear my ideas. So we met, and had a long, productive chat.

Our get-togethers would become weekly occurrences. We talked rugby: opponents, game-plans and so on. He said he wanted to involve me more in game-plans and preparation. As a former schoolteacher, maybe he knew that the best way to treat the troublemaker in the class is to give him responsibility! Soon I was watching footage of our next opponents and sending ideas to Girvan and Isa on Sunday nights.

My relationship with Stu grew from there. I hadn't got to know him that well in his first season, mainly because I'd missed so much through injury. I think he began to trust my judgement and understand my mentality more. I loved his coaching. His dedication to the job and work ethic was amazing. I used to love the videos he put together, using documentaries on other sports that were relevant to what we were trying to achieve. He used to challenge me on my leadership too, showing me clips of when I mishandled a referee. He made me aware of the positive and negative effects that my personality could have on the group. He taught me how to harness that drive to make a positive trait.

Another Stu was also a big help to me with a different set of problems I had around that time. My good mate Stuart O'Flanagan, later Leinster's team doctor, probably took more calls from me that summer than anyone else. I'd had a proper health scare after returning home from the Lions tour, when my nervous system started sending out loud alarm signals.

The first sign that something was up came in Manchester at the end of August. Mark, Jerry and I took Dad over to see Man U play Leicester, to celebrate his sixtieth birthday. We were having lunch before the game when my hands went pale and I started to feel like I was going to faint. I wondered if it was an allergic reaction to something I had eaten. I took an antihistamine and got through the rest of the day.

The following week I was at the airport heading to Portugal with the family when I had the same fainting sensation. On that holiday I had palpitations, stomach cramps, loose bowels. Normally I'd try and suck it up, but this was different. I called a couple of the Leinster medics to try and find out what was wrong with me. Professor John Ryan said he would carry out some tests as soon as I returned. Stuart O'Flanagan, my old Bective pal, tried to reassure me.

It turned out that I was suffering from Irritable Bowel Syndrome, the symptoms of which include cramping, diarrhoea or constipation, or both. It can feel like you constantly need to go to the jacks. It is not pleasant and it doesn't go away easily. I lost four or five kilos and spent a lot of time on the toilet that summer, sometimes in the middle of the night.

But IBS didn't explain the light-headedness, the cold hands or the palpitations. The next time those things happened, I got in touch with Jim McShane, another Leinster doc. Jim told me that it sounded like stress. But it couldn't be stress, I said. I'd finished the rugby season well; we'd settled in our lovely new home; it was the off-season and I was spending quality time with Laura and the kids. It was the first time in a long time that I felt relaxed.

Jim explained that stress often manifests itself as a delayed reaction. I'd been going non-stop, since for ever. Sometimes it's after the adrenaline stops pumping that the system collapses.

Stuart backed up this diagnosis and prescribed a radical overhaul of the way I managed my time, my body and mind. That started with learning to say no. If someone called and asked if I could make an appearance somewhere, I had to decline politely. When I organized my schedule, I was to leave a gap after every commitment. For example, if training was over at 3.30, I wasn't to tell Laura that I'd be home at 3.45. I shouldn't be constantly in a rush.

'You need to be good to yourself, Johnny,' Stu said. 'Put yourself first.'

Up to then, even the way that I recovered from training had been stressful. I went in for hard, vigorous massages or ice baths – things that increased cortisol, the stress hormone. I'd be in a plunge-pool, looking at my watch, wondering if I could get home to spend some time with my kids before they went to bed. Rather than recovering, I'd been making things worse. I was constantly in 'fight or flight' mode.

Stuart recommended more calming techniques to wind down after training: reading, acupuncture, mindfulness, meditation. He was especially keen on meditation. Everything was designed to settle the nervous system. We'd already been introduced to this with Ireland by Joe Schmidt, but I took a bit of convincing that it could make a difference. I had a 'fixed mindset' about stuff like that. Meditation? I was useless at it. We had mindfulness sessions in Carton House, in the team room before training. You'd be sitting there, eyes closed, with the guide encouraging you to focus on nothing except your breath, or on the sounds in the room, on the here and now. But in my mind?

We need to iron out a kink in that launch play.

Or:

I need to bring that physical therapy session forward by twenty-five minutes.

I was more suggestible now, though. Sometimes you learn things the hard way. When Stuart outlined the benefits of mindfulness, I was ready to listen. He explained how being mindful could calm the storm that was raging in my gut.

When he told me it could also make me a better rugby player, I was even more attentive. He was able to cite scientific studies about its effects, about improved productivity, creativity, energy, how it was recommended by so many leaders of industry.

In simple terms, to be mindful is to live in the present, to block out the past and the future. The opposite of what I was currently doing. How does that translate to rugby? It means that you don't dwell on what has been or what might be. You focus only on what is in front of you.

Like I say, I wasn't very good at this. I used to agonize over mistakes and their consequences. That season, with the help of apps like Headspace on my phone and a pair of headphones, I taught myself to stay 'present'. On the team bus going to the stadium, I was usually to be found lying on my back in the aisle, eyes closed, following the voice of my mindfulness guide – not staring out the window, Oasis blaring in my earphones, mind racing. For a long time, my mind was my biggest asset, always active on and off the pitch. But now it had all become too much. Becoming aware of this changed me for sure.

During the Six Nations that season, Rob Kearney said he'd never seen me so chilled. I just wished I'd known more about the mental side of the game sooner. It's something you have to work at, and it's easy to slip back into bad habits. But that season, being mindful made a huge difference to my rugby and to my life.

The trust between Stuart Lancaster and me grew that season. I remember telling him one week that I didn't think the team was in the right frame of mind before a Pro14 game against Benetton. I've always been good at that – knowing when people aren't switched on, knowing when to pick a fight with someone in training, to sharpen the mood. This time I didn't pick a fight or try to change the mood in the camp. I just told Stu I thought the lads were a bit flat, maybe complacent. Sure enough, we lost, at home. 'You called it,' he said afterwards.

I didn't follow the NFL, so it was Stu who told me about Tom Brady, the New England Patriots quarterback who was still going strong aged forty. He said he could see similarities between Brady and me.

I watched the stuff Stu sent me on Brady. There was a shot of him when he was first drafted, a long gangly guy with no muscle definition. You could see he was not very quick over the ground but had a quick brain. I guess this was the connection that Stu made – like Brady, I was a late bloomer but a student of the game who learned to become more professional; who was hard on those around him but learned when to encourage; who shared ideas with his coach.

Stu was strong on leadership, on communication and building relationships. He got us thinking about the different personality types within the group. One test we did, which involved answering one hundred multiple-choice questions, grouped everyone into four main personality types, differentiated by colour: blues are deep thinkers, analytical; greens are cool, laid-back and patient; yellows are extrovert and fun; and reds are strong-willed, drivers, highly competitive. When all the answers had been collated, Stu announced that we had lots of the various colours but only one pure red. There was a pause, as everyone looked over at me, and then we all exploded into laughter. It was funny for sure, but it was an eye-opener. I was now the outlier, and it was me that needed to change.

With Stu's encouragement, I took more ownership at Leinster. It was still a surprise when, for my first game of the season, against Edinburgh at the RDS, Leo approached me and asked me to be captain in Isa's absence – he was injured at the time. After what had happened a few weeks earlier, I actually laughed out loud. 'Are you serious?'

He was serious. And I was honoured. I was also excited about the team that was coming together. We had plenty of experience in the pack – Scott Fardy had arrived, Cian Healy was on top of his game, Dev Toner and Seán Cronin were current internationals – but we also had some exciting talents coming through in James Ryan and Dan Leavy, guys who brought energy and a bit of edge.

Meanwhile Robbie Henshaw had arrived from Connacht and James Lowe from the Chiefs in New Zealand. I loved playing with Lowey from day one. He brought a special energy to the team, especially in attack. I also learned pretty quickly that he beats defenders for fun, so every time the ball went to the left wing I would run an inside support line, knowing that there was a good chance I'd get the ball back. I picked up a few tries that season off him. We also had young guys like Garry Ringrose and Josh van der Flier who were ultra-professional in everything they did. It was a nice blend and it showed in our results. Before Christmas we won thirteen out of fifteen games.

We started to enjoy each other's company, too. It's a feature of most successful teams. That's what I remember of the Leinster side that dominated Europe around the turn of that decade – we won together and we celebrated together. So, when we had a good Champions Cup win away to Glasgow in October of that season, Laura and I invited everyone around for beers and pizza – I was captain that day, in Isa's absence. Celebrating wins became a bit of a tradition again that season, especially after European games on the road.

We became closer as a group. You can't measure the effect of those friendships on performances but I suspect they do make a difference when you're under the pump – as we were against Exeter on consecutive weekends. We won both games and ended up qualifying for the knockouts as top seeds.

It was all coming together nicely. If only people had known at the start of that season what was going on behind the scenes. I do appreciate looking back that I could have been more cooperative and a better leader. I'm forever grateful to Stu for talking sense into me and guiding me for the rest of our time together. Looking back I'm also very grateful to Leo and Guy. We all wanted the same thing, and their feedback gave me great learnings but also a crazy drive to win again with Leinster.

Stade de France, 3 February 2018

There are just over three minutes on the clock as Anthony Belleau stands over a penalty to the left of the posts. France are 13–12 in front. This is the first round of the Six Nations and already it looks like we have made a balls of our bid to win a Grand Slam.

The Slam was a stated aim among the team that year. Many of us had been involved in the back-to-back championship wins in Joe's first two seasons with Ireland and we were proud of that achievement. But we reckoned there was more in us than winning the title on points difference. We'd had a clean sweep of wins over South Africa, Fiji and Argentina in November. We'd had an infusion of special young talent – Ringrose, Ryan, Leavy, Van der Flier, Carbery, Jacob Stockdale.

So why not a Slam? And why not say it openly? The senior players agreed that we should come out and say it publicly, that the pressure of having to deliver on a stated goal would be good for us. Joe wasn't sure about this at first. He was still big on focusing game by game, day by day even. He also had humility at the top of his list of important traits for his teams.

Now, as Belleau stands over the kick, it looks as though Joe was right about the dangers of bigging ourselves up.

In the huddle behind the posts, I try to make sure everyone has understood the permutations. If Belleau converts the penalty, we need a try; if he misses, a penalty or a drop-goal will do it for us. We'll see how they set up to receive but I'm looking to target Teddy Thomas. In other words, Fergus McFadden, playing on the left wing opposite Thomas, is the man we need to win back possession. No better man.

I position myself behind the posts so that I can get my hands on the ball as soon as possible. Belleau pulls his kick wide.

77:30

I drop-kick the ball left as planned, low and shallow and at a good height for Ferg to catch it above his head. But Iain Henderson didn't hear my conversation with Ferg. He plucks the kick out of the air and piles forward. We are off.

78:10

After several narrow punches, I spread the ball across our 22 and Rob has to juggle to hold on to the pass. It is a miserable day in Saint-Denis and handling is a struggle. France are defending hard. They are fitter than previous French teams and the referee, Nigel Owens, seems blind to any of their transgressions.

But we have prepared for this with Joe. We have visualized extended periods of defence and attack. Our reference point is the All Blacks game of 2013. We'd have won that day if we'd been able to keep the ball efficiently and legally through multiple phases – coincidentally it was Nigel who pinged Jack McGrath for going off his feet. And we'd have won if we'd been able to hold our defensive shape for more than the 100 seconds it took the All Blacks to put Ryan Crotty over in the corner.

Joe set four minutes of full-on, uninterrupted effort as our target – 'killer defence' or 'killer attack' were the 'sausage bag' drills that he dragged us through. If we could keep going at 100 per cent for four unbroken minutes of maximum efficiency in training, we'd be able to handle any match situation.

80:00

As the match clock turns red, we are still in our own half, despite recycling the ball through about twenty-five phases. I can see Earlsy calling for a cross-kick on the right. He times his jump to perfection and his opposite number, Virimi Vakatawa, opts not to challenge for fear of conceding a penalty. Earlsy is dragged down beyond their 10-metre line. A big yardage gain.

80:40

John Ryan carries into contact near the French 10-metre line. Sébastien Vahaamahina clambers all over him to prevent release. I'm so convinced it's a penalty that I sit down to stretch out a bit of tightness in preparation for the kick. (People thought I was suffering from cramp, but I was just giving myself less to do before my penalty-kicking routine.)

But Nigel has clearly decided that this match is not going to be decided by a penalty kick.

81:40

The French are showing no signs of weakening. We need to send three or four into every ruck just to maintain possession. Punching close in is not working, so I go wide to Bundee Aki, but we lose metres as Belleau piles in.

82:25

Phase 39. Hendy pops up again, barrelling past a blue jersey and beyond the French 10-metre line once more. Jack McGrath cleans decisively so Conor has clean ball and the next runner – CJ Stander – can time his run. He gains us a precious two metres.

The ball is now midway between the 10 and the 22. The French are tiring but so are we. We've been attacking for close to five minutes – well past the four minutes we've been drilling with Joe. It's time. I give Conor a nod.

When you've been in a partnership as settled as ours, a nod is all it takes. He is now in the habit of looking at me just before he arrives at every ruck. There is no point in picking the ball and then looking for me, as every millisecond counts.

This time when he looks, he sees me step into the pocket and nod. Then he looks again, and again, as if to say: Are you serious? I'm standing forty-five metres from the sticks, so he knows that I'm on the edge of my range and we're on a wet surface.

Fortunately, the French don't expect me to go for it either. Max Machenaud is hovering behind the ruck rather than right at the hindmost foot.

Conor's pass is on the money, aimed at my right hip with speed. Every detail counts in these situations. Now all of the sessions with Dave Alred pay dividends, all of the reps in isolation after everyone else has hit the showers. Posture. Stay tall. I no longer have to think these things consciously because they have become ingrained through hours of practice. I just know I need to give it an extra little oomph to get it there.

82:38

As soon as I strike the ball, I'm confident that it's going to make it. But as I'm back-pedalling, I see that Nigel doesn't signal. The visuals are a bit deceptive at the Stade de France, with the crowd behind the posts so far back from the playing surface, so suddenly I look to the screen. Is Nigel going to the TMO? Then I look back towards the posts and I know – partly because there's a crowd of madmen galloping towards me.

Thankfully a photographer captured that moment, from behind me. I'm half-falling backwards as Bundee is the first to hop on me. You can see the euphoria on the faces of Ferg, Rob and Robbie Henshaw. I have the shot framed on the wall in my office at home. It's actually the only action shot in the house. I just love the way it captures my team-mates' joy at that moment. Four close friends chasing me with sheer joy in their faces. It is moments like this that make all the practice worthwhile.

The French TV coverage didn't do it justice, as the director was working for a local audience. The camera keeps cutting to Guilhem Guirado, their captain, who's sitting on the bench, head in hands. But I've seen the film from the camera above the pitch, aerial shots of this pile of Irish players heaped up on top of each other, celebrating like mad. And me at the bottom, half-smothered but indescribably happy.

*

The pivotal game of the championship was Wales – round three, at home. We were hyped for it right from the time we assembled in Carton House the weekend before. Joe was wired, too. You could hear the venom in his voice in our meeting that Sunday night.

We all had our personal motivations. Joe's record against Wales was his worst against all the Six Nations teams. Going up against his fellow Kiwi probably added an edge – Gats was always having pokes at him and us in the media about us playing a 'narrow' game.

I also had a score to settle with the Scarlets players who'd given me plenty of lip at the RDS in the Pro14 semi. Gareth Davies, the scrum-half, had been particularly gobby. Now he was in the papers saying that Wales were coming to Dublin for a bonus-point win.

Joe gave Davies a nickname that week: Bonus Point. For the entire build-up, whenever he'd be showing us Welsh clips, he'd say:

'Watch what Bonus Point does here.' Or 'This is where we can get at Bonus Point.'

We were wired. Maybe too wired. I completely overdid it in training that week and paid a price. On the Friday morning, as I bent over to place a ball on a tee, my back seized completely. Nightmare. I had about six hours of treatment, but I woke stiff and sore on the day of the game, a doubtful starter.

Adrenaline is amazing, though. By my reckoning, that 37–27 was one of my best games for Ireland, quite apart from being the game of the championship. Joe was full of praise, and there was nothing like kind words from him to lift the spirits – even if some people preferred to focus on the fact that I missed three of my seven shots at goal.

I also got some stick for taking a quick tap near the left

touchline when there was a kickable penalty with the game in the balance during the second half. Unfortunately, Jacob Stockdale hadn't read my thoughts – he was off getting sticky spray on his hands at the critical moment! Worse still, when I went into contact, I felt my hammy catch.

I bawled Jacob out of it. He needed to be alert – it's amazing how quickly defenders can switch off once a penalty is awarded in kickable territory. In fairness, Jacob paid his way that season with the number of tries he scored. Dan Leavy, Garry Ringrose and James Ryan were freakishly good too. The energy and self-belief that our youngsters brought was infectious.

I cajoled my body through the remainder of the championship. Luckily there was a two-week gap before Scotland, who had beaten England and France, and fancied themselves – as they generally do.

I barely trained for that fortnight, apart from mental training. Our mental skills coach, Gary Keegan, recorded an audio track for visualization purposes, to help me with place-kicking, taking me through the process from the moment the penalty is awarded: how I feel a sudden jolt of nervousness, how I regulate my breathing, get my heart rate down, how I receive the tee, how I place the ball on it and so on, right up to the moment that the ball bisects the posts. I listened to it a lot, listened to it in bed. If Gary only knew that his voice sent me to sleep! It worked, though. I kicked four out of five against the Scots, none of them easy, and we won 28–8.

That win secured us the title with a round still to go, but there were no celebrations. Winning a Slam in Twickenham was all that mattered.

All that stuff about how mindfulness transformed me that season? Not that week. I tried not to show the young lads in the side, but I was up the walls.

It got back to us that Eddie Jones had referred to us as the 'scummy Irish'. We used it in the build-up, of course, but it's not like we needed extra ammo. Also, I was paranoid about my hammy and my back. The forecast said cold and windy for Saturday: not good for place-kicking, not good for my back. I barely slept all week.

England surely knew that I wasn't 100 per cent, but we ended up using this to our advantage for CJ's try in the first half. As I popped to Tadhg Furlong and looped behind, Owen Farrell went after me, just as Joe predicted that he would. This left a hole for Bundee, who timed his pass to CJ perfectly.

I was off the field for a HIA when Jacob scored our third, to put us up 21–5 at the break. My back and ribs were seizing up, so I was never likely to go the distance. Ben Te'o, my old team-mate and friend, running over the top of me and smashing my nose was my last action. I was still able to enjoy watching from the touchline, safe in the knowledge that we were uncatchable.

We gave it a proper lash in London, and then had another party with wives, partners and families back in the Shelbourne the next day. It was an amazing sense of achievement: Ireland's third-ever Grand Slam, at Twickenham on St Patrick's Day. I'd been waiting nine years for this, having been side-stage for the 2009 Slam.

Two months later, as I was heading on to the pitch at the San Mamés stadium in Bilbao for my kicking routine, it was almost reassuring to hear a few hoots of derision from the Racing fans who turned up early. That's what you expect from French crowds. Subconsciously I almost wanted it. The Champions Cup final was my chance to prove to Racing that they hadn't seen the best of me. And of course there were other motivations: winning would bring us level with Toulouse on four titles, more than anyone else.

We did it, and yet I've never felt so deflated after winning a major trophy as I felt that day.

The rugby was crap – five penalty kicks to four, no tries, no quick ball, just a slog. It was no secret that Racing would try to stop us from playing, seeing as we were the best attacking side in the tournament. Beforehand Stu showed Wayne Barnes a few plays that we were going to use to check their rush defence, but he allowed them to live offside and kill ball all day.

Part of the reason I was subdued afterwards was that I'd had a clash of heads with Yannick Nyanga in the second half, and Isa took over the place-kicking towards the end. It brought on a migraine, so my vision was impaired for a few minutes, although the reason I gave the media was that I'd strained my groin. That was a porky, I'll admit.

This was at the post-match press conference, where I sat alongside Leo – captain and head coach, a picture of harmony. If only the media had known about the tension between us only months previously. Maybe some of them picked up on how often I mentioned Stu's contribution to our success. I didn't mean that to insult Leo. Stuart was the guy that turned around the club's fortunes, but he couldn't have done it without Leo. They were a perfect team.

The following night we had drinks in the Bridge in Ballsbridge, the pub owned by Jamie, Seánie and the Kearney brothers. There was still a double to be completed, so we hadn't planned to go completely wild, although when we arranged for the trophy to arrive things got a little wilder than we wanted. The following Tuesday we had a players' meeting where Isa and I spelled out the importance of finishing the job after so many previous near misses. It helped focus people's minds that Isa was finishing up, and we also owed it to Jamie, who had lost his battle with injury that February and who had been such an amazing servant to the club.

While we only squeezed past Munster in the semi, we played our best rugby of the season to beat the Scarlets in the Pro14 final. Having clinched the Slam in London, and then the Champions Cup in Bilbao, it was special to secure the double in Dublin before our fans.

It was amazing to think that only nine months previously I'd been at such a low ebb, worn down by IBS and by stress. Now, the prospect of a three-Test series in Australia was exciting. The Pro14 final was only my nineteenth game of the season for club and country. I was full of beans, to the extent that I was pissed off when Joe told me he'd be starting Joey Carbery in the first Test, in Brisbane.

I saw the logic, of course. We were just over a year out from the World Cup. Joey needed the experience of playing major Test opposition from the start of the game. But I was pissed off at Joey. The day after the Pro14 final, he had announced that he was leaving for Munster. I understood the reasons for moving, of course. I might have done the same thing in his position when I was younger. I had no problem with people doing what was best for them. Months previously, Joey had asked me for my advice, seeing as it was such a big decision. We got on pretty well in general and I was happy to help wherever I could. He told me that moving to Ulster was a possibility and then Munster had come up as an option. I told him to trust his instinct and to commit to whatever decision he made.

But that was the last I'd heard of it until now. He had told us he was staying. I wondered when he had made the call – and why he had waited until now to tell us, when he had picked up two winner's medals for Leinster. I wondered how Ross Byrne felt about all this, seeing as he'd committed to Leinster but had missed both finals.

I didn't like the way Joey was having such a laugh with all the Munster lads when we assembled in Carton House on the Monday before departure for Australia. It was all high-fives in the gym, right in front of the Leinster players that he'd just won a double with.

The Australia tour was one of the most enjoyable of my career. Australia's a little warmer and a little brighter than New Zealand at that time of year, especially in Brisbane, where we played the first Test. When the jet lag has you wide awake at 5 o'clock in the morning, there are places open where you can grab a coffee. Plus Joe was a little more chilled on that trip and we got to spend more down-time in each other's company.

I enjoyed it because it went well rugby-wise, too. It was a great series. We went one down in Brisbane, drew level in Melbourne and then it went down to the wire in Sydney, where we scrapped like dogs to hold on to our lead at the death.

That seemed like a regular pattern for us: winning matches by the quality of our defence in the dying minutes. That's what happens when you have the best defence coach in the world: Faz. It was the same against New Zealand that November, when the Aviva was as noisy and manic as I've ever experienced it – especially when Jacob scored that unforgettable try just after the break.

We didn't realize it at the time, but that Ireland team had just peaked.

*

Don't believe any elite sportsperson who tells you that awards don't matter. Trophies and medals are the most important, for sure. Whatever you win as a team is what counts – and in rugby, you are more dependent on team-mates than in most sports. But individual awards are nice. Of course they are.

We're talking about World Player of the Year. The big one. It often felt like we paid special attention to this award in Ireland because only one Irishman had won it – Keith Wood, back in 2001 – and especially because Brian didn't get it in 2009, when he seemed the obvious choice. How he didn't win it is beyond me.

It turns out that Brian was on the judging panel this year and he was on the flight out to Monaco a week after our victory over New Zealand. There was plenty of banter. He knew the result of the players' vote – every squad member from every Tier One nation had been asked to give his first, second and third choice – and the judges could use this to inform their own decision. The panel still had to meet for the last time to make their final decision.

The gig at the Salle des Étoiles was as glam as it gets for rugby. Laura was excited. I should have just relaxed and enjoyed the occasion – it's rare enough that we have a night away like this, without the kids. Somehow, though, I managed to turn it into a stress-fest.

My voice was the problem. Soon after we arrived in Monaco I had a meeting with World Rugby as a players' rep, discussing plans for a global season. I talked a little bit at that, then I had to do a fair bit of media on the red carpet, followed by a reception for several hundred people where everyone was shouting over one another. My voice went from hoarse to hoarser to . . . completely gone.

That's when I started panicking. *What if I have to speak in front of all these people?*

Laura told me not to stress. She was on her second or third glass of champagne at this stage. 'Don't worry, Jono. Worrying's only going to make it worse, love.' This only made me worse. I slipped outside, away from the noise, and called Stuart O'Flanagan back in Dublin. Only he couldn't hear me. No one could hear me. So I texted him. He suggested gargling with warm water and lemon. It didn't work. I tried hot whiskey. No luck.

Laura, Rob, and my advisor and good friend Ciarán Medlar were well on it by this stage, so my situation was hilarious as far as they were concerned. Fortunately, Rory Best had stayed sober as he'd been tipped off that we'd been chosen as Team of the Year. He agreed that if I was named as Player of the Year, he'd accompany me on stage and read some thank-yous on my behalf: to my team-mates, my coaches and especially to Laura.

And that's how it worked out. My name was called. I smiled and nodded, and Besty did the needful. As MC Alex Payne put it: 'For once, a speechless Johnny Sexton!'

There were more interview requests, but it was pointless. I was literally speechless. Twenty minutes after receiving the award, I was back up in our room. What should be a career highlight was a damp squib.

Things improved the next day, though. My voice was back, which helped. I'd booked a nice restaurant and four of us had a long and lovely lunch – Laura, Rob, Ciarán and me. Then we strolled around Monte Carlo till it was time to head to the airport, myself and Rob reminiscing about Leinster Under-16 summer training in Bective back in the day.

17

Just to recap, then. Ireland were ranked number one in the world and we had the best coach in the sport. Leinster were European champions and I had just joined an exclusive club that had some legendary out-halves among its membership: Jonny Wilkinson, Beauden Barrett and the guy I rank as the best ever, Dan Carter. I had a lot to be happy about.

I felt valued by my employers, too. The previous summer, just after the tour to Australia, I'd had a sit-down with David Nucifora, who wanted my thoughts on my plans going forward. We discussed his idea of Faz taking over from Joe, who'd decided to step down after the World Cup in Japan. Naturally, I was enthusiastic about the idea, especially when David told me that Faz was keen to keep me involved, too.

This was brilliant news. Say the IRFU hired a coach from outside the system, the new man might have wanted a post-World Cup clear-out, one that included getting rid of the thirty-four-year-old out-half. But Faz and I had a good relationship and he'd made it clear he wanted me to keep going, and not just for a transition period. My new IRFU deal would take me up to the end of the 2020/21 season, basically an eighteen-month extension. That would bring me close to my thirty-sixth birthday but we saw no reason to set limits. I had just completed a full season, twenty-two games in total, and my body felt good.

But could I relax and enjoy this special point in my career that Christmas of 2018? No: even then I found something to stress over. For all that the World Player of the Year award was wonderful, I felt sure that it came with a price attached.

I said as much to Laura while we were still in Monaco. She had innocently asked me if I'd ever dreamed of winning the award. Wait till you see, I told her. It will be used as a stick to beat me. She told me that I was over-thinking things, but I had this sneaking feeling that the rules had just changed.

I'd seen how the award had affected Beauden. He'd won it two years running. You'd think that would make him a national treasure in New Zealand, but no. It was like people were queueing up to have a pop at him as soon as he showed the slightest dip in form.

My hunch was right. It didn't take long for me to feel the heat. Initially, it came from Munster. After Leinster's game in Limerick at the end of that December, I became fair game for online abuse. And I was partly to blame, I admit.

I hadn't played in Thomond for six years and probably shouldn't have played that night. I'd been in bed with a bug over Christmas and I had some painful tendinitis in my knee. But I was now club captain and it was a big game. Leo and I agreed that I should play. We just didn't prepare like it was a big game. The squad Christmas party had taken a day's work out of our week. It's always hard to prepare during the Christmas period. Nothing about our prep was 100 per cent nailed on that week.

Our first mistake was forgetting to use the 'poker-face' routine that had been successful in Thomond Park on previous visits. It was something Joe had brought in to try and reduce the influence of the Munster supporters and certain players. No matter what happened on the pitch, good or bad, we would show no emotion, giving the Munster players – and therefore their supporters – nothing to feed off. We didn't bring the poker face with us on this occasion, and we paid for it.

Still, I didn't expect it to go as badly as it did. The game had barely started when Fineen Wycherley tackled me late and drove me into the ground. I reacted, pulling his scrum-cap off and generally throwing the toys out of the cot. In the middle of the tackle or the scuffle I managed to aggravate my knee issue. In other circumstances, I might have gone off for treatment, but you can't start a war and then just walk away from it.

Because of my reaction, referee Frank Murphy reversed the penalty and called me back to lecture me. Two minutes in, Thomond Park had their pantomime villain – and we had missed out on the chance to take an early lead.

Frank is actually an old Churchill Cup team-mate of mine, but we didn't get on well that night. He seemed to pick up on our every transgression while Munster were getting away with loads of stuff off the ball.

Soon there was another schemozzle near the touchline. For some reason Joey Carbery saw fit to run in and get involved. I yanked him out of it and he lost his balance.

Watching the clip later, I saw what a lot of people saw: shades of Croke Park 2009 and me yelling at O'Gara. Only I was no longer the young upstart. I was supposed to be setting a good example. I texted Joey afterwards to say that it was nothing personal. But when I thought about it, I was probably still pissed off at the way he'd left it so late to tell everyone at Leinster that he was leaving.

Munster won, but their supporters seemed to have more fun taking the piss out of us. At least that was how it looked on my Instagram feed. A few examples:

You really let yourself down tonight, Sexton. You're a disgrace.
You're a disgrace. Pack of thugs.
F**k off back to the Pale.
You've gone from World Player of the Year to World Dickhead
of the Year.

What really upset me was that Laura was upset. She thought that the Joey thing looked bad, and sent out the wrong message. She told me I had to be extra careful now, because I was Leinster captain, because of the World Rugby award.

This was fair enough, but I was still conflicted. My behaviour on the pitch showed how much I cared. I was just being me! What did the Munster fans want? For me to lie there and let Wycherley tickle my belly?

Some of the rush to judge me was based on the fact that we'd lost. We were still in it late on, despite playing most of the match without James Lowe, who was red-carded for a mis-timed aerial challenge. What if we'd won? Would my behaviour have been seen as courageous? Great leadership, setting the tone?

I care what supporters think, even people I don't know — though I wouldn't include Mr Keyboard Warrior in his Pyjamas from Tipperary, who had called me World Dickhead of the Year, and who had been blocked for his troubles. That's why it was so important for me to ignore as much of the media as I could. I really did care what people thought and said, so it affected me when I got exposed to it. I have always been that way, since I was a child.

I considered making a statement through Leinster, to defend myself, but then decided to call a few people for reassurance. Faz told me I'd done nothing wrong, that I was just being myself, that saying something publicly would only make it a bigger story. Paulie said pretty much the same thing. As a former captain, he had good insights on dealing with refs – when to speak, how to speak and what to say. Brian told me not to worry, that it would all blow over and to ignore the messages.

And yet it ate away at me, this idea that I'd let myself down. I wanted people to know that I'm essentially a good bloke. Over Christmas, we'd watched *The Greatest Showman* with the kids and, crazy as it might sound, I started identifying with the P. T. Barnum character, the guy who enjoys a bit of fame and celebrity and in the process loses sight of what really matters, which is running his circus.

Had I enjoyed all the adulation a bit too much? Coming up to that Christmas, it seemed like every second night was another awards night: RTÉ, *Irish Independent*, UK Rugby Writers. I knew that I had to keep my eye on the job at hand: Six Nations, then World Cup. I had a target on my chest now. We all did. Ireland, and Leinster – we were there to be shot down. This Munster flare-up had been well timed. Yes, it was a reminder.

I spoke to Stuart Lancaster about my dealings with Frank Murphy and specifically my body language. He said my physical behaviour was almost more important than what I said, and that I'd looked aggressive, confrontational.

I couldn't see a solution here. I'm no good at acting. I can't think one thing and show another. It's the way I am. But both Leo and Stu said pretty much the same thing. I'd have to work on my 'non-verbal communication'.

Stu was big on the concept of the red head / blue head and how those opposing mental states affect performance. I maintained that I could play with a red head but still make clear-headed, accurate (blue-headed) decisions under stress.

He just about accepted this. He merely pointed out that my body language could have an adverse effect on my own team-mates.

I can guess what you're thinking, though. If I called Farrell, O'Connell, O'Driscoll, Kearney and Lancaster, why didn't I call Schmidt? Why didn't I get Joe's feedback on that narky night in Thomond?

It's because I knew what he'd say and I knew I wouldn't like it.

Of course it wasn't just me who was being watched more closely now. After we'd beaten the All Blacks the previous November, their coach Steve Hansen said: Let's see how Ireland like being the number one side in the world. The implication was obvious. It's not easy when everyone else wants to knock you off your pedestal.

Hansen probably smiled when England came to the Aviva in the first round of the Six Nations and beat us 32–20. When you're top dog, everyone raises their planning and their performance by at least 10 per cent against you.

Losing to England supposedly sent us on a downward spiral, all the way to a heavy World Cup quarter-final defeat in Tokyo. It wasn't quite as simple as that, but it's fair to say 2019 did not provide many happy memories.

Joe tends to get most of the blame but that's unfair, and based to some extent on the fact that his relations with the media seemed to deteriorate. The players also have to take responsibility for failing to maintain the momentum that we'd built.

I don't know if Joe would admit to making a few mistakes. Everything is judged in hindsight. Everyone is an expert when they know the result. Joe is a genius, and he made decisions he thought were for the good of the team. Of course, it's natural to say now that we should have done this or that. I have looked back and said the same thing. Joe tried to change things up a bit, for example, to tell us before the Six Nations that everything was now secondary to the World Cup.

Some people thought that his early announcement of his departure after the World Cup was a mistake, as if it softened Joe's authority over us. Those people had clearly never worked under Joe Schmidt. Making the World Cup our sole focus didn't really work, though. But again that is in hindsight.

The idea of focusing on the World Cup was similar to the way we'd specified the Slam as our goal the previous season, forcing ourselves to think big. I guess Joe was also preparing us for some experimental selections to build squad depth – Robbie Henshaw played full-back against England when Rob was unavailable, for example.

But the danger with having a longer-term goal is that you can lose sight of what's immediately in front of you. This was Joe's mantra: the next game is the only thing that matters. As soon as we lost the England game, it felt like the bigger picture of prepping for Japan was forgotten anyway. Suddenly, it was all about salvaging the Six Nations.

The other mistake that we made was in not evolving our attacking game. Opponents analyse you more when you're the top side in the rankings, so you can't be a stationary target.

This came up for discussion at a meeting pre-Christmas but it was knocked back. Joe explained that the coaching group had decided that we would stick with the same attack plan – well-designed plays off set-pieces and a quick-rucking pressure game – but just get 10 per cent better at it. They felt we still had scope to improve what we were already doing.

People have asked me why the senior players didn't challenge Joe on this. We did, a bit. The Leinster guys enjoyed the way we trained under Lancaster and how we got comfortable playing unstructured rugby. We asked if we could work more in training on unstructured attack, to prepare us better for random situations. The misconception about Joe was he was this tyrant who you couldn't talk to. We spoke about everything and gave our opinion but we also trusted Joe to get it right. He had never let us down before.

There had been a good example in broken play during the New Zealand game, where I'd run to the short side and called one of our forwards for a pass 'out the back'. His pass was poor, though, and didn't go to hand. Just bad basics? Yes, but this had been the first time that week that this forward had been asked to make that type of pass in that situation, so it wasn't really such a surprise. We needed to make it a habit, and to make training so fast and unstructured that the game felt easy.

Joe's mantra was always about building good habits during the week so that things would come naturally on Saturday. Most of our game we had nailed: our starter plays, our defence off scrums, and so on. But we weren't as well prepared as we could have been for the random stuff that rugby can throw at you.

What prepares you for that is the type of training games we played with Stu at Leinster, where we worked in less structured situations to sharpen handling skills and spatial awareness. But was I about to tell Joe that his sessions compared unfavourably to Stu's? Joe was the best coach any of us had worked with, and the most successful one. And he was the boss.

International coaches aren't blessed with unlimited time, either. Was it possible to make changes with such short preparation windows? We had one camp in Portugal to prepare for the Six Nations, and a few people were nursing bumps after Challenge Cup games. It felt more like a recovery camp than preparation for war. And England came for a war. They were aggressive, sharp, on the money. We were sloppy – miscommunications and bad decisions in defence, poor execution in possession. And as players, we had to shoulder much of the blame for this.

It's amazing how one poor performance can plant a seed of doubt. We scraped a win in Edinburgh and then played terribly in Rome, winning 26–16. When I was replaced two minutes from the end, I vented my frustration by kicking a kitbag at the side of the pitch, for which I later apologized. It was a bad look.

But while I was frustrated, I realize now that some of my team-mates were suffering terribly from a lack of confidence. It was only later that I discovered how genuinely unhappy people were in Carton House at that time, how some guys dreaded coming into camp, kept their heads down in team meetings and were on the verge of panic attacks. Athletes are human after all. I was oblivious to it.

I guess I was the last guy they'd share their concerns with, seeing as Joe and I had a strong relationship. I always liked going into camp under Joe. I knew things would be organized and I knew my detail. It was like getting ready for an exam and I was comfortable in that environment.

And it wasn't all work. We had a good laugh in Belfast preparing for the France game, doing the Black Cabs tour and going out for a squad meal. We then produced our best performance for Joe's last game at the Aviva, winning with a bonus point to give us an outside shot at winning the championship on the final day.

Cardiff was a disaster, though. My record at the Principality with Ireland is poor, and that horribly wet day was the most miserable of the lot. By opting to keep the stadium roof open, we got what we deserved. And this was the players' fault, incidentally. Joe deferred to the senior players on that call. The problem was there were too many forwards in the leadership group.

I said we should let Wales have what they wanted and keep it closed. We were good enough to beat them with a dry ball. It would be like saying: We can beat you on your terms. I was outvoted by the forwards, who reckoned we would win a dogfight. It never even got close to being a dogfight. Wales got an early lead and defended it comfortably in the downpour, winning 25–7 to claim the Slam that Gatland had predicted for them.

I haven't had many more frustrating days on a rugby pitch. My restarts were a nightmare. It was as if all the rain went to make one huge pond in the middle of the pitch, and because Gareth Anscombe scored six penalties and one conversion for Wales, I had plenty of opportunities to drop-kick the ball out of the shallow end. It was like a comedy routine, except I wasn't finding it very funny.

Afterwards, Dad asked me why I hadn't moved along the halfway line, to a drier spot? Basically, because that's against the laws of the game, Dad. He meant well but it wasn't what I wanted to hear. I was narky at everyone, including the referee, Angus Gardner. After one decision against us, I threw the ball angrily in his general direction and was lucky it didn't clip him on the head.

While Anscombe was preparing for the shot at goal, I saw

myself on one of the big screens at either end of the stadium, just standing in the rain, pissed off. I remember wondering what the TV commentators were saying about me. I thought: *I know one thing. They aren't making excuses for me.*

That thought pretty much sums up my mindset for much of 2019: defensive. The mindfulness that had been so beneficial the previous year? The meditation, the breath-work? I was still practising it, but I was back in fight-or-flight mode the majority of the time.

I did try to be kind to myself at the very beginning of the year. Because my knee had flared up in the Munster game, I knew I wouldn't be playing until the Six Nations, so I decided to give myself a proper break – a couple of weeks off, no visits to the gym, a few meals out with Laura and friends. Some me-time! I deserved it. My rugby would probably benefit. I saw it as a mature decision.

As it turned out, one of those weeks was spent in bed with a bad chest infection. Then, on returning to work, I did a DEXA scan which showed that I had lost four kilos of muscle. Panic. The Six Nations was only three weeks away. I was told not to worry, to take on calories and do weights, and I'd be fine. But the prehistoric side of my brain tells me I need to do more, to punish myself to make sure I am ready.

It felt like I was struggling with my body for the rest of the year. Some of the injuries I got were purely accidental, like the thumb dislocation and the groin strain that restricted my pre-season to one World Cup warm-up game against Wales. But I had a succession of bangs and tweaks, meaning that I featured in only four games in the six months between the Six Nations and the World Cup.

They included a Champions Cup final and a Pro14 final,

which shows that Leinster were maintaining standards – well, almost. We were lucky to have squeezed past Ulster in the Champions quarter-final and were then outmuscled by Saracens in the decider in Newcastle. It's a massive regret – our fifth Champions Cup final and our first defeat. Such an opportunity, too. We had an opportunity to go in two scores up just before the break and didn't take it. Instead Saracens drew level on the stroke of half-time and that was a massive turning point.

Winning the Pro14 final at Celtic Park was our consolation. With the strength of our squad, we saw winning the Pro14 title as a basic necessity. The real bonus was the psychological points we scored over the Scotland contingent in the Glasgow side four months before we were to meet them in the World Cup opener in Yokohama.

It was all about the World Cup now. I was feeling quietly confident that summer. Finishing third in the Six Nations meant our bubble had burst, but it also meant we'd be flying in slightly under the radar. Being drawn in the same pool as Scotland, Japan, Samoa and Russia was favourable enough; being on the same side of the draw as New Zealand and South Africa was not. At least we had beaten both of them in our most recent meetings.

The other reason to feel hopeful was Joe. He was determined to finish on a high, with giving Irish rugby a parting gift: a World Cup semi-final, maybe more than that. His research was impeccable, as always. Two years previously he'd taken a squad to Japan (while some of us had been in New Zealand with the Lions), so he knew every hotel we'd stay in, every training base we'd use, and every stadium we'd play in.

On the basis that we were favourites to top our pool, Joe reckoned we'd more than likely get South Africa in the quarter-final and he already had a detailed game-plan to beat them, with various kick-plays to expose their back three and so forth. He was confident that Faz could get us in the right mental state to meet the enormous physical challenge that the Boks always present.

This all came out in the chats that we used to have that summer in Wilde & Green, a café roughly halfway between our houses. It's rare you get a relationship like that between coach and player, separated by twenty years in age but united by our obsession with rugby and winning.

On one level it was like teacher and pupil. As I anticipated, he'd criticized me for my behaviour in Thomond Park the previous Christmas, showing me clips and asking if my body language was appropriate for a captain. It still stung. I'd been hurt when Joe hadn't made me captain following Paulie's retirement. I understood his reason. He didn't want to load too much on my plate. That didn't stop it hurting. We had worked together for so long and being overlooked really hurt. I wanted it so badly, but I never told anyone except Laura.

But while I kept that to myself, he would still hear me out on other stuff. I told him the feeling among the players was that we had too many long team meetings with an overload of information. Joe countered by saying we'd had exactly the same number of meetings as in the Slam year and no one had complained then. Very true. Perhaps it's different when you're winning and the energy is generally positive.

I kept at him about working on our unstructured attack, about introducing unstructured matches in training that would improve general ball-skills. But he had pre-season already planned. Each week would have a theme. One week would be all about ruck. The next week would be all about defence. Next week about counter-attack, and so on. But I remember a few of the younger guys asking me that summer: Are we going to play any rugby, Johnny? They were used to Stuart's sessions where the ball was in play for fifty or sixty minutes.

Nobody was complaining when we hammered Scotland 27–3 in Yokohama. The only negative was that I re-strained my groin kicking and went off after fifty-eight minutes. With a six-day turnaround to the game against Japan in Shizuoka, Joe decided to rest me for that game. I wasn't happy. I knew my body well at this stage. I would be fit for Japan. I trained fully two days before the game and told Joe I was fit to play, but he was adamant.

'I need you ready for South Africa, Johnny,' he said.

He was obsessed about the Springboks. By this point, they had lost to New Zealand, so we were on track to meet them in the quarters, as Joe had predicted.

We knew Japan had some excellent individual players, but as a team they had looked very ordinary against Russia in the tournament opener. We weren't to know that their coach, Jamie Joseph, had put all his resources towards peaking against us. This sounds like being wise after the event, but I had a feeling the night before the game that we weren't mentally right.

Rob Kearney and I had just done some jersey presentations to World Cup debutants when Joe asked for the leadership group to stay behind. He'd been given two hotel options for the week of the quarter-final and wanted to discuss this with us, as we had to make a quick decision. I should have stepped in and handled the hotel issue. The other lads had a game the next day. This was an unnecessary loss of focus. I mentioned to Faz and Besty that I sensed complacency.

I'm not for a minute saying we would have won if I'd played that game. Japan out-ran, out-rucked and out-played us. Some of their offloading was sensational. They were fitter than us, too. I just think that if I'd been on the bench, I could have managed the last twenty. There was one attack in particular when we lost patience, and I was screaming from the stand for us to remain patient and to strangle them. Whatever. We lost. Despite big wins over Russia and Samoa, we finished second in the pool behind Japan. It would be New Zealand in the quarters.

We trained like superstars the day before that game. Joe's plan had been right all along. That was the best we had trained in a year. I remember thinking that we would be more match-sharp than the All Blacks. Their pool game against Italy had been cancelled because of Typhoon Hagibis so they'd had a two-week break since their previous game, a meaningless drubbing of Namibia.

I remember saying in a meeting: It's written for us. We have dipped from the highs of 2018 but now we're gonna turn up at Tokyo Stadium and prove to the world what a good side we are. Except we didn't. New Zealand wiped the floor with us. It finished 46–14: our worst World Cup defeat ever. They played like a team on a mission, like they owed us one. They were nowhere near as good against England in the semis. It was as though they maxed out against us.

It might have been a little different if a couple of moments had gone our way early on. Jacob Stockdale came close to an intercept. Jack Goodhue, their centre, managed to defuse an attack just when it looked like a try was on. It was unfortunate to lose Garry Ringrose after a clash of heads on twenty minutes. But the Kiwis cut us open with some clinical attacking. Two early tries for Aaron Smith and we were chasing the game. It's the worst position to be in against the All Blacks.

To concede seven tries was embarrassing, but the worst bit was that we just didn't play. Here we were on the biggest stage, in a tournament where teams like New Zealand and Japan were playing brilliant rugby, and we were running into each other or putting the ball on the floor. Our skills let us down.

Naturally we took a kicking in the media. Not that we were aware of it at first. We were somewhere in the Roppongi district of Tokyo, blotting out the memory. We were upset to lose, of course, but as is the way with losses we stayed together and had a few drinks. When you are staying in an industrial estate in the middle of Chiba and your tournament is over there isn't much to do apart from finding the bar, and when that closes to head back to various rooms for more drink.

Then: drama. Word reaches us that Joe is on the warpath. It's the middle of the night and the music is too loud and he's pissed off. People are legging it, half-giggling, half-scared that they'll be caught by the school principal. I am three sheets to the wind. When I meet Joe on the corridor, I greet him like a long-lost friend.

'Joe! How's it going?'

'Johnny, you need to get to bed.'

'No one's going to bed until Faz tells us, Joe. He's the boss now!'

This was hilarious for the lads who were hiding behind a wall in the corridor just across from us. They broke down laughing. Joe took it in good spirit too. We weren't about to fall out now.

I felt sorry for him when I saw all the flak he was getting

at home. Everyone was coming out of the woodwork to have a pop. Past players that had so much success under Joe were giving their negative opinion rather than protecting him. How short their memories were.

I called Joe soon after we got back from Japan, just to see how he was getting on. I told him that I'd contributed to the World Cup review that the IRFU was conducting, but that any criticisms I'd made matched the concerns that I'd voiced to him before the tournament. I also wanted to tell him that the criticism of him in the media didn't reflect how he'd be remembered by the Irish public.

When the dust had settled, I called over to see him with a bottle of wine and a letter of thanks. No coach has had more of an influence on me. Even at times during the Faz era, it was as if I saw the game through Joe's eyes out on the pitch. Before each game, I wrote down the same things that Joe taught me. *Play to space. Back yourself. If there's no space, put pressure on the other team.* That's the essence of his rugby philosophy. It might sound obvious now, and you might hear similar phrases from other coaches, but Joe was a pioneer. He owes Irish rugby nothing. What we owe him is incalculable.

18

Since retiring from rugby, I've often been asked to speak publicly about leadership. I enjoy doing it. I'm lucky to have experienced a wide variety of leadership styles, having worked with some of the best captains and coaches, so I've plenty to draw on.

Then there's my own experience of captaincy, first at Leinster and then with Ireland. Because I had to work at it, I believe I have more of an appreciation of what makes a good leader now. I learned the hard way through my mistakes. My natural approach to leadership was too direct for the younger guys in particular. Where did it come from? Well, consider my earliest heroes and role models:

Roy Keane – fiery Corkman with a short fuse.

Alex Ferguson – fiery Scot with a short fuse.

Michael Cheika – fiery Aussie with a short fuse.

Dad – fiery Kerryman with a short fuse.

The first person who really forced me to look long and hard at my interaction with team-mates was Stuart Lancaster. Joe had touched on it at times, but not the way Stuart did. Leadership was an area of special interest for him. He recommended articles, books and podcasts, and encouraged us to do psychometric tests designed to improve self-awareness and enhance relations in the workplace.

I reluctantly volunteered to do the 'Insights Discovery' test, a sort of multiple-choice quiz on your personality. The results formed a personality profile which, in my case, included some interesting observations:

Alert and outspoken, Johnny can see the fatal flaw in a proposal or position and often enjoys arguing either side of an issue from a position of devil's advocate.

Johnny is driven to achieve competence in all he does.

Johnny is seen by many people as independent and self-contained. He enjoys work that involves moving projects forward.

The funny part was the feedback that came under the heading: Strategies for Communicating with Johnny. It was hilariously accurate:

When communicating with Jonathan, DO NOT:
Try to control the conversation.
Underestimate his ability to decide for himself.
Criticize his ideas or take issue with his ideas.
Try to manipulate his point of view.
Wait for praise, or recognition.

I showed these to Laura and she laughed. 'Tell me something I don't know,' she said.

Joe used to make us do these sorts of questionnaires too. I'm thinking specifically of the one that Joe got us all to look at before Japan, where we were asked to mark each other out of 10 on a range of qualities from 'athletic profile', 'mental skills', 'commitment to role' and so on.

What jumped out at me was that the team-mate who had been assigned to rate me had given me just 4 out of 10 for 'Esprit de corps'. This translates roughly as 'group spirit' – I had to look it up, I admit. I guess he meant that I can be demanding and critical of others if I don't feel they're pulling their weight, maybe that I'm too single-minded. That was an eye-opener.

In my mind everything that I do is for the betterment of the group. Is that not esprit de corps? I could also mention the time that I've given to the welfare of my fellow pros, as a board member for the International Rugby Players over several years and for Rugby Players Ireland, most recently in helping to fight our corner when the IRFU proposed cutting our salaries by 25 per cent during the pandemic. Yes, I was trying to protect my income but I was also working on behalf of my fellow pros.

This feedback helped me to change. After I was appointed skipper at Leinster, I tried to make sure that we celebrated our successes as a group, often at my house, because I'd seen the value of those nights to teams earlier in my career. I also felt that I'd become more self-aware, especially in my behaviour around younger players, thanks to guidance from Stuart and Leo. Learning from their feedback off the pitch was becoming more important than feedback in training or matches. I was always able to take a slag and give a slag – and slagging is the everyday language of dressing rooms. It helps build team spirit. Or esprit de corps.

Yes, I barked at team-mates in the heat of battle, but when I watched the game back that night I was often mortified by the version of myself that I saw on screen and lost sleep worrying about what those team-mates thought of me. I had hoped that Faz saw the positive side of my competitiveness, the energy that it could provide. I desperately wanted him to choose me as his captain.

It was encouraging that he'd wanted to keep me involved post-Japan. But I was thirty-four and this was the start of a new World Cup cycle. I reckoned he might go for James Ryan, or Garry Ringrose, or Pete O'Mahony, who was an experienced skipper four years younger than me, with a better chance of lasting the course until 2023.

Then I did my right knee ligaments quite seriously at Northampton in early December, six weeks after we'd returned from the World Cup. I was suddenly in a race to be ready for the Six Nations. When some newspapers wrote me out of the first two rounds I was quickly on to Faz to tell him that this was rubbish. I was confident I could get fit for the opener against Scotland in Dublin. He reacted positively to this – but mentioned nothing about captaincy. Same when he held a mini-camp around Christmas. No word on the captaincy. I wasn't sure what to think when he texted in early January to see if he could call around for a coffee.

The moment he offered me the captaincy was special, not just because the honour was something I'd always quietly craved but because it was him that decided that I should be captain. I always admired him as a player growing up in that famous Wigan team. And I'd loved working with him since the Lions tour in 2013. He has played with some of the greats, so for him to decide that I was the guy to do it meant the world to me. The way that Faz did it was important too. There were no conditions of sale. It was just the two of us having a coffee in my kitchen. He was simple, heartfelt and positive and his words have stayed with me.

I want you to be captain, Johnny. I don't think it should be anyone else. You're the leader of this team.

Faz is a big admirer of Joe, but he recognized the need to put his own stamp on things and that meant changing the way we operated. It helped that we had a new training base in Abbotstown, a state-of-the-art facility on the Sport Ireland Campus. There was a new atmosphere, too. Faz put a smile back on people's faces after a disappointing World Cup. To introduce our new attack coach, Mike Catt, he showed us clips from the 1995 World Cup, when Jonah Lomu ran around, over and through Catty on numerous occasions. John Fogarty did the commentary and it was hilarious. A piss-take, but the perfect ice-breaker.

We looked forward to Faz's presentations. He knew how to use a humorous clip to get our attention but always linked it to a serious point, always improving our understanding of our roles and game awareness. The big difference was that we would no longer be passive learners. This was to be one giant collaboration – and that meant one giant culture shift for anyone who had worked with Joe.

Some of us – myself, Cian Healy and Dev Toner – had been under Joe's spell for ten years. Joe chose a group of senior players and encouraged us to be leaders. However, Joe's voice dominated meetings. I liked this. Only a few people would pipe up and there was always the possibility that they would be shot down if they were talking for the sake of it. This was a strength of the Joe system. No talk for the sake of it, no babble. Only clarity. As an out-half this was the dream. Everyone knew their role. End of.

Faz wanted us to come out of ourselves, though. Me included. Previously, I had chosen my moment in meetings, made sure that I knew exactly what I wanted to say and always tried to keep it punchy. Faz wanted more from me. Even when I thought I was doing it, he'd keep at me:

You're still not doing enough, Johnny.

But I've talked more this week than I've ever done in my life, Faz!

We need to hear you more, Johnny.

He was basically transferring ownership of the team back to the players. We had to be responsible for choosing how we went about our business, on and off the pitch, and that meant involving everyone. His mantra was that people had to be themselves in camp. Bring your personality with you, he'd say. Behave like you behave at your club because that's what got you to this point and it's a strength that we can use to our advantage.

Another thing he used to tell us was that there's no such thing as a stupid question. There were stupid questions, plenty of them! Sometimes I had to check myself from throwing my eyes up to heaven. But I got the point. People were taking risks, putting their head above the parapet, people who would have hidden previously in meetings. It was good for confidence.

The atmosphere became more relaxed, certainly. I wondered if it was too relaxed. Faz did away with the evening meetings and walk-throughs that had been staples of our routine with Joe. Once we left our new training base in Abbotstown and went back to Carton House, work was finished for the evening. Another novelty was that team announcements were brought forward to Tuesdays, removing the secrecy that previously added to the stress of match week.

But the biggest culture shift was in how we would play, or at least how we would attack. Under the Farrell philosophy, we would all be decision-makers on the ball. Yes, we would have a structure or a framework, but now everyone would be expected to react according to what they saw in front of them, not just me. Andrew Porter, Tadhg Furlong and the other lads in the front row, they now had to decide: Do I make a short pass left, right, or out the back, or do I step, attack a soft shoulder, offload?

This meant everyone had to improve their skills. From day one, we did ball-work in our warm-up, before training, after gym sessions when we were fatigued, plus extras. As much ball-time as we could get, basically. The new method also required a complete rewiring of everyone's brains. Joe had been all about grooving patterns to the point where players were pre-programmed. Now, they would be asked to make split-second decisions in the intense heat of a Test match. This would be challenging.

It was also exciting. Faz had a picture of where we needed to get to by the 2023 World Cup. He said we were never going to be the most physically dominant team but we could build a game to stress opponents and the basis of that game was decision-making. It was brave and it was a million miles from where we were coming from, so it took us a while to get the hang of it.

Scotland gave us a bit of a fright. It was a proud day for me, scoring all 19 points on my first day as the official skipper, but Stuart Hogg blew a try-scoring opportunity and we only won by 7. We beat Wales more convincingly but Twickenham was a sobering experience for us, even allowing for a few unkind bounces of the ball. My place-kicking was poor too.

The word 'pandemic' brings back strange memories. Minding the girls while Laura was home-schooling with Luca in the mornings, then bringing him down to the local park with a bag of balls, practising place-kicks into a kicking net in the back garden. We tried to beat the sense of Groundhog Day by having virtual poker sessions with a gang of St Mary's pals, chaotic virtual dinner parties (remember them?) with Earlsy, Murr, Pete, Bestie and all the wives/partners. When we were finally allowed back into camp, there was the constant testing, the protocols, the 'social distancing'. What a weird time.

Typically, Faz tried to use all that 'bubble' time to our

advantage. We spent so much time in each other's company that we got to know each other properly as people, to open up and admit fears and insecurities and vulnerabilities. That was a stressful time for many people, but for us it created a bond.

Be yourself, Faz kept telling us. Then he'd take me aside and say: Except you, Johnny. I don't want you to be yourself. I laughed, but he had a serious point. He wanted me to learn the skill of knowing what message each individual teammate needed at any particular time and also the way in which the message should be delivered, the tone of voice, whether it was in private or in front of the group. I had to be a chameleon, in other words.

This was new territory for me and it didn't come naturally. After the England match, we had a training game against the Ireland U20s in Donnybrook when I let fly at John Cooney. It was over a technical detail we'd been hammering home in meetings. When John repeated the mistake during the session, I was furious. He wouldn't take it. 'You can't speak to me like that,' he said. 'You're the captain now. You're supposed to set an example.'

As far as I was concerned, I was just doing what a captain does. Set standards. Let players know what's acceptable.

That little flare-up was embarrassing, though. At the end of the session, Faz took me aside and nodded in Cooney's direction. You need to sort that out, he said. I later made the phone call and apologized for the way I'd spoken, though it went against every fibre of my being.

It soon seemed like a minor matter, though. Towards the end of my first Six Nations as Ireland captain, my relationship with Faz was looking extremely shaky and I had serious doubts about whether I was going to continue as captain.

*

At the end of October we went to Paris needing a bonus-point victory to win the Six Nations title. This seemed very doable to me. We'd lost just one of our previous nine Tests against France. They were about to turn a corner, but it hadn't happened yet. Because of Covid, the Stade de France would be empty – another point in our favour.

But we got our prep wrong and I blame myself. Because we travelled the day before the game, I decided to can the captain's meeting that night to lighten everyone's load. It showed on the pitch. We had system errors and miscommunications and general sloppiness. I learned that you can't expect to win if you ignore your detail, especially on the road. Can't cut corners.

Still, with twelve minutes remaining we were just two scores behind at 28–20. I still believed we could win and was doing everything in my power to convince my team-mates. I was in the fight.

Ross Byrne had taken his tracksuit off, but I assumed Faz was moving me to centre, as he'd done in Twickenham.

At the next break in play, Wayne Barnes tells me I'm off. Ross is replacing me. I look up at the clock to check I have the time right and there are still twelve minutes remaining. Because of the slight time lag on the TV feed, I can see myself shaking my head in disbelief.

Disbelief and anger. And embarrassment. This is a game we can still win and Faz is replacing me? His captain? I respect Ross but he hadn't played a lot of tests up to that point. Getting the captaincy was one of the highlights of my career, because it was given to me by someone I respect so much. And that's why Paris was probably the lowest point of my captaincy.

I didn't say that to media, though I did admit that I'd been surprised and disappointed. What else did they expect me to say? But the next morning at the airport, Laura called me and said the media had gone to town on my head-shaking. I had undermined Faz – that was the headline. There was no holding back. Three former high-profile captains jumped on board. Keith Wood, Paulie and Brian all criticized me for showing my displeasure so obviously. I thought they might have supported me, protected me. *That's Johnny. He's fiery. He wears his heart on his sleeve. Of course he was disappointed.* But no. It was a pile-on.

Stu reassured me. He said he could see why I would feel the way I did. Laura was upset by the kicking that I was getting in the media, especially from former team-mates. Dad and Mark were fully behind me, too, of course. Their loyalty and unwavering support can sometimes mean they wear blinkers.

I knew I had to clear the air. I called Faz on the Sunday to apologize for shaking my head but at the same time to tell him how shocked I'd been. I'd thought that he, of all people, would trust me in that situation. He'd chosen me to lead. I explained how I felt embarrassed.

Faz kept it simple. He accepted my apology. He said undermining me was the last thing he had intended. He'd just thought we needed fresh legs and he also wanted to show some faith in Ross. The important thing was that we had to move on from it, he said. We agreed on that much.

I still wondered if our relationship had been broken. Would he now pull rank on me for the autumn Nations Cup matches that had been scheduled to fill the gap in the rugby market? From a selfish point of view, it was probably no harm that I was injured for two games where we struggled – the 18–7 defeat in Twickenham and a scratchy 23–10 win over Georgia. I just couldn't be sure where I stood. Was he ready to cut ties, to move on without me? This was where my mind was taking me.

One thing I would say from this period was that I really battened down the hatches. I learned who was in my corner and who wasn't. During the weeks I was off injured I could really reflect. I concluded that it was my fault he took me off. I'd given him a reason. I wasn't playing well enough. I wasn't leading well enough. People talk about the last few years of my career being rejuvenated by not getting picked for the Lions that year, but really this was the event that sparked it all. I made a deal with myself that I wasn't going to leave any stone unturned in my own prep or the team's prep. I wanted to succeed as a captain. I wanted it more than I ever wanted anything else in my career.

Faz had plenty on his mind around then. Even before we lost the first two games of the 2021 Six Nations, people in the media were beginning to ask if he was the man for the job. The way that we stuck together through that shit-storm was the foundation for the success that came later.

The week after we lost the tournament opener in Cardiff was one of the toughest of my career. With ten minutes remaining, I suffered a concussion caused by an accidental knee to the side of the head from Justin Tipuric. As I was led from the pitch by Dr Ciaran Cosgrave I sort of reached out to hold Ciaran's arm, a small movement but one that got a lot of air-time over the following days.

We had an eight-day turnaround before we played France in Dublin, which meant I could be available if I hit certain markers on the return-to-play protocols during the week. By midweek, I was hitting those markers – but it wasn't as simple as that. There were external pressures. A French radio station interviewed my old neurologist, Jean-François Chermann, who somehow thought it appropriate to say that he believed that I'd had 'somewhere in the region of thirty concussions' during my career.

I wasn't surprised that the French media might chase a headline like this in the week of a Test match. But I was gobsmacked that Chermann could be so unprofessional. Whatever about his opinions on what constitutes a concussion, what about doctor–patient confidentiality? I rang him and hinted that I might be taking the matter further. He quickly made a public retraction of his comments but the damage had been done. Nobody ever sees the apology or retraction on the back page.

I was torn between playing and pulling out. I passed HIA 2 and HIA 3 and trained on the Thursday afternoon. But I had a groin niggle and was constantly second-guessing myself about how I felt mentally. I was stressed about the stories in the media and how they were affecting my family.

I decided that if I still had doubts by Friday, then I would pull out, which is what happened. Faz still made sure to let everyone know what he felt about the media coverage in France. 'It stinks, on so many grounds,' he said. 'I'll leave it at that.'

France won 15–13 – their first win in Dublin in ten years, and they celebrated accordingly. We were zero from two. Even if we won our final three games, the highest we could finish was third, the same as 2020. This wasn't what I'd imagined when I took over the captaincy.

Our response was phenomenal. It's almost amusing to think that Faz's position was under a bit of pressure or that my relationship with him was a little rocky or that journalists were telling me to retire graciously. It's amusing, because we won twenty-seven of our next twenty-nine games.

*

One of the reasons often given for our upswing in fortunes is that I wasn't selected for the Lions tour to South Africa. Supposedly I benefited from having a summer off. I'd needed a mental break and getting a full pre-season with Leinster did me good. Whatever. I don't buy it.

If I'd toured with the Lions, the IRFU would have made sure I got a proper rest and a full pre-season. I could have delayed my return as long as I needed. The only benefit I got from not touring was that it motivated me to prove Warren Gatland wrong. Does the fact that he admitted he got that selection call wrong make me feel better? No.

We'd never had a very close relationship, but I was convinced he would bring me, based on the fact that we had been successful on previous tours. Gatland has always said that Six Nations form was his main selection guide and I had finished the Six Nations strongly. Our performance in the final game, when we gave England a 32–18 spanking in the Aviva, was a turning point for the team.

I'd set a few personal targets to achieve before the end of my contract: to reach one hundred caps, to captain Ireland to a Grand Slam and Leinster to another double. I also craved a third Lions tour. There's an exclusive club of players who have played in three or more Test series for the Lions and I desperately wanted to be in it.

Competition was tight, I'll admit. I expected that Gats would go with Owen Farrell and Dan Biggar, players who had delivered for him before. Quality players and proven winners. Finn Russell was the darling of the media during that year's Six Nations but he didn't look like a Gatland player to me. I reckoned that if Gats chose three out-halves and if he was true to his ideals, I was in.

It didn't help that I suffered a second concussion two

months after Cardiff. This was in Exeter, in a Champions Cup quarter-final. Dave Ewers, their flanker, absolutely emptied me – the heaviest hit that I've ever taken. It was a shoulder to the chest, causing a whiplash so violent that it damaged my inner ear.

Weirdly, I was initially OK to carry on. I felt fine once I was in motion, but then, as I paused before taking a conversion, I felt dizzy. I got the conversion but then alerted the medics, who took me off. Apparently it's very common for an inner ear problem to affect your balance only when you slow down. Running around I was fine, but I couldn't stand still without feeling like falling over.

This was mid-April, three weeks before the European Cup semi-final in La Rochelle and four weeks before Gats announced his Lions squad. The day after Exeter, the only part of the HIA that I was failing was the Tandem Test, where you walk with one foot immediately in front of the other, eyes closed, arms by your side. As soon as I closed my eyes, I lost my balance.

I flew to the UK to see Tony Belli, a global expert in traumatic brain injury and sports concussions, who conducted a battery of tests, did scans and prescribed exercises to improve my vestibular system. Once I was able to pass the balance exercise, he was happy to declare me fit for La Rochelle, though he did say another week's recovery would help. On Faz's advice, I contacted the Lions medical staff to let them know that I'd be fit for the final, if Leinster made it.

They didn't, but the rational part of me said that Gats would still be guided by my form in the last three rounds of the Six Nations and what I'd achieved for the Lions in 2013 and 2017. When I saw the squad, it felt like he'd been guided by someone else. Eight Scots in the squad? Based on what?

Fourth in the Six Nations, with a win in Paris on the final day, when France handed them the result by chasing a bonus point when the game was over.

I never heard from Gats. He wasn't obliged to call me, of course. I didn't expect a call. Being picked for the Lions is an honour, a privilege and not something you should ever think you are guaranteed. I still get the occasional urge to call him and find out, off the record, exactly what was said in the selection meeting. You'd probably think I'd be over it by now. It kills me to this day.

His official line was that he didn't think I'd last the rigours of a series against the Springboks. I heard another rumour that the Lions had been told I was too much of an insurance risk, that there was a danger that they would be liable for an expensive payout if I got another head injury while on tour. Whatever. I didn't pay attention to the rumours. I wasn't selected, end of story.

I stayed fit in case I was needed, but didn't play in the Rainbow Cup – another Covid tournament rustled up to fill a gap. Leo wanted to use it more as a development exercise, which was fair enough. I then regretted the decision when I heard that Russell had injured his Achilles early in the tour.

Faz was soon in touch to see if I'd heard anything from Gats. A few former Lions team-mates also texted from South Africa to check if I was on my way out. I was in a corporate box at Lord's Cricket Ground, watching England play Pakistan, when I saw the news that Marcus Smith had received the call. Two more beers, please, barman.

People say I was lucky. They say it was the worst Lions tour ever, that the players were imprisoned in their hotel by Covid restrictions, and they lost a boring Test series 2–1 in empty stadia. I supposedly dodged a bullet. I don't buy that, either. I reckon the Boks were there for the taking and if the Lions had won the series, that's the only thing people would remember. I would have given anything to be out there.

6 November 2021 – Ireland v. Japan, Aviva Stadium

Rituals are comforting, especially in the week of a big game. And this was a big week for me – my hundredth cap for Ireland, twelve years to the month since my first. Because of the occasion, there were potential distractions. A ritual keeps everything in place, removes uncertainty.

It always started with my match bag, with making sure I had all my bits and bobs in place. I wasn't always good at this sort of thing. I remember the panic before a Test early in my career when I discovered that I didn't have the right gumshield, and having to rush home from the team hotel on the morning of the game. One poor game later and you convince yourself that it was down to this small error.

My bag-packing process started as early as the Sunday before a Test match, when our laundry was returned to our rooms at Carton House. The first thing I always looked for were my shoulder pads. I kept the same pair since we played South Africa at Croke Park in 2009, all the way to the end. They originally came as part of an undergarment recommended to me by Dave Alred, with bands inserted to pull your shoulders back so that you could retain good posture while place-kicking. I liked the pads because they made it look like I had a proper pair of shoulders. By the end, I simply had those same pads strapped on to my shoulder before games. Superstitious? Maybe a little.

So I packed the shoulder pads, a couple pairs of cycle shorts, my match kicking tee and a back-up tee – I only used them on match-day and the day before. Then came my match boots, kindly designed specially by Adidas for the occasion – white, with green stripes, and some special symbols: the initials of Laura and the kids, a shamrock and '100'. I was delighted when those boots raised €24,000 at auction for Debra Ireland, a charity I've often supported, which cares for sufferers of a horrific skin blistering condition called epidermolysis bullosa.

I had a box for my gumshield. In that box I also had the Miraculous Medal that Richie Hughes gave me in school, some rosary beads that I nicked from my granny's house in Listowel, a stone from Daddy John's grave and, on match-days, my wedding ring. My notebook went into the bag too, though I obviously used it at different times during the week, and my tracksuit. That was pretty much it. I usually had it packed by Monday evening, in the corner of my bedroom, ready to go. It was part of my mental prep, really.

Before one game with Leinster, I asked John Fogarty, the scrum coach, to dispose of the caffeine gum I had been chewing as I didn't want to throw it on the grass. I played brilliantly that day and so we continued the ritual right through to my last game for Ireland. After every warm-up he'd take the piece of gum and put it in his pocket. Then he'd give me a hug or a high five, or slag me about something or other. Fogs is a legend, an energy-giver. Our interactions put me at ease and probably showed younger players in the squad that I wasn't such an ogre after all.

Faz likes to mark special occasions and the Japan game was special for Tadhg Furlong and Dan Sheehan, too – one making his fiftieth Ireland appearance, the other his first. Getting players' families involved was difficult with Covid – even though crowds were allowed back for our games that

November, we were still being kept in a strict bubble. Faz rose to the challenge, though.

With everyone gathered in the team room, he started off by saying how devastating it was that we couldn't have families in to share the occasion. But we had video messages on the big screen from Mum, Dad, Mark, Gillian and Jerry Jr, and from all the previous centurions. Paulie and Church were on site, so they did the jersey presentation.

Then there was a lovely video from home, with Amy and Sophie wishing me well, and finally Luca, with an angry face on him. 'Good luck on Saturday, Dad,' he said. 'They told me I couldn't be there because I'm not allowed. But I'm like you. I don't take no for an answer . . .' That's when he walked into the room, with my hundredth jersey in hand, and the place erupted. There were hugs and there were tears. I was overcome.

It turned out that in the preceding weeks Luca had done every PCR and antigen test necessary to be there, with the assistance of Faz and our managers, Mick Kearney and Ger Carmody, plus our video analyst Vinny Hammond. It was so thoughtful of them.

The performance on Saturday matched the build-up. No one outside the group saw a 60–5 victory coming. Japan had most of the side that had beaten us at the World Cup and they'd pushed Australia close two weeks previously. This was our first game in seven months.

It felt like Faz came of age as a head coach that summer, though. He went to another level. He took control of our phase attack, tightening up our shape and our option-taking and getting us to play at pace. He also picked a lot of Leinster players to start, which gave us real cohesion.

The irony was that Faz's attack shape was so similar to the one that Japan had used against us in Shizuoka, with multiple potential first receivers off Jamison Gibson-Park, all with a variety of options. The key was speed of ruck ball, and the guy who gave us that was Paulie.

He'd come into the coaching team for the Six Nations and he was the last piece in the jigsaw. He was seen primarily as a lineout guru, but he made a difference in a lot of areas. He sharpened up our breakdown work on both sides of the ball. Essentially he brought back a bit of Joe. Joe always said the ruck is the heartbeat of any team and Paulie transformed that part of our game. He also brought our discipline back to Joe levels, going hard on anyone who allowed the opposition easy access into our third of the pitch. Bringing Paulie in allowed Simon Easterby to move to defence coach, which he was brilliant at. We suddenly had a new voice in two key areas.

Paulie's influence could be seen in our performance against England the previous March, but the Japan game was when everything suddenly clicked. They had no answers to our furious speed and skill. The best moment for me came early in the second half, when Jamison put me away to the short side of the scrum and I scored in what used to be the Wanderers corner of the ground. I was mobbed by every single member of the team.

After the game I did a TV interview at the side of the pitch and I couldn't hear the questions because the cheering was so loud. There were only around 30,000 people in the Aviva that day but it seemed like the loudest I've heard it. I'd never felt so much love on a rugby pitch. Not having any crowd for the previous two years really made me appreciate it. Some of my best friends in the game, Ferg and Rob, retired in an empty stadium. Church got his hundredth in an empty stadium. So for me to get this reception on my special day made me feel emotional and grateful. I also felt a bit for my mates who weren't so lucky.

19

What does a perfect ending look like? Every professional sportsperson knows there's no such thing, but that doesn't stop us from chasing it. It's partly Brian O'Driscoll's fault. It felt like he hired a scriptwriter to design his exit. First, he was man of the match in a 50-point win over Italy for his farewell Test at the Aviva, followed by a special presentation on the pitch. The following week we secured the Six Nations title in the Stade de France. And then, for his final game at the RDS, Leinster clinched a Pro12 title. He deserved it all for being the greatest Irish player ever.

Coming into my own final lap I had targeted another double with Leinster, this time as captain. I wanted another Grand Slam. And I wanted us to win the World Cup. Forget making it to the semis for the first time. I wanted the whole lot. You don't get into sport to be second-best.

The great thing about playing for Andy Farrell is that you genuinely believe it is all attainable. He makes you believe. His skill for creating that sense of belief in a group is remarkable.

There were a couple of themes he kept returning to. The first was the idea of us making the country proud. Faz had introduced this theme before, during Joe's time – I particularly remember on the eve of the game against Scotland in Yokohama, when he spoke so powerfully about his experience of playing for England at Croke Park in 2007, how his team-mates had felt like they were taking on an entire nation and all of its history.

Now, he showed us clips of Irish Olympians returning home with medals and how the Irish public had responded to their success. I'm old enough to remember how glorious failures like the football World Cups of 1990 and '94 caused a gush of national pride, the players waving from open-top buses and O'Connell Street heaving. Faz got us to imagine what the reaction would be like if we achieved our potential. Imagine if we won the World Cup. What it would do to the country. How it would inspire young boys and girls. His words gave you goosebumps.

The other notion that fuelled our self-belief was backed up by the work that we did with our mental skills coach, Gary Keegan. Gary and Faz introduced the concept of us becoming strengthened by the setbacks we encountered along the way, rather than being weakened by them. They wanted us to get to the point where we almost welcomed adversity because we knew it would bring out the best in us.

Irish people aren't really wired to think this positively. I don't know if it's our history, but we tend to brace ourselves for the worst. I know that I was feeling a bit defeatist at half-time against the All Blacks in November of 2021. When Codie Taylor scored a try completely against the run of play, we were trailing 10–5 and I'm thinking: *This feels familiar. Another opportunity missed against these guys.*

Faz's messages in the dressing room were simple but somehow very convincing: Keep hammering away. Keep doing what you've been doing and you will be rewarded. Sure enough, in the next ten minutes, both Rónan Kelleher and Caelan Doris scored tries and we held our lead till the end. Another huge win for us.

Faz's excitement about the quality of players coming into the side was also contagious. He'd occasionally ask me about certain young players in Leinster. My default response was: He's good but he needs to improve x or y. Faz came at things from a different angle. It was like he only saw the potential in people.

I remember we discussed Rónan Kelleher when he had only played a few games for Leinster. I gave my usual response and he'd say something like: 'The size of him! Wait till you see, Johnny. By the time we get to the World Cup, this kid is going to be world class.' It was the same with Caelan Doris or Hugo Keenan or Dan Sheehan. He looked at them and saw diamonds in the rough. It was his job to polish them.

He's excellent at spotting talent and at marshalling his resources. He realized that Andrew Porter was too good to be sitting on the bench behind Tadhg Furlong so switched him back to loose-head and put him into the starting side. He saw that Connacht had a gem in Mack Hansen and picked him. Suddenly Mack was plucking a restart out of the sky at the Stade de France and running down the wing to score. Easy.

I had to watch that game from the stands because of a hamstring niggle. When a TV director spotted me and my face appeared on the screens in the stadium, there were boos from the French fans, which I took as a compliment. Eighteen months out from *their* World Cup, we were seen as a threat. We lost that game 30–24 and the French won a Slam, but we came away with a Triple Crown – not what we'd aimed for, perhaps, but another building block.

Saturday, 2 July 2022, Auckland

We are in the medical room and the Independent Match Day Doctor is asking me the usual questions – the first stage in a Head Injury Assessment. My answers are sharp, impatient.

My heart rate is up at around 170 and I'm in a rush to get this done and get back out on the pitch.

What venue are we at today?

Eden Park, first Test.

Which half is it now?

Near the end of the first half.

Who scored last?

New Zealand (We'd been trailing 7–5, attacking just outside their 22 when the move broke down and suddenly Sevu Reece is running under the posts at the other end. Nightmare!)

What team did you play most recently?

The Māori, in Hamilton, our first game on tour. I wasn't playing, though. Look, there's nothing wrong with me.

Calm down, Johnny. Who won?

The Māori won. Next?

Next is a test of my immediate memory, where I hear ten words and have to try to recall them . . .

Plug – lamp – apple – table – pigeon etc.

I have to concentrate hard for this. It's not because I'm concussed. I took a glancing blow, nothing more. There's a tiny bump at the side of my head but it's superficial. I was raging when word came on that I had to get a HIA.

The reason I need to concentrate is because the match is so distracting. This medical room in Eden Park is only fifteen metres from pitch-side and I've just heard a huge roar. The All Blacks have obviously scored again. F**k!

What's next?

Tandem gait test. This is actually tricky in the middle of a Test match when the blood is up. Then, another huge roar. Jesus, they can't have scored again? FFS!

The doc moves on to a numerical cognition test. But there's only one piece of arithmetic that really matters. Those two big roars for the tries plus two smaller ones for the conversions adds up to a half-time scoreline of 28–5.

The medics tell me that I won't be going back out for the second half. They say they aren't able at this stage to rule out a concussion. The injury is not deemed Category 1, which would have meant a minimum twelve-day stand-down and the end of my tour. If I pass my HIA2 (within three hours of the knock) and HIA3 (after two nights' sleep), I could be OK for the second Test, in Dunedin. But they're going to err on the side of caution for now. I feel the urge to argue, but there's no point.

We lost 42–19. Faz said he wanted New Zealand to be a tough tour, one that would make a World Cup campaign seem almost easy by comparison. That's why he added in two midweek matches against the Māori, just to stretch us. Well, we were stretched.

At one stage, the whole trip was in danger of snapping. We had a lot of cases of Covid in the camp, with some guys isolating in their rooms. We also had a run of injuries at prop so bad that Mick Kearney, our manager, had to make contact with Michael Bent, an old Leinster team-mate, who had retired to the farm in Taranaki and was dabbling with a bit of club rugby at weekends. Thankfully we didn't need him in Auckland, but he togged out and did the warm-up. It was that tight.

There is no tougher place to tour than New Zealand in July, especially when you're losing. You're leaving long summer evenings in Ireland for very short days, when the sun drops like a stone at around 5.30 p.m. – if the sun is visible, that is. Usually it's raining. Faz still managed to keep the mood upbeat. There wasn't much that needed fixing, he said. A few set-piece tweaks and tightening up our defence in transition and that was all. The series was still there to be won.

Next stop Dunedin. Our hotel was the same as the one we used in 2011. It looked as though it hadn't seen a lick of paint in the intervening eleven years, or a hoover. We made this a reason to laugh, rather than to mope. Seeing the positives in every situation was becoming a habit for us.

It wasn't an easy week for me, though. There was uproar when Faz told the media that I was still in the mix to play the second Test – a clear case of people not understanding World Rugby's concussion protocols. Faz told me I should step down if I had any doubts at all. And I did have doubts. Say you feel tired – is this jet lag, or something more sinister? Or you leave your phone in the team room by mistake. Is that normal? You can overthink things.

But by Thursday my mood was improved. I felt better when I was training. That's always a good sign. I decided to make a decision and stick with it. I would play. I ended up playing probably the best game of my international career, two days shy of my thirty-seventh birthday. And we won – Ireland's first Test win on New Zealand soil.

It was a mad game, one that tested our ability to stay in the moment. New Zealand had three cards before the break – one red and two yellows – and we probably should have had a penalty try as well. But when Beauden Barrett scored on the stroke of half-time, our lead was just 10–7.

We'd had something similar in Twickenham earlier that year, where England had a red early on but were galvanized by it, before we finished strongly. We finished strongly here, too. By the time I was replaced, seven minutes from the end, our lead was 23–7. I was able to enjoy those final minutes, safe in the knowledge that we were uncatchable.

I'd kicked 13 points off the tee but it was more my option-taking and execution in attack that pleased me, my pass selection at the line. In defence the New Zealanders tend to go man on man, with each defender watching his man rather than the ball, so they rarely get a two-man tackle in. I went 'front door' on a couple of occasions and put Tadhg Beirne and Andrew Porter through holes.

I was happy with my game awareness, too. When we won a penalty while they had two props in the bin, I took the scrum option, knowing the law stated that they would have to go to twelve men. My only mistake was in not making absolutely sure that referee Jaco Peyper enforced the law. He didn't do a headcount so the All Blacks got away with using an extra man. But once Ports extended our lead with his second try, they never looked like hauling us in.

It felt amazing to have made history. And it felt especially sweet for those of us who'd been there for the Hamilton Horror Show a decade earlier – Pete, Earlsy, Murr, Church and myself.

The All Blacks weren't lessened in my eyes, though. They have always been the greatest challenge in rugby as far as I'm concerned. Because we've beaten them a few times, Dan Sheehan's generation may see it differently, but I still looked at them as they set up for the haka and felt a sense of awe. Maybe it was because I had a better record against the Springboks, and hadn't ever played in South Africa, but for me, New Zealand never lost that aura – even when they were trailing us 22–3 in Wellington a week later.

Suddenly the series was ours to lose. That's a negative way of looking at it but I needed to emphasize in the dressing room how quickly that lead could be eaten away. I reminded the lads about the game in Dublin in 2013, how we'd been 19–0 ahead and lost. I knew a storm was coming. We needed to score next.

We didn't. By the fifty-third minute, our lead was back to seven points and Ports was in the bin, with Josh van der Flier also off the pitch to make way for a replacement prop. When we got a penalty on halfway I kicked for goal to try and kill a minute, but it rebounded off the crossbar. Chaos. Soon Will Jordan was knifing through in open play and it was a foot race between me and him. No contest.

At least we were now back to fifteen men. And in the huddle while the conversion was being taken, we were calm and clear. *The restart is going short and down the middle, and Hugo will be on it. No better man. If we score next, we win the game.*

And that is pretty much how it went. Hugo's chase forced the error and won a scrum. Jamison, Hugo and Bundee all made good ground off a dominant scrum and Ardie Savea conceded a penalty at the breakdown. Corner or points? Our maul had already set up a try for Josh before the break, so we went again. This time Rob Herring took a punt by spinning away on his own, and it worked. Try.

I watched the final historic seconds from the touchline along with all remaining squad members and staff, hugging everyone that came near me. Pete was in tears. Amazing scenes.

What we'd achieved – winning a three-Test series in New Zealand – had never been done by any visiting team in the professional era. Better still, we'd won from behind. 'The hardest thing to do in rugby, by a country mile,' as Faz described it.

Harder than winning a World Cup? At the time, as we serenaded the surprisingly large number of Ireland supporters in Wellington that night, anything seemed possible.

The day before the Wellington Test, I'd received a friendly WhatsApp warning from Laura, who was back in Dublin managing a heavy load: minding three kids under the age of eight during the school summer holidays.

Whatever happens tomorrow, leave it in New Zealand!

The days after you return home from tour can be tricky. It's brilliant to be back – the excitement on the kids' faces is always magical – but switching immediately into Dad mode is difficult. Apart from the jet lag, you've become used to an almost exclusively adult, male environment where every day is mapped out for you in advance. Suddenly it's time to leave all that behind.

You switch off your phone and make an extra effort to be 'present', but after a while your wife will catch you with that faraway look on your face, as you mentally replay a contentious breakdown decision.

It's definitely easier if you've just won. Beating the All Blacks meant we were back at the top of the world rankings, but I felt we could get better. Newish players like Dan, Mack, Ports and Caelan already looked world class, while experienced players were further improving under the influence of Faz and his coaching group: guys like Bundee, Robbie, Jamison and Tadhg Beirne, who'd had a sensational tour.

And me? Could a rugby player improve in his late thirties? Some people seemed to think so. The week after we got back from New Zealand, someone sent me a screenshot of a newspaper article by Warren Gatland, where he was picking a notional Lions Test team to play the following week. He'd selected me as his out-half:

'Quite simply he has earned the right to be there, even at the age of 37,' he wrote. 'I think Marcus Smith is something special but if I want to win a game next week, Johnny has to start.'

I guess I'd proved him wrong. My aim was to keep proving him wrong all the way to the World Cup. The key was staying fit. I was confident that my ability to read a game and make the right decisions was as sharp as ever. I just needed to keep 'investing in my body', as Jamie Heaslip would have put it. Jamie led the way with his attention to detail on prehab and rehab and it showed in his career stats. Ever since the injury problems I'd experienced during my time in Racing, I'd tried to follow his example. I also picked the brains of the likes of Paulie, Brad Thorn, Peter Stringer and Donncha O'Callaghan, who had good longevity. They were so professional in everything they did that it would have been mad not to learn from them.

It starts with nutrition, hydration and sleep hygiene and includes rehab work above and beyond the excellent care I received from Leinster and the IRFU. My go-to man for the latter part of my career was Enda King, the former Cavan footballer who is a rehab specialist, sports physio and strength-and-conditioning expert. He is brilliant at identifying a problem and prescribing an exercise to target a specific area. Often as part of my prep for pre-season I'd spend a full week with Enda, doing three sessions a day, whether in the Sports Surgery Clinic in Santry or more recently at the Aspetar Clinic in Doha. That summer of 2022 was no different.

All you can do is reduce the risk of injury, though. You can't avoid it. And I didn't avoid it on that last lap. In the fourteen months between that Test in Wellington and our World Cup opener against Romania in Bordeaux, I featured in just nine games – five for Ireland and four for Leinster, with two of those off the bench. Fortunately, the five Tests were all significant.

First was a 19–16 victory over South Africa at the Aviva in November, when my heavily strapped right quad held on to kick an important penalty from wide on the left with seven minutes left, one that kept us two scores ahead.

There were setbacks, though. Two weeks later, about an hour before kick-off against Australia, I had to pull out with a calf strain. Training all week with a dead leg meant I was overcompensating, and my calf on the opposite leg paid the price. Against Connacht on New Year's Day, I stayed too upright in my attempt to stop Jarrad Butler and our heads collided. I cracked my cheekbone and had to wear a protective mask in training when I finally made it back to prepare for the Six Nations opener in Cardiff.

Warren Gatland had just been reappointed as Wales coach, so I knew what to expect when I did my captain's press conference at our training base in Quinta do Lago, four days before the game: my non-selection for the Lions. It was old news, but that didn't stop people asking about it, and I was honest about how it had affected me.

I find it difficult to sidestep a straight question, which is probably why the media seemed to like to interview me. I didn't always like doing the interviews but understood it is part of the job! It took me a while to get used to the fact that someone could slate you in print and act like they're your best buddy the next time you see them. But I always tried to be respectful, and honest. A few people have told me that such honesty would make me a good pundit, but I let it be known during my career that I wasn't interested. If being honest means saying something critical about a former team-mate to a huge TV audience, then thanks but no thanks.

Look at the Cardiff scoreline now – 34–10 – and it's surprising to recall how nervous I was in the lead-up. I was short on game-time. I was aware of my cheekbone, naturally. Plus there was so much expectation.

Even though I hadn't formally announced anything, everyone knew this was my last Six Nations, my last chance to lead Ireland to a Slam. There was a lot of external noise about Gats inspiring Wales. Faz then ensured some extra noise by agreeing to have the roof closed at the Principality Stadium. He welcomed the extra pressure that this would bring. On top of that, Jamison and Church were ruled out on the eve of the game.

But we blew them away. We scored three tries in the first twenty minutes – starting well had become a habit for us. By half-time we led 27–3. I had never seen the Principality so subdued. With the late changes not affecting us, it showed that our mental strength work and preparation were improving all the time. The strength of our squad was improving too. When you lose a player like Jamison and replace him with a quality player like Conor you know you are in a good place.

People have complained about the Aviva occasionally lacking atmosphere. Not for the France game in 2023. The hype was huge – 1 v. 2 in the world rankings, the forerunner for a possible World Cup quarter-final – and the game delivered in a huge way. The ball-in-play time for the first half alone must have broken records. We started brilliantly again – Hugo scoring a belter off a variation of an old Joe play we'd planned to use off dropout receptions, with Finlay Bealham in the pivotal handling role – and we outscored France by three tries to one before the break. We struggled to shake them off, though. With ten minutes left, they were only 6 points behind before finally, a brilliant pass from Caelan gave Garry a sniff and he finished superbly. Caelan was immense that day. Many of us were. We needed to be.

This was a second bonus-point win and a big psychological boost, especially given the impact of our bench: Craig Casey and Ross Byrne had shown up well in the final quarter. The negative for me was a fresh injury. I strained my groin when Uini Atonio fell on top of me in the forty-seventh minute – a bit frustrating that, given that he shouldn't have been on the pitch. How he escaped a red card for a high challenge on Rob Herring was beyond me.

I was fortunate with the schedule, though. A fortnight later we were in Rome, followed by another two-week break before Edinburgh, when there was so much at stake, and not just for us. The Scots had already beaten England and smashed Wales so they were chasing a Triple Crown, and on the occasion of Stuart Hogg's hundredth cap.

Yet when I think back to that game, the memory that jumps out is of the laughter in our dressing room at half-time. It's not funny when team-mates suffer injuries, but the number of setbacks we'd had in the first forty was verging on comical. Within the space of eleven minutes we lost three forwards: Caelan, Dan and Hendy. Towards the end of the half, it was also clear that Rónan (Dan's replacement) was in trouble.

Cian had played a bit of hooker in school so Faz had cleverly listed him as being capable of playing in all three front-row positions. He scrummaged at hooker. Meanwhile, Josh did the lineout throwing, and did it ridiculously well; he'd been doing a bit of practice on the side, apparently. His performance reinforced the idea that we had all bases covered, that we could handle whatever adversity came our way. For all our setbacks, Scotland never scored after Huw Jones's early try. It finished 22–7. Our medical list was long but we felt almost bulletproof.

England had just suffered their biggest ever defeat at

Twickenham, to France. They now stood between us and a Slam. Ireland had won only three of those, and never done it in Dublin. It would be my final Six Nations appearance, on St Patrick's weekend. My scriptwriter was doing a decent job.

One of my favourite action sequences comes from that Slam game against England. I'm not actually visible in it. None of the players are. It's shot from the West Stand in the Aviva and it zooms in on Laura, Luca, Amy and Sophie, sitting in the crowd as I'm lining up my first shot at goal, eighteen minutes into the game.

It's forty metres out, into the shallow end of the stadium, directly in front of the posts, and the all-time Six Nations individual points-scoring record is at stake. Laura is twisting her wedding ring, which she says she does for all my kicks. Luca and Amy are taking deep breaths, in through the nose, out through the mouth, as if they are mimicking me as I stand over the kick. It cracks me up every time.

Luca had been talking about the record all that week, which didn't really help. He didn't hear about it from me. I was trying not to talk about it. Not publicly, anyway.

I had to think about it, though. I had to prepare myself mentally, to make sure that an individual record didn't have a negative effect on me or the team. I had to get it out of the way, almost. And I had to talk about it as the journos were asking me about it in my captain's press conference.

I'd been talking about it previously, although in a different way, with Mark, my brother. The previous December, Harry Kane had been standing over the penalty that could have given him the England goal-scoring record, against France in the World Cup quarter-final. Only a few minutes previously, he'd slotted the penalty that brought him level with Wayne

Rooney. But this time he blasted the ball over the bar and France went through. Had he known about the record? Had that awareness affected him?

I didn't want that happening to me. Most of the pressure revolved around the fact that this was a Grand Slam game against England. The record was maybe 1 per cent of that pressure, but I had to ensure it didn't become a distraction. So I put even more time than normal into my mental prep, reading and rereading the mental cues I had written in my notebook.

Breathe.

Routine.

Distracting thought? Accept it as natural and let it go.

Process.

Forget the outcome. Commit to the process.

Breathe.

Pick your target behind the posts. Focus on your target.

Posture.

Pick the exact spot on the ball. Focus on that spot.

Commitment to the process is key. Be obsessed with the process and not the outcome.

Then you hear the announcement on the PA: 'Your new Six Nations points-scoring record-holder: Jonathan Sexton!'

Up in the stand, Laura is hugging Amy and Sophie, while Luca is punching the sky. I love it.

That kick broke a record, but England were still ahead 6–3. I knew they'd turn up. No team with Owen Farrell in it was going to hand us a Slam, especially given that he was playing against his dad's team. Whatever it meant to my family, imagine what that weekend was like for the Farrells?

England had come for a scrap and Owen was in the thick

of everything. At one stage in the first half, I was hit late by Alex Dombrandt. When I appealed to the ref I put my hand to my head to show that I'd been clipped. Quick as a flash, Owen was in with: 'Shouldn't he be getting an HIA then?' I would have tried the same. We both laughed when we caught each other's eye.

England were unlucky to lose Freddie Steward to what was never a red card, but as in Twickenham the previous year, going down a man galvanized them. I encouraged the crowd to get behind the team, but it had to come from us. Dan Sheehan obliged, finishing brilliantly off a rehearsed line-out play. What a rugby player.

The occasion got to us, undoubtedly. It was only ten minutes from the end, when Dan scored his second try, that we could breathe a little more easily. When I kicked the conversion from wide on the right, I jumped and punched the air. Before the tournament I'd flown Dave Alred over specifically to work on wide-angle place-kicks. In the Scotland game I had four of them, and now I had another massive one from the exact spot we had worked on. I knew it was a huge kick to go more than two scores clear. My extra bit of preparation with Dave paid off.

A couple of minutes later, when England's maul crashed over our try-line, I was at the bottom of the pile, in pain, having ruptured my adductor off the bone. I knew it was bad.

As Ciaran Cosgrove helped me from the pitch, I was too busy quizzing him about my recovery time to fully appreciate the crowd's ovation. He looked at me in disbelief. 'Jesus, Johnny, your recovery can wait!' I let a special moment pass me by. My last time walking off the Aviva pitch.

There were plenty more moments to cherish that day. This was the fourth time I'd experienced a championship win but the first time in Dublin. I loved the slow lap of honour, seeing my folks in the crowd, so many familiar and happy faces.

I loved the messages of congratulations I received from previous Ireland out-halves like Ollie Campbell, Mick Quinn and Eric Elwood but also from legends in other sports like Paul McGrath, Shane Lowry and Joe Canning. They reinforced Faz's mantra about making the entire country proud.

We got to share the celebrations with our families the next day. In the Shelbourne, we watched the Ireland Under-20s clinch their own Slam – another special achievement for the Sextons, as Mark was attack coach.

The party went on. There was no talk of the World Cup. It was important to enjoy that moment. As I kept telling the lads: This is for keeps. When we meet in thirty years' time, we'll still be celebrating this. No one can take it away from you. That's the beauty of winning.

Before the Six Nations had even started, Laura had asked me which I'd prefer: a Grand Slam or a fifth European title with Leinster? I replied that I didn't need to choose. I could have both.

Not now, I couldn't. It emerged soon after the England game that I'd need an operation on my groin. I'd hopefully be recovered in time for 16 June, when we began our World Cup prep with Faz. But my Leinster career was over. The surgeon didn't guarantee me anything. He explained that at my age, the race to be ready for the World Cup would bring challenges.

It felt like a huge anticlimax. In April, I gave an interview to the *Sunday Times* where I said I wished that the forty games I'd played for Racing had been played for my home province. I wished I'd been a one-club man, in other words. I guess it was my way of sending some love to the Leinster supporters.

Our defeat in the 2022 Champions Cup final in Marseille had been painful: La Rochelle nicked victory with the final play. I'm not begrudging them their success. They outscored us by three tries to none and edged the physical battle on a hot day in a noisy stadium. But it's also true that we had little luck. Twice within the space of sixty seconds in the third quarter we were undone by freakish bounces. The turning point was Brice Dulin's drop-goal attempt back-spinning wickedly into my arms, just as I stepped on to the goal-line, forcing me to run the ball back, unsuccessfully. But that wouldn't have happened but for the ball brushing against Jimmy O'Brien's leg a minute earlier, just before rolling into touch-in-goal. If not for that, we'd have had a scrum feed-back on halfway, with an 8-point lead. I know, I know. If my aunt had balls, she'd be my uncle. I'm just saying we were short on luck in the 2022 final.

When the plan to play the 2023 final at Tottenham Hotspur Stadium had to be put back a year, the Aviva was chosen instead. Perfect. I had presented the squad with a theme for the new season: 'Let's bring it home'. The video guys put a short piece together, with images of the Aviva and clips of us playing games in the stadium, and 'Take Me Home, Country Roads' as the backing track. I thought it struck the right note.

But now, facing into the business end of the European Cup, I was out injured. Leo tried to keep me involved. I sat in on Monday meetings. But it's hard to pass comment on games when you haven't been involved. I felt I needed to let Ross Byrne take ownership of the situation. For most of the week, I was out in Abbotstown with the Ireland physios.

I did feel our form had been mediocre, in the URC and in the European Cup, and that mistakes and bad habits were being brushed over. I felt these things could come back to bite us, but I said very little. I felt detached. This was natural, given that I'd only played in one Champions Cup match all season – twenty minutes off the bench against Gloucester in the pool stages.

All of which begs the question: If I felt so detached, how do I explain my behaviour on the day of the final? That's exactly what Laura and Mark asked me later on. You were barely eligible for a medal if Leinster had won. Why get so incensed about a game you weren't involved in?

I thought about that question a lot. I was obsessed with winning a fifth European title. I'd mapped out the year in my head, lifting the trophy at home in the Aviva in my last game for Leinster. This was a dream scenario. That opportunity being taken away from me made me very bitter. It had been an emotional week too. Leo had asked me to present the jerseys on the eve of the game and I'd been on the verge of tears. But that's no excuse. What happened is a huge regret, all the more so as Luca witnessed everything.

That was the day of his First Holy Communion, too. We hosted a family get-together earlier that day. I'd had a few beers watching Man U beat Bournemouth with Dad and Mark, which probably didn't help. Laura dropped me and Luca down near the stadium. After twelve minutes, it looked like we were, indeed, bringing the cup home: three tries in the bag and Tawera Kerr-Barlow in the bin. What could possibly go wrong?

By the break, La Rochelle were back in it at 23–14. I went downstairs to go to the loo. There were a few lively words with some of the La Rochelle coaching staff outside the match officials' room – Leo had sent Seánie O'Brien down to keep them away from Jaco Peyper. It was minor stuff, though. The real trouble started in the second half.

There were two of Peyper's decisions that I took exception to. One was against Caelan for what was a perfectly legal poach, the other against Jimmy O'Brien, supposedly for hitting an opponent in the air when in reality, he made a perfectly fair offensive jump-and-catch just outside their 22.

In the first half, I'd been sitting alongside Tony Spreadbury, EPCR's Head of Match Officials, and we'd been having good banter. Now I turned to him and said: 'Those are two massive game-changing decisions. They should be for us to relieve the pressure and he has got them 100 per cent wrong. It's a fucking joke.'

I was down pitch-side for the final seconds as we chased the match-winning score. On the final whistle, some of the La Rochelle players that had been replaced celebrated in my face, which probably riled me up further. I turned to Spreadbury and said: 'Tony, I fucking told you those decisions would cost us.'

As I walked out to console the Leinster guys, I couldn't stop myself from saying something to the match officials, who were standing together on halfway. 'It's a fucking disgrace that you guys can't get the big decisions right.'

They couldn't have heard my exact words with all the noise, but they would have known from my body language that I wasn't complimenting them. For the presentations, Luca and I were standing near the Leinster players. I looked over at the officials occasionally and shook my head, muttering away under my breath. I was still fuming. I cursed them when they were receiving their medals but Luca was the only one who could have heard me.

I'd cooled down a bit by the end of the ceremony. I decided it might make sense to say something conciliatory, but Christophe Ridley, one of the assistant refs, politely advised me that they couldn't engage with me.

I was twitchy that evening. There was a clip doing the rounds on social media, showing me pointing my finger at the match officials on the pitch, and it was getting a lot of traction. The next day I texted Spreadbury to see if he would take a call, as I wanted to apologize for my behaviour. I explained how emotional the occasion had been for me – though I knew this didn't excuse my words or actions. He said that he understood totally. There had been no need to call. He wished me well with my recovery from injury and we left it there.

So I had apologized to Jaco Peyper's boss but I wondered: Should I contact Peyper, too? By Tuesday, the incident was getting even more coverage on social media, especially in South Africa and France. Already the thought had crossed my mind: *Could this affect the World Cup?*

I rang Faz and David Nucifora. They reassured me. It was against the code of conduct for players to contact refs directly, but if there was anything in the ref's report we would have heard about it by then. Soon David Nucifora called with further reassurance. Don't worry, he said. I've done worse.

I felt more confident as we boarded a flight to Spain on a family holiday. But three weeks later, as we were on our way home, I received a call from Faz that made my blood run cold.

'EPCR has sent a letter to the Union,' he said. 'They're up to something.'

20

Getting into conflict with people wasn't anything new. It's one of the themes of this book: conflict with coaches, opponents, team-mates and the odd schoolteacher. It has caused me grief over the years, but often created energy that produced positive results. This conflict was different, though. I had virtually no control over the outcome. It also caused massive disruption in my preparation for the World Cup.

Even before leaving the Aviva pitch, I knew that I'd been completely out of order. In the next day or two I made a string of apologies: to Laura, to Luca, to Faz, to Leo, to David Nucifora and Kevin Potts, the IRFU's CEO, to Tony Spreadbury – to anyone I felt deserved an apology. I wanted to apologize to EPCR and to the match officials, too, but I was forced to wait for a tortuous quasi-legal disciplinary process to run its course. The period from crime to sentencing lasted all of eight weeks. Very early in the process it began to feel like a witch-hunt.

It felt as though EPCR and the match officials saw an opportunity to make an example of me. I had the impression that they were deliberately taking their time to build as strong a case as possible, but also to make things uncomfortable for me. The possibility that my World Cup would be disrupted – or even that it might not happen at all – was frying my brain.

According to EPCR, there were three separate incidents:

1) the inflammatory comment 2) my supposedly 'intimida-
tory' behaviour during the presentation ceremony and 3) my
approach to them after the presentations. There had been
talk of investigating the half-time tunnel kerfuffle, too, but
this was quickly thrown out as none of the match officials
had even been aware of any such incident. Leinster were also
in the dock for their failure to keep me under control.

Before they issued the misconduct charge on 12 June,
EPCR sent a letter to Leinster seeking details from my version of events. We duly obliged, and then received another
letter seeking further detail. It felt as though they were giving
me a chance to hang myself.

Paranoid? Of course I was. The longer the process took,
the more time there was for conspiracy theories as to who
was actually leading the witch-hunt. I couldn't help but notice
how much coverage the case was getting in the South African media, though this was perhaps to be expected, given
that Jaco Peyper is South African.

I was fortunate to receive excellent legal representation,
from solicitor Derek Hegarty and barrister Michael Cush
SC. Obviously I intended to admit to and apologize for my
misconduct, but I was confident that whatever suspension I
might receive for disrespecting the officials would be reduced
given that I had no 'previous'. After eighteen seasons as a
pro, my disciplinary record was spotless.

At the eight-hour hearing, conducted by video conference
on 13 July by an independent disciplinary panel, I admitted
that I'd often 'pushed the line' with officials but had never
actually been disrespectful. Out-halves and captains who try
to influence referees are just doing their job.

By the time of the hearing, the Ireland squad had been
back training for a month, which was a handy distraction.

Training was hard but fun and the mood was upbeat. The slagging that I took was merciless. Whatever song was playing in the gym at Abbotstown, Jack Crowley and Craig Casey found a way of slipping 'Jaco' into the lyrics as they sang along. In training matches, Faz or John Fogarty would award outlandish penalties against me, just to wind me up. Cue general laughter. I sucked it up. I had no option.

Maybe the lads believed that I'd only get a slap on the wrist, or that I'd be banned from just one of our three warm-up Tests, against Italy, Samoa and England. Maybe they reckoned that taking the mickey out of me was the best way to keep me sane. It was a release, all right, but only a temporary one. Once a session was over and I switched my phone back on, I'd see multiple emails, all relating to the case. It was a nightmare.

The EPCR team were able to produce a huge amount of footage of me, from a variety of angles – from Hawkeye and from the various broadcasters who covered the final. Edited cleverly and seen in conjunction with the statements of the match officials, they made it sound like I had been coursing them around the pitch with intent to intimidate. I hadn't been.

There were detailed statements from all four match officials, all incriminating against me. Jaco Peyper said he had received no apology from me after the match – despite knowing that I was forbidden from contacting him directly. When asked about the phone call he'd received from me on the Monday after the game, Tony Spreadbury said he'd taken it as a personal apology, not intended for the officials.

Michael Cush assured Peyper that I had 'apologized unreservedly' for behaviour that had been 'completely unacceptable'. He was also able to show the panel that I had been invisible and inaudible to the officials at the time when I was supposed to have been eyeballing and cursing them.

In fairness to Christophe Ridley, he described my approach after the presentations ('Incident 3') as 'measured and not confrontational'. This was my attempt to apologize. The disciplinary committee still reckoned that Incidents 1 and 2 counted as misconduct, with the latter aggravating the former. I was banned for six games, reduced to three for good behaviour – in other words, our three World Cup warm-up games. Leinster received a suspended fine.

I had to laugh when former players said that I'd been let off lightly. During the hearing my solicitor went through almost all comparable cases and found examples where players and coaches had done far worse than me but received bans of one or two matches. We decided not to appeal, though. The whole business had taken up too much time already and caused enough stress.

In retrospect, missing the warm-up games wasn't fatal. At the time, once I was fit enough to play in practice games, I was ravenous for any action that I could get. At a training camp in the Algarve in August, we had a training run against the Portuguese, who were surprisingly strong. Roy Keane was a guest at the session along with Niall Horan and Pádraig Harrington. 'I was trying to figure out which side were the Grand Slam champions!' Roy joked afterwards.

Roy and I actually had a good chat about the whole EPCR thing. He said that if he'd operated under the same disciplinary standards, he'd have been banned for his entire career. I'd put it behind me by then and was only looking forward to France. Subconsciously, though, I think the experience had made one thing clearer for me: I wouldn't go into coaching after retirement.

My reasoning was simple. As an occupation, coaching is more results-driven than playing, and in rugby the result is too often dependent on the 'interpretation' of the officials. Is there any sport where the officials are more influential? Is there any sport where the application of the laws is as inconsistent as it is in rugby?

I know that reffing is a bloody tough job, and I acknowledged this at the disciplinary hearing. I'm aware that rugby is a sport of so many moving parts and grey areas. There is an ongoing game of cat-and-mouse between law-makers and those coaches who find loopholes to exploit. The balance can't be right if the world champions are content to spend more time without the ball than with it.

At the time of writing, World Rugby have just introduced another batch of law-trials, to improve the game as a spectacle and cut out some of the 'dead' time caused, for example, by so many scrum resets. But these trials will only work if refs apply the law consistently in other parts of the game for the entire match.

We need to give the ref the licence to apply the laws rigorously, regardless of how high the penalty count gets. I have heard players say their coaches tell them to live on the edge, because refs won't referee the game strictly for the whole eighty minutes. But if referees apply the laws consistently, teams – and coaches – will soon get the message and the spectacle will benefit. Teams playing positive rugby should benefit, too. Shouldn't that be the general idea?

I'd had great plans for a farewell appearance at the Aviva on the occasion of our final warm-up, against England. I imagined how I'd lead the side out with Luca, Amy and Sophie accompanying me. Instead, because of my ban, I wasn't even allowed near the pitch. As my team-mates enjoyed reminding me, I was a menace to society.

Things happen for a reason, though. The England game was Earlsy's hundredth cap. It was his day. He deserved it to be all about him. He scored our fifth try with an acrobatic dive in the left corner. The stadium gave him a standing ovation and a roar that summed up what he meant to Ireland. Luca was one of Ireland's three mascots, so I had my representative. Besides, I'd already had a special moment at the Aviva, on the day that we had won the Grand Slam. My send-off could be at the World Cup, I thought to myself.

I was just apprehensive about what sort of a reaction I would get from the Ireland supporters who travelled to France in their tens of thousands. I was genuinely nervous before the pool opener in Bordeaux. Part of it was playing my first game in six months and not knowing how my body would handle the collisions and the 37-degree heat. Three weeks before departure, I'd had some tightness in my hammy from overdoing it in training, then a calf niggle.

Apart from that, there was the lingering sense of having let people down after the Champions Cup final. Had I been forgiven?

I found out an hour before kick-off at the impressive Stade de Bordeaux. Straight after the coin toss, I walked up the tunnel and into the heat, the first player on to the manicured playing surface. I did my normal half-lap before settling into my passing and kicking drills with Mike Catt. And all the way around the side of the pitch, all along the dead-ball line and back up the far side, men, women and kids in green were going nuts, roaring encouragement.

For me. What a lift. I tried to cherish it all knowing I didn't have too many more match days ahead of me.

During pre-season, we'd talked about the energy we could take from our travelling support. The younger guys, who were going to their first World Cup, kept asking for detail from previous tournaments, like kids begging for bedtime stories. Earlsy, Murr, Pete and myself – and Church, before he was cruelly injured on the eve of departure – were able to give them plenty of material. We told them about the hordes of campervans in Dunedin in 2011, the incredible noise at the Millennium when we beat France in 2015, or the way Irish fans had packed out Wembley for the Romania game the same year, and the huge numbers who travelled to Japan in 2019.

Having this World Cup so close to home was a big advantage but I told the lads that we had to honour our side of the bargain and to keep on winning. It hasn't always been this good, I said. We've got to make this count.

The game against Tonga in Nantes also felt like a home game. I had another nice moment scoring the try that broke Ireland's all-time points-scoring record. So much better to do it with a try, where you can celebrate with supporters and team-mates, rather than kicking a penalty and running back with a straight face.

Faz emptied the bench early that night, so I only got forty minutes, to go with sixty-six minutes against Romania: not really enough to prepare you for the Springboks after six months out. Adrenaline is amazing, though. I got an extra little surge of it when I ran out again, an hour before kick-off, to find that the Irish support had doubled or even tripled in size. Yes, I could hear a few boos from the South African supporters, but there was no competing with our fans. They had come to participate, not just to be there. They helped us to create a momentum that honestly felt unstoppable.

When you win despite certain parts of your game mal-functioning, it's a big boost to your self-belief. For once we didn't enjoy the strong start that had become our trademark, partly because we coughed up a few attacking lineouts – big opportunities missed in what would be the joint lowest-scoring game of the tournament. It was a testament to all the great work Simon had put into our defence over the last couple of years.

You could see how pumped we were by the aggression of our tackling – Rónan Kelleher emptying Damian Willemse at the start, Garry smashing Manie Libbok, Eben Etzebeth getting choke-tackled by James Lowe and a few others. That night, we were on it, physically.

The Springboks weren't exactly shy of contact themselves. In the second quarter, Damian de Allende ran a hard line in my direction on our 22. I went low, leading with the right shoulder. Oof. Following the initial numbness, came a burning sensation down my right arm.

For about thirty seconds, while I received treatment, I feared that my tournament was over. With that numbness, you're unable to tell initially if it's a bad shoulder injury or a stinger. A stinger is unpleasant, but it's the best possible result in this circumstance. I was soon back in the defensive line, watching our scrum lock out under enormous pressure, near our try-line. A big moment.

I was proud of my thirty-eight-year-old body that night. In my seventy-two minutes on the pitch, I made the second-highest number of tackles – eleven – and was on the receiving end plenty of times, often in the act of passing, when you're not always fully braced for impact. It was a proper Test match.

We won 13–8. We had some luck, for sure. South Africa

missed four shots at goal and we kicked three from three. They had an attacking lineout with the last play of the game and normally they are very clinical in this area. We held out.

After the final whistle my only mild disappointment was that they played our new anthem – 'Zombie' by the Cranberries – while we were still shaking hands with the Boks. I wanted to relish it properly, while walking the perimeter, applauding the fans and picking out familiar faces. I was incredibly sore but we were facing into a two-week break before the final pool game against Scotland, and four days before we reassembled at our base for the tournament: the city of Tours, three hours south-west of Paris. A few beers were called for.

That two-week break between games came about because of an extended World Cup schedule, designed for reasons of player welfare. Some commentators said it dragged the tournament out too long. No one in our camp was complaining.

The beauty of having the competition so close to home was that family members could commute. It helped that Aer Lingus were our official sponsors, and we were also very grateful to Hannah Hanlon and Geraldine Armstrong of the IRFU for making everything run so smoothly for the wives, partners and kids who regularly flew in and out.

My initial plan was to spend a few days in Paris with Laura and Luca and to revisit a few old haunts from the Racing days. But we'd grown to love Tours, a picturesque medieval city in the Loire Valley, so we headed back there for our mini-break along with a few other families.

We'd heard so much about how poor the team hotels had been at previous World Cups in France. Our team hotel in Tours was lovely – only a short bike ride or a tram journey from the town but with plenty to offer in itself. The team room was actually a big marquee that doubled as an amusement palace: table-tennis table, pool table, PlayStations and a dodgy box so we had access to whatever TV we wanted, plus a well-stocked, state-of-the-art coffee station. Most importantly, the IRFU had forked out for a Trackman: an indoor golf simulator. Some of the games of 'Bullseye' we played were ridiculously competitive.

This was our team room but it was also a family room. That's how Faz wanted it and how we wanted it – a place where partners or kids could wander around freely and feel at home on the weekends when they were over. It was the tightest group that I've ever been a part of.

By the Thursday after the South Africa game, partners and kids had returned home. We were back to work. I was proud of the way that I led the squad in the build-up to Scotland. It's easy to brush over flaws when you're winning, but you'll get caught out eventually – I'd seen it happen at Leinster. So I was fairly blunt about what needed to be improved. People outside the group had already written us into the quarter-finals as pool winners. We couldn't afford any complacency.

I probably needn't have worried, though. The very fact that the Scotland game was Pete's hundredth cap almost guaranteed that we'd be switched on. We had a four-try bonus wrapped up by half-time and led 36–0 before the Scots scored two late tries. They'd been dominated on the pitch and they were dominated in the stands. We acknowledged our supporters afterwards, but the celebrations were much more muted than they had been after the South Africa game. As far as we were concerned, we'd only just arrived at the business end of the World Cup.

I'm still convinced that we were the best team at the tournament, that our world ranking was accurate. I know I'm biased. And I know that South Africans – and others – will tell me to look in the record books. But it wouldn't be the first time that the best side in a sports tournament didn't end up winning it.

People have asked me if we were nervous before the quarter-final, if we felt 'the weight of history on our shoulders', if we did anything differently from previous games. Yes, we were nervous, but no more so than before any other game. Revisit the first couple of minutes and it's the All Blacks who look incredibly jittery. I don't believe history had any relevance. This was a different team from previous sides, with its own methods, its own psychology and personality. We didn't do anything differently on that day.

We just didn't play to our optimum, or even at 90 per cent capability. It's virtually impossible to do that throughout a tournament. It's inevitable that at some stage you'll dip a little. We chose a bad day to dip.

At 90 per cent plus, it's easier to take variables out of the equation – variables such as the bounce of a ball or a referee's bias against your loose-head's technique, even when he is dominating his opponent in the scrum. Ninety per cent plus is what you need to overcome a New Zealand side who played probably their best game in two years, after that jittery start. They had been coached well, too. All three of their tries had their origins in the video analysis room. The All Blacks' attack coach that day? Joe Schmidt.

Afterwards I read that Faz should have replaced me before the end. My legs had gone, they said. It's true, my legs did go during that final 37-phase attack, which lasted all of five minutes and fifty seconds, during which I touched the ball a lot of times. But it's not as if Faz could have replaced me in the middle of that attack. And if you go back and have a look at the minutes just before we started that attack, all of my contributions were positive. New Zealand just shut the game down very cleverly during the period that Codie Taylor was in the bin, and we didn't get any breaks.

I was glad that Faz allowed me to stay out there and give every last drop. And I was proud that we stayed in the fight and came so close to pulling off what would have been one of the greatest comebacks. When our maul was going forward again with about eight minutes to go I was thinking we had done it. Jordie Barrett getting his body under the ball as Rónan Kelleher lunged for the line was a moment of brilliance. Fair play to him.

At my captain's meeting the night before the game, I'd said it as plainly as I could: We've gone past the stage where heroic near misses are good enough. We needed to fulfil what we'd seen all along as our destiny. And we didn't do that.

I struggled to contain my sadness afterwards, but the healing process began even while I was still on the pitch in Saint-Denis. The TV cameras were on me and Luca when he looked up and told me: You're still the best, Dad.

One of the beauties of extending my career was that Luca is old enough to appreciate what we achieved in my last couple of seasons, to have experiences that he will remember. I was so proud of him, that he knew exactly the right words to say at that moment. He must get his emotional intelligence from his mum!

I found Laura at the front of the stand where she was sitting with the other wives and partners. She hugged me and told me she was proud of me. The following morning,

I spoke to Amy and Sophie on FaceTime and Amy, too, found the right words. 'We're sad that you lost but we're happy that we're going to see you tomorrow, Daddy,' she said. My heart melted.

Even Dad knew what to say. He told me not to worry about the penalty I'd missed on sixty minutes. We'd been awarded a penalty try only four minutes later, so his point was that the miss didn't affect the outcome. This was open to debate, but I knew that he meant it only to console me. I knew also that I'd made him and Mum proud.

There were other words that helped me to process my disappointment, to cope with the blunt fact that, unlike previous disappointments, there was no rebounding from this one. Faz said some very complimentary things about me in the dressing room and then to the media. When I got the chance, I reciprocated, and not just out of courtesy.

He is unique, the only coach I've come across who has the full package – man-manager, strategist, tactician, technician, communicator, motivator and great bloke, all rolled into one. Just as I had done with Joe four years previously, I called over to him when everything had died down, with a gift and a letter of thanks.

The 'afterlife' was so different. As a pro athlete, every minute of your working day is mapped out for you. My new employers, by contrast, allowed me the flexibility to shape my own working schedule, whether at home or in the office. I also have the flexibility to accommodate my new sporting addiction: padel.

I knew I would find it difficult when the Six Nations rolled around. Our stunning victory in Marseille caused a weird cocktail of feelings – pride mixed with something like jealousy. I was genuinely touched when Paulie spoke about my legacy living on, how I'd shown younger guys 'how much they have to care about how they prepare'.

I was proud of and happy for Jack Crowley, who had shadowed me for my final lap and pumped me for info and then stepped forward in his first full Six Nations. And I made sure to meet a few of the lads for a couple of beers on the Monday evening after they won the title.

All that helped me, and so did the warmth and affection that I felt from so many rugby supporters. As I mentioned at the start of the book, this was the inspiration for my retirement message on Instagram around a fortnight after we came home from the World Cup. I didn't expect my statement would attract so much comment, that it would become news, almost.

I saw it as an opportunity to thank those supporters properly, to express how much I appreciated their kind words. It was also my way of thanking everyone else who had helped me over the years: coaches, teachers, mentors and teammates at Bective, Mary's – school and club – Leinster, Racing, Ireland and the Lions. I thanked my family and I had a special word for Laura and the kids and their unconditional love. I am so lucky to have them in my life.

I concluded by returning to the team and our support staff and the amazing journey that we'd been on together. 'The sadness and frustration we couldn't progress further remains,' I wrote. 'They will for a long time to come but the overarching feeling is the pride I felt playing with such a committed and talented group of players, the best group I have been lucky enough to be a part of, on and off the pitch . . .'

This was how I wrapped it up: 'Four years ago we sat down

as a squad and spoke about what we wanted to achieve. Our main motivation and objective was to inspire the nation. I think we achieved that. We lost, but we won.'

Not everyone would let me away with those last words. Writers in some of the Irish media took issue with my assertion that we had inspired a nation, or with the way I claimed 'victory' after we had lost.

Their words rankled at first. I wasn't just referring to the World Cup in my statement. I was talking about the team's journey over the last few years. I thought of what we had achieved during my time as captain – the historic series victory in New Zealand, the Slam, the record-breaking run of victories – and I am unbelievably proud. I still believe we inspired the Irish sporting public, not just rugby fans. That was clear to see from the scenes in Paris and throughout Ireland during the World Cup.

I got what the writers were saying, though. I'd said pretty much the same thing myself, on the eve of the quarter-final: We have gone beyond the stage of heroic defeats. We needed to win. We didn't.

Part of me found that repulsive, in the same way that I found it repulsive after a cup defeat in school when Mum tried to console me on the car journey home and I snapped at her.

The only difference is that this time, I had no comeback, no next match. I was retired, finished. When winning is an obsession and you lose, it normally torments you for weeks and sometimes longer. It fuels your next goal, your next competition. I didn't have that any more. I wrote what I felt and how I felt was very different to any previous reflection. Of course it was. I wasn't the obsessed person I had been for the last twenty years. I had to find comfort in what was in the past. I found it in the memory of those crowd scenes at the Aviva and in Saint-Denis, in all those messages and letters I received.

You make sense of it all by counting your many blessings and by finding new distractions. And then you move on.

Acknowledgements

Writing an autobiography is a big undertaking. Thank you to Peter O'Reilly for his patience with a project that started in 2017. It was a big help having an experienced writer to structure my thoughts and tell my story. The relationship we built during the year we spent putting together my first book, *Becoming a Lion* (2013), really helped me open up to Peter for this book. Thank you, Peter: I didn't always enjoy getting coaxed into the difficult conversations, but you did a great job. I also enjoyed your company through the many hours we spent together.

Ciarán Medlar's feedback was invaluable, as ever. I first approached Ciarán eighteen years ago to ask for his advice on financial matters, but he is now my first port of call whenever I need advice on anything, and he is also a good friend.

Thanks to Conor Ridge and Brian Moran in Horizon Sports for all their work on my behalf off the pitch, allowing me to concentrate on my rugby.

It's only when you become a parent yourself that you appreciate fully all the love and support that you received from your own parents, all the sacrifices that they made. Mum and Dad, I can't thank you enough, especially for instilling good values and principles, ones that I try to instil in my own kids.

To Mark, Gillian and Jerry, thanks for putting up with me! I know it can't have been easy, especially when the three Sexton boys were sharing a cramped bedroom in Rathgar, but I love you guys.

I am genuinely blessed to have come under the influence of some remarkable teachers and coaches – at St Mary's (school and club), Leinster, Racing, Ireland and the Lions. There are too many of you to mention by name but please accept my heartfelt gratitude.

To my team-mates, thanks – all of you. It was only towards the end of my career that I realized there were different ways to drive and maintain high standards, different styles of communication, all of which could be effective. Part of me wishes I could go back and change the way I did things for large parts of my career, but another part of me accepts that this is just my journey. I'm sure I could be difficult to work with at times, but I hope you saw me as a loyal team-mate who always put the side first.

Most of all, thanks to Laura and to Luca, Amy and Sophie. Particularly Laura, who was with me through it all. Your support through the tough times meant I never had to do it alone. I am so lucky to have you.

Peter O'Reilly

I'm very grateful to Johnny for trusting me to help tell his story. This project started back in 2017 and took longer than expected, simply because his career kept extending so impressively. This meant I often got to witness and document his unguarded reaction to the various highs and lows in real time, which was both fascinating and a privilege.

Johnny's exceptional memory for detail meant that I didn't need to carry out many supplementary interviews, but a few people's contributions deserve special mention. Thanks to Laura Sexton, Johnny's wife, for her astute observations and also for her warmth and hospitality. Clare Sexton, Johnny's mum, provided great insights on the early years in particular. Richie Hughes, his English teacher and rugby coach at St Mary's College, was wonderfully helpful. I'm indebted also to those team-mates and colleagues who shared recollections and corroborated details.

Thanks to Michael McLoughlin and Brendan Barrington at Sandycove for their professionalism, guidance and encouragement.

Finally, much love and appreciation to my wife, Cliodhna, for her intelligent feedback and constant support, and to our children – Lucy, Michael and Katie.

Index